Healing in the Early Church

The Church's Ministry of Healing and Exorcism from the First to the Fifth Century

Peter

Wishing you God's rich blessing
as you continue your healing ministry
and thank you for your & your parish's
support for me in the Philippines.

Best wishes,

Andrew

STUDIES IN CHRISTIAN HISTORY AND THOUGHT

A full listing of all titles in this series
appears at the close of this book

STUDIES IN CHRISTIAN HISTORY AND THOUGHT

Healing in the Early Church

The Church's Ministry of Healing and Exorcism from the First to the Fifth Century

Andrew Daunton-Fear

Foreword by David F. Wright

Paternoster:
thinking faith

MILTON KEYNES · COLORADO SPRINGS · HYDERABAD

First published 2009 by Paternoster

Paternoster is an imprint of Authentic Media
9 Holdom Avenue, Bletchley, Milton Keynes, MK1 1QR, UK
1820 Jet Stream Drive, Colorado Springs, CO 80921, USA
OM Authentic Media, Medchal Road, Jeedimetla Village,
Secunderabad 500 055, A.P., India

www.authenticmedia.co.uk
Authentic Media is a Division of IBS-STL UK, a company limited by guarantee
(registered charity no. 270162)

15 14 13 12 11 10 09   7 6 5 4 3 2 1

British Library Cataloguing in Publication Data
A catalogue record for this book is available from the British Library

ISBN 978-1-84227-623-5

Typeset by the Author
Printed and bound in Great Britain
for Paternoster
by AlphaGraphics Nottingham

STUDIES IN CHRISTIAN HISTORY AND THOUGHT

Series Preface

This series complements the specialist series of *Studies in Evangelical History and Thought* and *Studies in Baptist History and Thought* for which Paternoster is becoming increasingly well known by offering works that cover the wider field of Christian history and thought. It encompasses accounts of Christian witness at various periods, studies of individual Christians and movements, and works which concern the relations of church and society through history, and the history of Christian thought.

The series includes monographs, revised dissertations and theses, and collections of papers by individuals and groups. As well as 'free standing' volumes, works on particular running themes are being commissioned; authors will be engaged for these from around the world and from a variety of Christian traditions.

A high academic standard combined with lively writing will commend the volumes in this series both to scholars and to a wider readership.

Series Editors

In memory of
my beloved aunt and godmother
Sister Anastasia
(1900-1991)
who devoted her life to healing
ministry

and

Professor William Frend
(1916-2005)
who, as my teacher at Cambridge,
imparted to me
a great love of the Early Church

Contents

Foreword

In most phases of the history of the Christian church it is difficult to miss the dimension of divine healing, that is, healing attributed in a more or less direct way to the power of God. The ministry of Jesus himself is shot through with this same dimension. He could be summarily described as someone who 'went about doing good and healing all who were oppressed by the devil' (Acts 10:38). The ascription of illness, whether physical or psychological, to the devil immediately raises all manner of questions for modern readers, but at the very least it signals the instinctive conviction of Christians in every age that illness stands over against the good purpose of God for all human beings and that healing, however carried out, is a service always fraught with divine significance, whether the person experiencing it or the one effecting it acknowledges God or not.

From this perspective, a special importance has to attach to the ministries of healing attested in the first centuries of the church following the generation of Jesus and his apostles. Here in this book Andrew Daunton-Fear has provided us with an exemplary survey of healing in the early church. It is sympathetic, in that it is written by someone with first-hand involvement over a number of years in healing ministries in the contemporary church, and it is scholarly, being abreast of the best recent research and writing on the church of the Fathers. These twin qualities, of the insights of an insider and the reliability of an expert in Patristics, must be essential for any treatment of this subject which invites our serious attention – and not one without the other.

The place of healing within the life of the Christian church has undergone something of a resurgence in recent decades. The reasons for this are various. Widespread now is an enhanced perception of the human person as a unity, encompassing body as well as mind and spirit, rather than an uncomfortable composite of essentially disparate elements, with its essence residing in the soul to the detriment of the flesh. Sacramental or quasi-sacramental specialized ministries of healing have been recovered, not only in the more 'catholic' Christian traditions. Then there is the massive and still-multiplying impact of the fastest-growing brand of global Christianity which might be conveniently described as charismatic. This vast wave of burgeoning churches in what used to be called the Third World but now is increasingly referred to as the South or the Majority World – for so it indubitably is in terms of world Christianity – is marked by almost incredible diversity. For many Christians in the weary realms of the old Christendom its salient interest in healing has often been disenfranchised in advance by the sensationalist excesses of TV evangelist-healers with their slick professionalized campaigns and parallel preoccupation with fund-raising. It is crucially important for western Christians, pressurized daily by secularist mentalities, to be exposed to a scholarly account of the dimension of healing in the first age of the Jesus movement.

It is no less important for that account to be measured, responsible, informed by current expertise in the writings of the Fathers and other sources, and yet at the same time sensitised by personal experience where otherwise an anti-supernaturalistic *Tendenz* might hold sway. This is a very welcome high-quality study which deserves a wide readership in circles far beyond the reach of patristic studies, not least, we might hope, in that Majority World where increasingly the centre of gravity of global Christianity resides.

David F. Wright
Professor Emeritus of Patristic and Reformed Christianity,
University of Edinburgh

Acknowledgements

I would like to express my particular thanks to Dr. Graham Gould who supervised my Ph.D. research at King's College, London; to the Rt. Rev. Michael Turnbull, his successor as Bishop of Rochester the Rt. Rev. Michael Nazir-Ali, and the Parochial Church Council of my parish of Barming in Kent, who were willing to let me devote one day a week to research from 1992 until my degree was awarded; to Marion Brookfield who so patiently typed and retyped my thesis; to Lesley Bates, Genesis Langbao, the Rev. Dr. Russ Parker, the Rev. Professor John Richardson, Allan Thompson and Catherine Young who in different ways have helped my work forward to publication; and to the members of my family and close friends who have been a constant source of encouragement. I would like to say also how much I have appreciated the quiet and pleasant setting of my home at St. Andrew's Theological Seminary, Manila, where I have been teaching since 2003, for facilitating the updating of my work. Finally, I am honoured and delighted that my monograph has been accepted by Paternoster Press for publication in their Studies in Christian History and Thought series, and I wish particularly to thank Dr. Anthony R. Cross for his great patience in helping me to put my typescript in a form suitable for printing and for most kindly preparing the index.

It is sad indeed to record that David Wright, Professor Emeritus of New College, Edinburgh, whose Foreword I so much value, died before he could see this book published.

Andrew Daunton-Fear,
November 2008

Abbreviations

ACW	Ancient Christian Writers
ANCL	Ante-Nicene Christian Library
ANF	Ante-Nicene Fathers
Bauer	W. Bauer, *A Greek-English Lexicon of the New Testament and Other Early Christian Literature,* 2nd edn., rev. W.F. Arndt and F.W. Gingrich (Chicago, 1979)
BHM	*Bulletin of the History of Medicine*
BJRL	*Bulletin of the John Rylands Library*
CCSA	Corpus Christianorum, Series Apocryphorum
CCSL	Corpus Christianorum, Series Latina
EEC	*Encyclopedia of the Early Church,* ed. A. di Berardino, 2 vol. (Cambridge, 1992)
FOC	Fathers of the Church
GCS	Die griechischen christlichen Schriftsteller
HTR	*Harvard Theological Review*
JECS	*Journal of Early Christian Studies*
JEH	*Journal of Ecclesiastical History*
JTS	*Journal of Theological Studies*
Lampe	*A Dictionary of Patristic Greek,* ed. G.W.H. Lampe (Oxford, 1961)
Loeb	Loeb Classical Library
MPG	Migne Patrologia Graeca
MPL	Migne Patrologia Latina
NPNF	Select Library of Nicene and Post-Nicene Fathers of the Christian Church
NTS	New Testament Studies
OCD	*The Oxford Classical Dictionary,* ed. S. Hornblower and A. Spawforth, 3rd edn. (Oxford, 1996)
ODCC	*The Oxford Dictionary of the Christian Church,* ed. F.L. Cross, 3rd edn. by E.A. Livingstone (Oxford, 1997)
ODJR	*The Oxford Dictionary of the Jewish Religion,* ed. R.J.Z. Werblowsky and G. Wigander (Oxford, 1997)
PGM	Papyri Graecae Magicae
SP	*Studia Patristica*
SC	Sources Chrétiennes
Scot.JT	*Scottish Journal of Theology*
TU	Texte und Untersuchungen
Tyn. Bull.	*Tyndale Bulletin*
VC	*Vigiliae Christianae*
ZKTh	*Zeitschrift für Katholische Theologie*

Introduction

The pages of the New Testament tell us of Jesus Christ and his apostles healing the sick and driving evil spirits out of people, but what happened next? Did the Church in the post-apostolic era continue these activities? If so, what methods were used? Did the number of miracles increase or decrease? How long did they remain a feature of church life?

Various writers in modern times have, in part, addressed these matters. Evelyn Frost in her *Christian Healing: A Consideration of the Place of Spiritual Healing in the Church of Today in the Light of the Doctrine and Practice of the Ante-Nicene Church* (London, 1940), as her subtitle indicates, places the evidence for healings and exorcisms within the context of a discussion of the patristic understanding of the nature of man and other matters. She also seeks to evaluate the evidence against modern medical knowledge. But her study is not exhaustive, and of course medical knowledge has greatly developed since then.

S.L. Rayner's unpublished dissertation 'The Early Church and the Healing of the Sick' (Durham University, 1973) is a fine study, setting the Church's healing work in the first six centuries against the background of Greco-Roman medicine, but it by no means covers all the relevant patristic passages and rarely refers to the Greek and Latin. In his *Christian Healing after the New Testament: Some Approaches to Illness in the Second, Third and Fourth Centuries* (Lanham, 1994), based on his 1988 doctoral dissertation at MacQuarrie University, N.S.W., R.J.S. Barrett-Lennard has made minute studies of writings of four of the Fathers and eleven fourth-century letters. Subsequently he has spread his net a little wider. For the post-Nicene period R.A. Greer's *The Fear of Freedom: a Study of Miracles in the Imperial Church* (Pennsylvania, 1989) surveys the field admirably.

The matter of exorcism was tackled by R.M. Woolley in his *Exorcism and the Healing of the Sick* (London, 1932), published posthumously, a work impressive both for its scope and penetrating insights. It ranges beyond the New Testament and the writings of the Fathers to the Apocryphal Acts, Pseudo-Clementines and early church orders. Furthermore he extends his study to the fifth century and even beyond.

But in quite a small monograph he is unable to deal exhaustively with all the material. K. Thraede's lengthy article 'Exorzismus' (in *Reallexikon für Antike und Christentum*, 1969) draws extensively on the German literature and provides valuable information about the non-Christian cultic scene. But his interpretation of Christian exorcism, largely assimilating it to the pagan variety, is subjective and questionable at many points. The more recent monograph of Eric Sorensen *Possession and Exorcism in the New Testament and Early Christianity* (Tübingen, 2002) fascinatingly traces roots of exorcism in ancient Mesopotamia and Persian Zoroastrianism and offers explanations as to why Christian exorcism broke through hostile prejudice to achieve popularity in the Greco-Roman world. But he does not examine the Christian material in much detail and his explanations are open to question. A further contribution has now been made by Graham H. Twelftree in his recent book *In the Name of Jesus: Exorcism among Early Christians* (Grand Rapids, 2007). This is fundamentally a scrutiny of the New Testament for evidence about exorcism in the first-century Church. The author extends his study, however, to cover patristic evidence up to AD 200, but not with the same thoroughness and only to provide a 'lens'[1] through which to look back at the New Testament, amplifying what it says. This is indeed a strange approach which scarcely allows the developing patristic scene to speak for itself, and he makes some uncharacteristically careless judgements.

On individual modes of healing, C.L. Maconachie's doctoral dissertation 'Anointing and Healing' (Greenwich University, 1990) provides a useful survey of the biblical background and the evidence for anointing in the Church up to the fifth century. R.A.N. Kydd's doctoral thesis 'Charismata to 320 AD: A Study of the Overt Pneumatic Experience of the Early Church' (St. Andrew's University, 1973), upon which his briefer popular study *Charismatic Gifts in the Early Church* (Peabody, 1984) is based, concentrates primarily on prophecy but also discusses pertinently key references to gifts of healing. B.W. Amundsen's article 'Medicine and Faith in Early Christianity' (*BHM*, 1982) provides a brief but valuable study of the Fathers' attitude to medicine.

The purpose of my own work is to provide a much more comprehensive survey of healing in the Early Church than is to be found elsewhere. It is based on my doctoral thesis 'The Healing Ministry in the Pre-Nicene Church' (London University, 2000) and further reading. Whilst it remains a systematic and rigorous study I have rearranged the material and tried to make it accessible to the non-specialist. The thesis's detailed study of the New Testament gospel miracles has been

---

[1]   Twelftree, *Name of Jesus*, 31, 205 *et passim*.

replaced by a summary. From the Apocryphal Acts and the writings of the more prolific Fathers, such as Origen, I have quoted representative material rather than tediously recounting all the overlapping passages. I have also updated my work, taking into account more recent material.

My first chapter summarises the healing ministry of Jesus as presented in the four canonical gospels and contrasts it with healing sought through miracles, magic and medicine in the Greco-Roman world of his time. Chapter 2 looks principally at the rest of the New Testament for information on the Church's earliest healing work. Chapters 3, 4 and 5 review in some detail the pre-Nicene material on healing and exorcism. The arrangement is chronological, but subdivided geographically and then by author. Besides the patristic writings I have looked also at the Odes of Solomon, the five main Apocryphal Acts, the Pseudo-Clementines and some rabbinic evidence. Chapter 6 presents representative post-Nicene material from the fourth and early fifth centuries showing the paths along which the Church proceeded after persecution had finally stopped. No doubt much more remains to be said about this period but I hope I have, with the aid of Woolley, Greer, Barrett-Lennard and others, effectively opened up a field which others later may make the subject of more detailed studies. The Conclusion assesses both my findings and the adequacy of the conclusions reached by other secondary authors.

Though no attempt is made in this book to assess the historical value of the miracle stories of the canonical gospels, it is important to recognize that contemporary scholarship has moved far from the approach of D.L. Strauss who, in his *Life of Jesus* (German original: *Leben Jesu,* Tübingen, 1835), offered naturalistic explanations for the various miracles, and of Rudolf Bultmann who, in his *History of the Synoptic Tradition* (tr. from the 2nd edn. of the German: *Die Geschichte der synoptischen Tradition,* Göttingen, 1931), declared the miracle stories to be 'imaginary scenes illustrating in some concrete occasion a principle which the Church ascribed to Jesus',[2] and claimed we can in no instance penetrate back to actual history. More recent studies, most notably that of R. Latourelle, *Miracles of Jesus and the Theology of Miracles* (French original: *Miracles de Jésus et Théologie des Miracles,* Paris, 1986), and the detailed work of Twelftree in his earlier writings *Jesus the Exorcist* (Tübingen, 1993) and *Jesus the Miracle-Worker* (Downess Grove, Il., 1999), display a large measure of confidence in the historical value of these stories.

---

[2] R. Bultmann, *The History of the Synoptic Tradition,* 2nd edn. (Oxford: University Press, 1968), 41.

Those who, like Bultmann,[3] in the name of science wish to rule out the possibility of miracles today, do well to realise that Quantum Theory has now replaced Newtonian physics with its fixed 'laws of nature', and scientists no longer speak of rigidly determined events but merely statistically probable ones.[4] The 'laws' anyway were descriptive rather than prescriptive. Former theoretical physicist John Polkinghorne writes:

> The history of science is full of the unprecedented and unexpected... The problem of miracles is the problem of finding a wider framework in which they can find a coherent place.[5]

And elsewhere:

> We cannot exclude the possibility that in normal circumstances, of which we have no previous direct experience, novel phenomena will occur... Absolute and complete truth is beyond our grasp.[6]

And he concludes that modern science does not draw the bounds of possibility so tight as to allow no scope for the particular action of a personal God.

                                        *   *   *

Let me conclude on a personal note. Studying healing in the Early Church has enabled me to bring together two of my greatest interests, Patristics and the contemporary healing ministry. In dedicating this book to my aunt Sister Anastasia and my former teacher Professor William Frend I acknowledge my indebtedness to two without whose influence this study would, I am sure, never have been undertaken. I hope that those who come to it out of interest in history may be encouraged to consider further the healing ministry today, and those who have come to it out of a love for just that ministry may discover themselves so fascinated by the Early Church that they want to find out more. For both categories of reader I have been so bold as to place in an appendix what I suggest are some 'pointers' or guidelines from the Early Church material and my own experience, for healing ministry today.

---

[3]   'New Testament and Mythology', tr. R.H. Fuller, in *Kerygma and Myth*, ed. H.W. Bartsch, 2nd edn. (London: SPCK, 1964), 4-5.
[4]   See, for instance Mary Hesse 'Miracles and the Laws of Nature' in *Miracles*, ed. C.F.D. Moule (London: SPCK, 1965), ch. 3.
[5]   J. Polkinghorne, *The Way the World Is* (London: SPCK, 1983), 55.
[6]   J. Polkinghorne, *Science and Providence* (London: SPCK, 1984), 24.

CHAPTER 1

Jesus and His Contemporaries

The Healing Ministry of Jesus

According to the four gospels of the New Testament Jesus was famed for a spectacular healing ministry. Some twenty-two stories (excluding parallel accounts) depict his healing powers: in three instances he raises the dead[1] in four he exorcises evil spirits,[2] and in the remaining fifteen he cures a wide variety of physical sickness or malfunction: blindness (three times),[3] paralysis of the body (twice),[4] leprosy (twice),[5] fever,[6] a withered hand,[7] a haemorrhage,[8] deafness with speech impediment,[9] a bent back,[10] dropsy,[11] a detached ear,[12] and a near death condition.[13] Many more healings and exorcisms are referred to in summaries.[14]

---

[1]   Mk.5:21-24, 35-43, Lk.7:11-17, Jn.11:1-44.
[2]   Mk.1:21-28, 5:1-20, 7:24-30, 9:14-29. Because Mark is generally agreed to be the earliest of the gospels, where there are parallel accounts of the same story, references to the miracles in his gospel will be sufficient here. The allusion to Jesus' casting out a dumb spirit in 'Mt.12:22-23/Lk.11:14 (Matthew says the man was blind as well) is not a full story. It may be a 'generalized memory' of Jesus' exorcisms from Q (a posited second source of material generally believed by New Testament scholars to have been used by both Matthew and Luke) adapted by these evangelists.
[3]   Mk.8:22-26, 10:46-52, Jn.9:1-7.
[4]   Mk.2:1-12, Jn.5:1-19.
[5]   Mk.1:40-45, Lk.17:11-19.
[6]   Mk.1:29-31.
[7]   Mk.3:1-6.
[8]   Mk.5:25-34.
[9]   Mk.7:31-37.
[10]   Lk.13:10-17.
[11]   Lk.14:1-6.
[12]   Lk.22:50-51.
[13]   Mt.8:5-13, Lk.7:1-10, cf. Jn.4:46-54.
[14]   Mk.1:32-34, 6:56 *et passim.*

These acts of power substantiated Jesus' message that the kingdom of God was indeed at hand,[15] accredited him as the Messiah,[16] and showed his compassion for those in need.[17] He repeatedly put people's needs before religious restrictions. Five of the stories tell of healings on the Sabbath,[18] a point of contention with the scribes and Pharisees since their oral law stipulated healings should only be performed on the Sabbath if a person's life was at risk.[19] And he refused to be deterred by the possibility of incurring ritual contamination. He was quite prepared to touch a leper[20] or the bier carrying a dead person[21] in the course of healing them, and did not berate the woman with the haemorrhage for touching him.[22]

During his temptations Jesus declined to use miraculous means to dazzle crowds into following him[23] and this same attitude is evident in the accounts of his miracles. Indeed so insistent are his attempts not to publicize them, particularly in Mark's Gospel, that the German New Testament scholar W. Wrede developed the influential theory that this was part of an editorial ploy by Mark to explain why so few Jews had become Jesus' followers. Wrede called it the 'Messianic secret'.[24] Nevertheless it is quite possible to explain Jesus' injunctions to silence in terms of his concern for the well-being of his patients, his desire to discourage false ideas about himself and inhibit any response to him divorced from genuine repentance and faith.[25]

In two of the healings Jesus specifically links the malady with the person's sin[26] but, unlike rabbinic Jews,[27] he refuses to do this invariably.[28]

---

[15] Mt.4:17, Mk.1:15; Mt.12:28/Lk.11:20 state that exorcisms indicate the kingdom of God has come upon the people.

[16] Mt.11:2-6, Lk.7:18-23.

[17] Mt.14:14, Mk.1:41 (?), Lk.7:13, cf. Jn.11:35.

[18] Mk.3:1-6, Lk.13:10-17, 14:1-6, Jn.5:1-18, 9:1-41.

[19] The application of spittle to eyes is proscribed in *y.Shabbath* (Jerusalem Talmud) 14, 14d, 17f. Kneading was forbidden on the Sabbath – *Shabbath* 7.2, and this would include making clay (Strack-Billerbeck I, 623-29 discusses these).

[20] Mk.1:41, cf. Lev.13:45-46.

[21] Lk.7:14, cf. Num.19:11-16.

[22] Mk.5:33-34, cf. Lev.15:25-27.

[23] Mt.4:5-7, Lk.4:9-12.

[24] *The Messianic Secret*, tr. J.C.G. Grieg (Cambridge: University Press, 1971) from the German original (1901).

[25] See J.D.G. Dunn, 'The Messianic Secret in Mark', *Tyn. Bull.* 21 (1970), 92-117; C.D. Marshall, *Faith as a Theme in Mark's Narrative* (Cambridge: University Press, 1989), 99, commenting on Mk.5:43.

[26] Mk.2:5-12, Jn.5:14.

Before he heals Jesus looks above all for faith in the person afflicted[29] or his or her companions.[30] Quite often he demands an action that will call forth faith from the sick person, for instance: "Rise, take up your bed and walk",[31] "Stretch out your hand".[32] Lack of faith at Nazareth is said to have inhibited his healing work there.[33]

Jesus' healing methods were simplicity itself: a word of command,[34] touch,[35] and sometimes the use of spittle.[36] The desired results were almost invariably instantaneous. In just one instance he had to lay his hands twice on a blind man before he fully recovered his sight (Mk.8:22-26), an incident, it seems, Mark used strategically within his narrative to reflect the gradual awakening of Jesus' disciples to his true identity.[37]

In raising the dead, Jesus simply addresses a word of command to the lifeless body to get up[38] or come out of the tomb,[39] with immediate results, to the amazement of all present. In the case of Lazarus he first prays, but his prayer is not a petition, but a thanksgiving for the assured result, an illustration perhaps of the principle he gave his disciples in Mk.11:24: "I tell you, whatever you ask for in prayer, believe that you have received it and it will be yours." It is noteworthy that Jesus did not raise those who had long been dead. In each case the death was recent and, it seems, premature.

The four exorcisms related by Mark are varied indeed. The setting of the first is a synagogue (1:21-28). Did the possessed one appear at first

---

[27] 'A sick man does not recover from his sickness until all his sins are forgiven him', *b.Ned.* 41a (Babylonian Talmud); cf. Ecclus.38:9-10, Jas.5:14-16.

[28] Jn.9:2-3.

[29] Cf. Mk.5:34, 10:52.

[30] Mk.2:5, 5:36.

[31] Mk.2:9.

[32] Mk.3:5.

[33] Mk.6:5-6.

[34] Jn.5:8; cf. previous two notes.

[35] Lk.13:13, 20:50 *et passim*.

[36] Mk.7:33, 8:23, Jn.9:6, which is seen by some commentators as an indication of magic – J.M. Hull, *Hellenistic Magic and the Synoptic Tradition* (London: SCM, 1974), ch. 5; Morton Smith, *Jesus the Magician* (Wellingborough: Aquarian Press, 1978), 92.

[37] The first to suggest this appears to have been A. Richardson, *Miracle-Stories of the Gospels* (London: SCM, 1941), 86; cf the statement of the early second-century bishop Papias of Hierapolis that Mark, as a disciple of Peter, had recorded accurately all that Peter had remembered of Jesus' sayings and doings *though not in order* (Eusebius, *H.E.* 3.39.15).

[38] Mk.5:41, Lk.7:14.

[39] Jn.11:43.

devoutly religious? The second occurs in a graveyard (5:1-20) and tells of one infested by multiple spirits ('Legion'). In both cases the possessing spirits seem drawn to Jesus like a moth to a flame, crying aloud his identity and expressing their fear of his power over them. Such unwelcome publicity he will not tolerate and immediately commands the spirit(s) to leave. In the second case there is a prolonged conversation during which Jesus asks the spirit's name and the spirit pleads not to be sent out of the region, negotiating to depart into a nearby herd of pigs. The particularly bizarre features of this story have led many to doubt its historical value,[40] but would it not be fitting in Jewish eyes for 'unclean spirits'[41] to enter 'unclean' animals?[42] That Legion does not depart at once, and that both in the synagogue story and that of the dumb spirit (9:25-30), even after Jesus' command, the spirits convulse their victims one last time before departing, are surely signs of the authenticity of the events, for who would *invent* stories allowing evil spirits such width of manoeuvre in the presence of the divine Messiah? One further point: in the story of the dumb spirit, Jesus charges it to come out of the boy "and never enter him again" (v.25). In view of his warning elsewhere that an exorcised spirit might later return with companions to the person from whom it had been driven out,[43] it may be that this injunction was a common feature of his exorcisms. Finally, the story of the Syro-Phoenician woman's daughter (Mk.7:24-30) tells us that Jesus could exorcise from a distance.

Such a wide range of both physical healings and exorcisms lends some credibility to the suggestion of M. Dibelius that one of the purposes of the transmission of these stories was to give practical guidance to Church members in their exercise of gifts of healing.[44]

But how did Jesus' approach compare with that of other healers of his day?

---

[40] Including M. Dibelius, who considered it a tale of non-Christian origin, *From Tradition to Gospel* (London: Nicholson, 1934), 87-89, and R. Latourelle, who saw the matter of the swine as 'a literary device to show that henceforth demons no longer have any power over human beings unless Jesus allows it', *Miracles of Jesus*, 117.

[41] Mk.5:2.

[42] Lev.11:7.

[43] Mt.12:43-45, Lk.11:24-26.

[44] M. Dibelius, *Tradition to Gospel*, 84, 86-87 (quoted below p. 32); cf. Twelftree, *Miracle Worker*, 97, 109, *Name of Jesus*, 117-18, 130 *et passim*.

The Contemporary Scene

H.C. Kee, in his valuable study *Medicine, Miracle and Magic in New Testament* Times,[45] gives us a useful framework within which to investigate this subject. We shall look first at miracles, then magic, and finally medicine, whilst recognising the boundary between these categories is not always clearly drawn.

Miracle

In his 1980 Bampton Lectures A.E. Harvey pointed out that, in the period 200 BC – AD 200, the number of miracles attributed to named historical individuals is astonishingly small.[46] There are the two credited to Vespasian,[47] a few attributed to a small group of charismatic Jewish figures, most notably Hanina ben Dosa,[48] and those purportedly performed by Apollonius of Tyana.[49]

The Roman general Vespasian (later emperor), Tacitus tells us, was in Alexandria in Egypt in AD 70 awaiting favourable weather conditions for travel, when he was petitioned by a blind man, a devotee of the god Serapis, to moisten his cheeks and eyes with spittle and so cure his blindness; likewise by a man with a crippled hand who asked him to tread on it and thereby cure it. Vespasian at first ridiculed these petitions but then consulted physicians. They declared the power of sight in the first had not been completely eaten away and would return if the obstacles were removed; in the other man the joints, they said, had been displaced and could be restored by healing pressure. Perhaps the gods had chosen Vespasian for this divine favour. And so, smiling graciously, he now granted the requests, and the treatment was in each case successful. But how far can such medically advised 'treatment' be called miraculous?

The case was rather different with Hanina ben Dosa, who likewise lived in the first century of our era. The rabbinic literature attributes others with miracles such as rain-making, but to him healings. Two stories are related in the Babylonian Talmud *Berakoth* 34b:

---

[45] Cambridge: University Press, 1980.
[46] A.E. Harvey, *Jesus and the Constraints of History* (London: Duckworth, 1982), 103.
[47] Tacitus, *Histories* 4.81; cf. Suetonius, *Vespasian* 7.
[48] See G. Vermes, *Jesus the Jew,* 2nd edn. (London: SCM, 1983), ch. 3.
[49] Philostratus, *Life of Apollonius.*

1. The son of Rabbi Gamaliel (perhaps St. Paul's teacher)[50] was suffering from mortal fever so the distraught father dispatched two of his pupils to find Hanina. When they arrived at his home he had retired to an upper room. Emerging he said, "Go home, for the fever has departed from him." Incredulous, they asked if he were a prophet. He denied it and explained: "If my prayer is fluent in my mouth I know that he [the sick man] is favoured; if not, I know that it [the disease] is fatal." The envoys recorded the day and hour of these words and returned to Gamaliel, who at once confirmed that that was when his son's fever had departed and he had asked for water to drink. There are obvious similarities between this story and that of Jesus' healing the nobleman's son (Jn.4:46-53) but also differences.

2. Rabbi Johanan ben Zakkai's son also fell ill. The father sent forHanina and requested, "Hanina, my son, pray for him that he may live." Hanina put his head between his knees and prayed, and the son lived. His posture for prayer recalls that of Elijah on Mount Carmel praying for rain (1 Ki.18:42).

The Jewish scholar G. Vermes draws the cautious conclusion:

> It would appear...that the logical inference must be that the person of Jesus is to be seen as part of first-century charismatic Judaism and as the paramount example of the early Hasidim or Devout.[51]

But, while Hanina, like any pious Jew, prayed for the sick, Jesus used direct commands and simple actions in his cures. Hanina made a mere ripple in Jewish history, but Jesus founded an enduring world religion.

The life of Apollonius of Tyana in Cappadocia (Asia Minor) occupied, it seems, most of the first century AD. His biographer Philostratus depicts him as a 'divine man', an itinerant Neopythagorean philosopher with supernatural knowledge and power to drive away demons.[52] In one case (*Life of Apollonius* 3.38) a letter from him containing alarming threats is said to have effected the deliverance; in another (4.20) his gaze tortures a possessing spirit and, at his command, it departs, knocking down a statue. A third story (6.43) tells of a boy who, after being bitten by a dog, exhibits dog-like behaviour. Apollonius has the dog fetched to lick around the wound it caused and the boy recovers. After the sage has prayed and made it swim across the river, the dog is likewise cured. Another story tells of a bride from the

---

[50] Ac.22:3.
[51] G. Vermes, *Jesus the Jew*, 79.
[52] See below my Conclusion pp. 160-62 for a discussion of 'demon'.

family of a Roman consul who appeared to have died in the hour of her marriage. Apollonius stops her bier, touches the girl and, calling to her secretly, wakes her from 'seeming death'. There are resemblances here to Jesus' raisings of both the son of the widow of Nain (Lk.7:11-17) and Jairus' daughter (Mk.5:21-24, 35-43). Philostratus, completing his biography c.AD 220, may well have known both stories, but here he comments that there was some debate as to whether the girl was really dead and says he is not competent to decide.

Not only, in fact, was Philostratus' work completed over a century after Apollonius' death, his chief source of information Damis was probably his own invention.[53] Moreover his narrative reads like a romantic novel at times totally in the realms of fantasy.[54] It is therefore dubious whether his work is of any serious historical value.

Besides these few named individuals credited with miraculous healings there were in antiquity healing cults. The Egyptian goddess Isis was known as early as the fourth millennium BC. She became viewed as the law-giver, the guarantor of the stability and continuity of human life, and then as the mistress of the seas. Later she was associated with Serapis as a healer. In the first century BC Roman historian Diodorus Siculus writes of her:

> As for Isis, the Egyptians say that she was the discoverer of many health-giving drugs and was greatly versed in the science of healing; consequently, now that she has attained immortality, she finds her greatest delight in the healing of mankind and gives aid in their sleep to those who call upon her, plainly manifesting both her very presence and her beneficence towards men who ask for her help.[55]

Her cult spread around the Mediterranean. A catalogue recording donations at the Serapion at Delos in the south Aegean, dating from the second century BC, mentions many gold and silver eyes and fingers and sometimes ears and feet, suggesting perhaps that these parts of the body had been healed there.[56] A text discovered at Maronai in Greece tells of one who attributed the restoration of his sight to Isis, though it does not

---

[53] See G.W. Bowersock's introduction to C.P. Jones' translation of the *Life* (Harmondsworth: Penguin, 1970), 11.

[54] For instance when telling of the Indian sages' storing winds and rain for their country in stone jars (3.14) and of the elm tree in Egypt talking in an articulate feminine voice (6.10).

[55] *Bibliotheca* 1.25.2-3.

[56] H.C. Kee, *Miracle in the Early Christian World* (Yale: University Press, 1983), 126.

tell us how it happened.[57] We do not know how serious these medical conditions were, or how many of those who sought healing actually found it. We may infer from Diodorus' statement, perhaps, that petitioners slept in her temples praying for a healing encounter with this goddess.

This was indeed the procedure in the pre-eminent healing cult of the ancient world, that of Asclepius (Lat. *Aesculapius*). Originally it seems a human physician from Thessaly,[58] perhaps as early as 600 BC he was worshipped as a god, the son of Apollo and Coronis, born at Epidaurus. The site at Epidaurus has been excavated revealing a considerable complex and testimonies of healings found inscribed prominently on columns for visitors to read. They relate stories from c.300 BC to the second century AD, attesting many cures. Prominent are cases of blindness, paralysis, injury from weapons and stomach problems. Usually the sufferer has slept in the *abaton,* the special chamber of the god, and in a dream received treatment from Asclepius or one of his sacred snakes or dogs. For example:

> A man had his toe healed by a serpent. He, suffering dreadfully from a malignant sore in his toe, during the daytime was taken outside by the servant of the Temple and set upon a seat; when sleep came upon him, then a snake issued from the abaton and healed the toe with its tongue, and thereafter went back again to the abaton. When the patient woke up and was healed he said that he had seen a vision: it seemed to him that a youth with a beautiful appearance had put a drug upon his toe.[59]

Another example shows how scepticism was deplored:

> Ambrosia of Athens, blind in one eye. She came as a supplicant to the god. As she walked about in the temple she laughed at some of the cures as incredible and impossible, that the lame and the blind should be healed by merely seeing a dream. In her sleep she had a vision. It seemed to her that the god stood by her and said he would cure her, but that in payment she must dedicate to the temple a silver pig as a memorial of her ignorance. After saying this, he cut her diseased eyeball and poured in some drug. When day came she walked out sound.[60]

---

[57] Y. Grandjean, *Une Nouvelle Arétologie D'Isis à Maronée* (Leiden: Brill, 1975).

[58] See the discussion in E.J. and L. Edelstein, *Asclepius: a Collection and Interpretation of the Testimonies,* vol. II (Baltimore: John Hopkins Press, 1945), 1-22.

[59] Edelstein, *Asclepius* I, 423, case 17.

[60] Edelstein, *Asclepius* I, 423, case 4.

In some cases the dreams depict such violent treatment that they must have seemed absolute nightmares. Case 23 relates that a woman's treatment involved her head being cut off and later replaced. Case 38 tells of a man with crippled knees. In a dream he sees himself taken outside the temple. The god yokes his horses to a chariot and, after circling round him three times, drives over him. The man gains instant control of his knees!

Presumably these testimonies were written up by the priests of the cult using evidence from those who claimed healing. Payment is mentioned in a number of them but charges were not exorbitant. 'A cock to Asclepius' became almost proverbial; such slight requirement ensuring the cult was popular with the poor.[61]

Asclepius was viewed as the patron of Greek medicine. Some of his temples were associated with a nearby medical school. Excavations at Cos have revealed an operating theatre with beams, levers, knives and apothecary equipment.[62] The cult spread all over the Greco-Roman world, reaching its zenith in the second century AD and posing a challenge to Christianity. By the third century the Church began to gain the upper hand.[63]

What is one to conclude about the alleged cures? The Edelsteins, noting the positive attitude to the cult of respected second-century physicians Rufus and Galen, declare this is 'ample proof of the actuality of the dreams and of the effectiveness of the cures'.[64] One suspects the situation was more complex, some of the cures being psychosomatic, some medical. The Church Fathers were forthright in their condemnation of the cult. Origen says that Asclepius' healings are probably not genuine but, if they are, they are due to evil spirits, assisted by 'Egyptian magic and spells'.[65] Arnobius contrasts the throngs of suppliants at Asclepius' temples who return home unhealed with Christ who healed all who came to him for help.[66] Eusebius defends Constantine's destruction of the temple of Aigai in Cilicia on the grounds that it had drawn people away from the true Saviour Christ into error.[67]

---

[61] Edelstein, *Asclepius* II, 116.
[62] See S.M. Sherwin-White, *Ancient Cos* (Göttingen: Van den Loeck & Ruprecht, 1978).
[63] Edelstein, *Asclepius*, ch. 6. When, for instance, the temple at Pergamum was destroyed by earthquakes between 253 and 260 it was not rebuilt.
[64] Edelstein, *Asclepius* II, 147.
[65] Origen, *Against Celsus* 3.24-25, 36; cf. Tatian, *Oration* 18.1-3, qu. below p. 53.
[66] Arnobius, *Against the Nations* 1.49.
[67] Eusebius, *Life of Constantine* 3.56.

Magic

R. Lane Fox cautions us from drawing a sharp line between practitioners of magic and the conventional cults:

> In antiquity magic was itself a religious ritual which worked on pagan divinities. It was not a separate technology, opposed to religious practice. To the ancients, magic was distinguished from respectable rites and prayers by the malevolence of its intentions and the murkiness of the materials which it used.[68]

Egypt was the reputed home of magic,[69] and its priests renowned for their ability to exorcise. Their procedure consisted of first an invocation of the god whose power they sought to harness. A string of names was often used to make the appeal effective. Then the demon was ordered (Gk. ὁρκίζω or ἐξορκίζω – 'I bind by oath') in the name of the god to come out of the person, a succession of sonorous nonsense syllables being added for effect. There was an accompanying ritual. Finally the cure was sealed by giving the delivered person an amulet (charm).[70] Much of our information comes from the Greek Magical Papyri (PGM) which date from the second century BC to the seventh century AD. Jewish elements are found throughout the collection, and Christian elements become common from the fourth century.[71] The most comprehensive collection of these papyri has been made by H.D. Betz.[72] Though comparatively little space in these manuscripts is devoted to

---

[68] R.L. Fox, *Pagans and Christians* (Harmondsworth: Penguin, 1986), 36.

[69] E.A.W. Budge, *Egyptian Magic* (London: Kegan Paul, 1901), though Herodotus (*History* 1.101) says that the word μαγεία (magic) was first used of the craft of the μάγοι (magi), one of the six tribes of Media, a priestly tribe, and Pliny declares magic undoubtedly arose in Persia with Zoroaster (*Nat. Hist.* 30.2). Undoubtedly Media-Persia was another ancient locus of magic. See Hull's discussion, *Hellenistic Magic*, ch. 3.

[70] For more details see Kee, *Medicine, Miracle and Magic*, ch. 4.

[71] See below my ch. 6, 'Magical Practices', no. 19, for an exorcistic text which clearly exhibits the procedure just outlined and which also incorporates Jewish and Christian elements. Whilst this text dates from the fourth century of our era it was probably adapted from earlier MSS (Hull, *Hellenistic Magic*, 20; Twelftree, *Name of Jesus*, 263).

[72] H.D. Betz, *The Greek Magic Papyri in Translation including the Demotic Spells* (Chicago: University Press, 1986, 1992). While Betz omits predominantly 'Christian' magical texts M. Meyer and R. Smith have published a collection of these principally from the fifth century and onwards as *Ancient Christian Magic: Coptic Texts of Ritual Power* (San Francisco: Harper, 1994).

exorcism or healing, PGM VII.193-214, 218-21 contains a list of twelve remedies for various physical ills: a scorpion's sting, discharge from the eyes, migraine headache (2 cures), coughs (3 cures), hardening of the breasts, swollen testicles, and fevers (3 cures). The remedies are stated briefly and without any reference to demons or exorcism. Four are explicitly said to be amulets but, as five more require the writing of magical characters on a piece of papyrus, parchment, rag or olive leaf, sometimes specifying that this then be placed on the affected part of the body, these too are clearly intended as such. Of the remaining cases, two involve the use of oil:

> For migraine headache: Take oil in your hands and utter the spell,
> "Zeus sowed a grape seed: it parts the soil;
> he does not sow it; it does not sprout." (199-201)

> For fever with shivering fits: Take oil in your hands and say seven times,
> "Sabaoth" (add the usual, twice).
> And spread on oil from the sacrum to the feet. (211-12)

Clearly oil is viewed here as a healing agent (symbolically at least) and, combined with a powerful divine name, is expected to produce results. The final cure involves the knotting of a cord with the utterance of 'Kastor' (Castor, son of Zeus?) and 'Thab' (an Egyptian deity?).

Whilst a scorpion's sting could scarcely be attributed to a demon resident in the victim (and the cure by applying an inscribed parchment appears today ridiculous), fever was certainly viewed then as of demonic origin,[73] and so headache and perhaps the other ailments referred to could be similarly attributed.

The range of physical ills for which these magical cures are offered is somewhat limited. Betz includes a few more spells against fever and headache later in his collection of magical papyri,[74] but for broken bones and many other physical conditions none are prescribed. These may well have been left to medical treatment.

Jews had been in Egypt since at least the sixth century BC, when the remnant of the kingdom of Judah not exiled to Babylon fled there, taking with them the unwilling prophet Jeremiah.[75] They evidently prospered for, by the first century AD, two out of the five quarters of

---

[73] There were numerous categories of fever spirits in the ancient world, see Hull, *Hellenistic Magic*, 102.

[74] PGM CXV.1-7, CXIXb.1-5, CXXVIII (against fever); CXXII.53-56 (against headache).

[75] Jer.43:4-7.

Alexandria were predominantly Jewish.[76] Magic, though explicitly forbidden by the Torah,[77] had been practiced in Israel[78] but now, in the cultural milieu of Egypt (and indeed in the Hellenistic world beyond), Jews developed a considerable reputation for their magical practices.[79] The account given by Josephus of a late first-century exorcism seems to bear this out. Josephus is supplementing the biblical information about Solomon, telling of his esoteric powers:

> And God granted him knowledge of the art used against demons for the benefit and healing of men. He also composed incantations by which illnesses are relieved, and left behind forms of exorcisms with which those possessed by demons drive them out, never to return. And this kind of cure is of very great power among us to this day, for I have seen a certain Eleazar, a countryman of mine, in the presence of Vespasian, his sons, tribunes and a number of other soldiers, free men possessed by demons, and this was the manner of the cure: he put to the nose of the possessed man a ring which had under its seal one of the roots, prescribed by Solomon and then, as the man smelled it, drew out the demon through his nostrils, and, when the man at once fell down, adjured the demon never to come back into him, speaking Solomon's name and reciting the incantations which he had composed. Then wishing to convince the bystanders and prove to them that he had this power, Eleazar placed a cup or foot basin full of water a little way off and commanded the demon, as it went out of the man, to overturn it and make known to the spectators that he had left the man. And when this was done the understanding and wisdom of Solomon were clearly revealed... (*Jewish Antiquities* 8.45-9)

A considerable literature grew up attributing to Solomon (and indeed Moses) esoteric powers,[80] enabling Jews to use at least quasi-magical techniques with a clear conscience. The novelistic document the *Testament of Solomon* (Christianized now but presumably from a Jewish original)[81] says that a ring was given to Solomon by God after prayer, and that it had the power to control the demons led by Beelzeboul, who were trying to disrupt the building of the temple. It had a seal engraved on precious stone. The root referred to is presumably *baaras* which Josephus says, in his *Jewish War* 7.180-5, has the power to expel 'so-

---

[76] Cf. W.H.C. Frend, *The Rise of Christianity* (Philadelphia: Fortress Press, 1984), 34.

[77] Dt.18:9-14, cf. Ex.22:18, Lev.19:31, 20:27.

[78] 2 Ki.21:6, Is.3:3, Jer.27:9, Ezek.13:18-19 *et passim*.

[79] Pliny, *Nat. Hist.* 30.2.

[80] See M.E. Mills, *Human Agents of Cosmic Power in Hellenistic Judaism and the Synoptic Tradition* (Sheffield: Academic Press, 1990), chs. 3, 4.

[81] *Ibid.*, ch.4.

called demons' which are 'the spirits of wicked men' that can possess and kill the living unless help is forthcoming.

In the light of all this it is not so surprising to hear Justin Martyr saying in the mid-second century that, besides invoking the 'God of Abraham, God of Isaac, God of Jacob', Jewish exorcists employ incense and spells just like their Gentile counterparts.[82]

Medicine

As the ancient Greeks developed philosophy, mathematics and the arts, so also they developed medicine. Against the popular belief that health and sickness were in the hands of the gods (or demons) material means were developed for alleviating sickness, showing that in practice it was viewed as having natural causes which could be treated. As early as the fifth century BC surgery, pharmacology and regimen (dietary control) were all practiced.[83] The first great figure of medical history is Hippocrates, well-known to Plato, who saw him as a philosopher who sought to understand the human body as a whole organism.[84] A large quantity of amorphous medical literature was attributed to him from which, in the second century of our era, Galen attempted to draw out a unified philosophy:

> To the four elements and their respective qualities: fire (warm), water (cold), earth (dry) and air (moist) there correspond in the human body four 'humours': gall or yellow bile (warm and dry), phlegm (cold and moist), black bile (cold and dry) and blood (warm and moist). In a healthy body the humours and their qualities are correctly proportioned. By disease the proportion is upset. Hippocratic therapy sought, through diet and drugs, to correct the imbalance according to the principle 'contraries are cured by contraries'. Thus, for example, a cold moist condition was treated with what was considered warm and dry. Normality was viewed as being 'according to nature', abnormality as 'contrary to nature'. Hippocrates taught in addition that climate and seasons are determining factors in the incidence of sickness and that the air can carry disease and spread epidemics. The Hippocratic surgeon relied on anatomical knowledge but he was more concerned with bones than soft tissue. Some Hippocratic practitioners, known as the Dogmatists, held rigidly to the

---

[82] *Dialogue with Trypho*, 85.3.

[83] O. Temkin, *Hippocrates in a World of Pagans and Christians* (Baltimore: John Hopkins Press, 1991), 10.

[84] Plato, *Phaedrus* 270 C-D.

philosophy of the humours, others, the 'Empiricists', looked more at practical considerations such as hunger, cold and lack of sleep.[85]

From the foundation of the Museum or Royal Academy there by Ptolemy I in the third century BC, Alexandria became the foremost centre in antiquity for the study of medicine.[86] Regular dissections were for a while performed there upon live human beings - criminals, whose lives were thought to be expendable! But, before long, Alexandrian medicine became split into competing sects, each dedicated to its founder and his particular philosophy. Their quarrels only served to hinder the advance of knowledge.

Most Hippocratic physicians were aware of the limitations of their art and would allow prayer and, believing in the divine origin of dreams, 'incubations' (sleeping in temples) for chronic cases when their art proved ineffectual.[87]

The Romans distrusted the theoretical side of Greek medicine and it gained ground only slowly among them. They tended to lampoon physicians, amongst whom admittedly there was much quackery and ignorance.[88] Their greatest contributions to maintaining health came from their practical bent. They built public baths with well-drained latrines; they appreciated the value of good ventilation, and constructed aqueducts for transporting pure water over long distances; for sick soldiers they built *valetudinaria* (elementary hospitals). The remains of surgeons' shops have been found with various medical instruments, for surgery was widely practised, but without anaesthetics. Tools were made of iron or, better, copper as advocated by Hippocrates. But with regard to anatomy, it seems, the Roman physician learnt largely by experience.

In the Old Testament indications of a medical profession are very slight indeed. It was the priest to whom anyone with a 'leprous' skin condition must resort, and no medical treatment was prescribed (Lev.13-14). Sickness was seen as God's punishment for sin;[89] he alone was the source of all healing[90] and for it he must be approached with repentance and prayer. In 2 Chronicles 16:11-12 King Asa is disparaged for turning

---

[85] This is my summary based on Temkin, *Hippocrates*, ch. 2.

[86] E.D. Phillips, *Greek Medicine* (London: Thames & Hudson, 1973), ch. 6 provides a useful survey of its work.

[87] L. Edelstein, 'Greek Medicine in its Relation to Religion and Magic' in *Ancient Medicine: Selected Papers of Ludwig Edelstein*, ed. O. and C.L. Temkin, tr. C.L. Temkin (Baltimore: John Hopkins Press, 1967), 239-45.

[88] J. Scarborough, *Roman Medicine* (London Thames & Hudson, 1969), ch. 7.

[89] Lev.26:14-16, Dt.28:15, 21-22, 27-28, Num.25:1-9 *et passim*.

[90] Ex.15:25-26, Dt.32:39.

to physicians rather than to God. However, by the early second century BC, influenced no doubt by Hellenism, Ben Sirach is urging his Jewish readership to honour the physician and not to despise medicines used by the pharmacist, for the Lord created them. While the sick person must pray, repent of his sins, and offer sacrifice, the physician too will be praying to God in order to make a correct diagnosis (Ecclus.38:1-14). Evidently Jews did avail themselves of medical help. We know this from the story of the woman with the twelve-year haemorrhage who approached Jesus (Mk.5:26) but also from the fragmentary remains of a report by a health officer found among the Qumran documents. It is now known as *4Q Therapeia* and dates probably from AD 30-50. In it Greek medical terms are transliterated into Hebrew.[91] It may well be then that, by the time of Jesus, all Jews who could afford it freely resorted to such medical assistance as they could find.

General Conclusion

Against this general background of healing in antiquity it is easier to appreciate the impact of Jesus' healing ministry. According to the gospel record, unlike physicians, he offered no questionable course of treatment, and provided almost invariably instant cures free of charge. Unlike magicians, he coerced no reluctant powers into his service, and his activities were beneficent not malicious. Unlike the healing cults, distant and forbidden anyway to pious Jews, it appears no-one returned from him uncured. In contrast to other Jewish exorcists, he required no aids in his exorcisms, achieving effective results simply by word of command. It is unlikely then that the evangelist is exaggerating when we hear Jesus' spectators crying out in wonder, "We never saw anything like this!"[92] And Jesus is quickly compared with Elijah[93] though, in the number and scope of miracles he is reported to have performed, he had no peer in antiquity.

According to the gospel record, on occasion he shared his power to exorcise and heal with his disciples.[94] Nearing the end of his ministry he declared that they would do the same or even greater works of power than he, and encouraged them to pray to the Father in his name and expect their prayers would be answered.[95] Why then do Matthew[96] and

---

[91] A translation of the fragment and a conjectural reconstruction of the whole report by J.H. Charlesworth are to be found in an appendix to Kee, *Medicine, Miracle and Magic.*
[92] Mk.2:12 *et passim.*
[93] Mk.6:15, 8:28, cf. 1 Ki.17-18.
[94] Mk.6:7, 13, Lk.10:9.
[95] Jn.14:12.

Luke,[97] in their accounts of his Great Commission to them to evangelize the world, make no mention of miracles? It seems to be their way of stressing that, as in Jesus' ministry,[98] miraculous works must be subordinated to the proclamation of the word.[99]

---

[96] Mt.28:18-20.

[97] Ac.1:8, cf. Lk.24:44-49.

[98] Mk.1:38-39, Jn.14:11.

[99] Though Twelftree seems to make a fair point when he says that 'keep everything that I have commanded you' (Mt.28:20) would surely include what Jesus had *practised*, including exorcism (*Name of Jesus*, 160). If so, it would of course embrace all his healing work.

CHAPTER 2

The Era of the Apostles

The Acts of the Apostles

It has been argued that the Acts of the Apostles must have been written before AD 64[1] since it does not record the death of the apostle Paul. Scholarly consensus today, however, favours a later date, AD 80-90,[2] to allow Luke's Gospel to be written first. For the present study it matters little. Of considerably more importance is assessing the historical value of Acts. M. Dibelius considered that in Acts Luke just put forward what he felt to be typical, altering and generalizing what really happened.[3] In his influential commentary E. Haenchen declares that he thinks Luke largely invented the miracles he attributes to Paul to show the Gentile mission was according to God's will.[4] But, on the contrary, Paul's own references to his work as an apostle (Rom.15:18-19, 2 Cor.12:12) imply that everywhere he went he both preached and performed miracles – an impression reflected in the narrative of Acts.

While one must allow Luke's creative hand, to some extent, in the sermons in Acts, it would be extraordinary if his general approach in his second book diverged markedly from that in his gospel. As in the gospel he relied on eye-witnesses and preachers of the word (the apostles themselves?) and sought to report events accurately and in order (Lk.1:1-3) so we should expect he was concerned with accuracy in Acts.

---

[1] F.F. Bruce, *Commentary on the Book of Acts* (London: Marshall, Morgan & Scott, 1954), 22.

[2] Bruce, *Acts of the Apostles: the Greek Text with Introduction and Commentary*, 3rd edn. (Grand Rapids, MI: Eerdmans, 1990), 18; E. Haenchen, *The Acts of the Apostles: a Commentary*, tr. from the 14th German edn. (Oxford: University Press, 1971), 86.

[3] M. Dibelius, *Studies in the Acts of the Apostles,* ed. H. Greeven, tr. from German (London: SCM, 1956), 136-37.

[4] Haenchen, *Acts*, 113.

Confirmation for this has come from Sir William Ramsay[5] who, from archaeological discoveries in Asia Minor, verified Luke's use of official titles; from H.J. Cadbury,[6] who noted his precision in stating geographical locations; and from A.N. Sherwin-White,[7] who has affirmed his knowledge of the intricacies of Roman law. It appears from Col.4:14, Phmn.24 and the 'we' sections[8] of Acts that Luke was a close associate of Paul. He must have obtained much information direct from him. For the rest, where he had no access to the people he mentions, he may well have visited the churches with which they were associated to glean information.[9] We may surely assume, then, that there is historical value in the miracle stories of Acts.[10] As Jesus was first empowered by the Holy Spirit at his baptism and then began his powerful preaching and healing ministry (Lk.3:21-2, 4:14-15), so the Holy Spirit was the source of spiritual power of the apostles and the wider Church (Acts 1:8).

Eight healing stories, including one of exorcism and two of raising the dead, are described in some detail. There is also the incident where Paul, bitten by a viper, does not die (28:1-6). In addition there are seven healing summaries and four punishment miracles which result in the discomfort or death of the individuals concerned.

Scholars have noted various parallels between miracles attributed by Luke in the gospel to Jesus and in Acts to Peter, and again within Acts between those of Peter and Paul.[11] The implication is that Luke sees in Peter's ministry some reflection of the ministry of Jesus, and in the experiences of the 'Apostle to the Gentiles' God's rich blessing in like measure to that experienced by the 'Apostle to the Jews'.[12]

---

[5] Sir William Ramsay, *The Bearing of Recent Discovery on the Trustworthiness of the New Testament* (London: Hodder, 1915), 96-97, ch. 7.

[6] H.J. Cadbury, *The Making of Luke-Acts*, 2nd edn. (London: SPCK, 1958), ch. 17, though the author is qualified in his acceptance of their historicity in some cases.

[7] A.N. Sherwin-White, *Roman Society and Roman Law in the New Testament* (Oxford: University Press, 1963).

[8] Ac.16:10-17, 20:5-21:18, 27:1-28:16.

[9] Cf. Haenchen, *Acts*, 86.

[10] For further consideration of the historicity of the Acts narratives see I.H. Marshall, *Luke: Historian and Theologian* (Grand Rapids, MI: Zondervan, 1970), 67-76.

[11] See G.W.H. Lampe, 'Miracles in the Acts of the Apostles' in *Miracles*, ed. C.F.D. Moule (London: Mowbray, 1965), 175-78.

[12] Cf. Gal.2:6-10.

Exorcism

The only exorcism recounted is in 16:16-18. It took place at Philippi on Paul's second great missionary journey (c. AD 50), and is part of a 'we' passage. Paul and his companions are going to a place of prayer by the river outside the city, when they are accosted by a slave-girl possessed by a 'pythonic spirit' (πνεῦμα πύθωνα),[13] a spirit associated in the Hellenistic world with oracles and ventriloquism.[14] Like the spirits who recognised Jesus' identity (Mk.1:24, 5:7), this one recognises their spiritual status and cries out, "These men are servants of the Most High God, who proclaim to you a way of salvation." This happens day after day and eventually Paul can tolerate it no longer and, like Jesus (only in the name of Jesus), turns and says to the spirit, "I command you in the name of Jesus Christ to come out of her", with immediate effect. Since her fortune-telling abilities, and hence her owners' lucrative trade, are gone Paul and Silas are accused of anti-Roman practices, beaten and put in gaol. The conversion of the Philippian gaoler and his family is the beneficial outcome.

Healings

(1) In 3:1-10 a miracle is recorded from the earliest days of the Church. Peter and John are going into the temple to pray and, as they come to the gate called Beautiful, a beggar, lame from birth, asks for alms. Peter, telling him to look at them, confesses he has no money but what he has he will give. Then he commands, "In the name of Jesus Christ of Nazareth, walk." He gives him a helping hand and the man leaps up healed. Then, walking, and leaping, and praising God he accompanies them into the temple. The onlookers are awed.

G.W.H. Lampe[15] sees this story as a fulfilment of the prophecy of the new age in Is.35:6. He and others have seen in it a parallel to Jesus' healing of the paralytic let down through the roof (Lk.5:18-26). Like Jesus (only in the name of Jesus) Peter issues a simple, direct command to walk. The man's healing is attributed to faith in Jesus (v.16). The

---

[13] Such people were believed to have supernatural prophetic powers by virtue of being possessed by the Greek god Apollo embodied, it was believed, in a snake at the oracular centre at Delphi (Bruce, *Acts* (1990), 360; cf. Twelftree, *Name of Jesus*, 146).

[14] Cf. Plutarch, *Obsolescence of the Oracles*, 414e.

[15] Lampe, 'Miracles', 174.

outcome of the miracle is the gathering of a considerable crowd to hear Peter preach (vv.11-12).

(2) In 9:17-19 Saul (Paul), who has been blinded for three days as a result of his encounter with the heavenly Christ on the road to Damascus, has fasted for three day. Ananias, a disciple specially commissioned in a vision by Christ, comes to him, lays his hands on him that he may regain his sight and be filled with the Holy Spirit. Immediately something like scales falls from his eyes and he regains his sight. He rises and is baptized.

This brief account shows how one who is not a church official could heal after a vision and commission by Christ. The healing is connected with the laying on of hands. That Paul should also receive the Holy Spirit implies that, after his encounter with Christ, in a period of reflection he has come to repentance and faith. He is certainly ready for baptism, which is administered forthwith. This is the first instance of healing accompanying Christian conversion.

(3) 9:32-35 tells of Peter at Lydda healing Aeneas, a man paralyzed and bed-ridden for eight years. He instructs him, "Aeneas, Jesus Christ heals you; rise and make your bed." He gets up at once. The residents of Lydda and Sharon turn to the Lord.

Again we see a simple, direct command given to the sick man on the basis that Jesus Christ is healing him. Aeneas shows faith in obeying. The miracle engenders faith in many more people.

(4)14:8-20 relates a healing during Paul's first great missionary journey. While Paul is preaching at Lystra in Galatia he sees a man, crippled from birth, listening. He detects he has the faith to be healed (Gk. σωθῆναι, 'saved', indicating perhaps spiritual as well as physical healing[16]) and commands in a loud voice, "Stand upright on your feet." He springs up and walks. The crowd concludes the gods Hermes and Zeus have visited them.

This may be the Pauline equivalent to the Petrine healing in Acts 3, but the story is very different. This time faith in the recipient is actually mentioned as a precondition of the healing. Again a simple, direct

---

[16] Cf. Lk.8:48, Ac.16:31.

command is made and obeyed with immediate results. Surprisingly any reference to the name of Jesus is absent,[17] but perhaps this is because the healing took place within the context of preaching. The dramatic impact of the healing suggests that such a miracle was highly exceptional, perhaps unique. The observers' false interpretation of it shows that miracles were not always an asset to evangelism. Archaeologists have in fact discovered the combination of Zeus and Hermes in local dedications.[18]

(5) The last healing story, in 28:7-10, occurs on Malta where Paul, his
   fellow passengers and the crew of the ship that carried them have
   been shipwrecked. They are entertained by Publius, the chief man of
   the island. His father is sick with fever and dysentery and Paul prays,
   lays his hands on him and heals him. The rest of the sick on the
   island are brought to Paul and healed. They show great gratitude.

This is part of a 'we' passage, indicating Luke has witnessed what has happened. It appears to be an abbreviated account, for only one of many healings is described. Nevertheless we see Paul employing the laying on of hands. As in the case of Jesus, one healing leads to requests for many more (cf. Mk.1:32-34).

Raising the Dead

(1) In 9:36-43 we hear of the raising of Tabitha, a woman noted for her
   charitable acts, at Joppa (present-day Jaffa). Peter, at nearby Lydda,
   is sent for. When he comes he puts the mourners out of the room,
   kneels and prays; then turning to the prone figure says, "Tabitha,
   rise." She sits up. He gives her a hand and lifts her up. What has
   happened becomes known throughout Joppa and many become
   believers.

This moving story has obvious parallels to the raising of Jairus' daughter. Like Jesus, Peter excludes the crowd of mourners; like Jesus he addresses a short, direct command to the dead person. The parallel is so close that Morton Smith claims the later story is merely a variant of the earlier one with 'Tabitha' a mispronunciation of *talitha*.[19] But the

---

[17] Though Codex Bezae (D) and a few other MSS add the words: "I say to you in the name of the Lord Jesus Christ."

[18] Bruce, *Acts* (1990), 323-24.

[19] Morton Smith, *Jesus the Magician*, 95.

overall stories are very different, and the verbal similarity of the command is not with the Lucan account of the earlier story but with the Aramaic of the Marcan account, ταλιθα κουμ ("little girl, get up", Mk.5.41). Tabitha (a person's name meaning 'gazelle') is not a little girl but a grown woman. It is quite surprising to read that Peter did not command 'in the name of Jesus Christ' but, unlike Jesus, he knelt down and prayed first. This is the only request in Acts for an apostle (or anyone else) to travel to raise someone dead and we may perhaps infer that the death was premature. It was also, as in the gospel cases, recent. Clearly the miracle aided the work of evangelism in that area.

(2) 20:7-12 relates Paul's bringing back to life the young man Eutychus at Troas. It is the last night before Paul is leaving on his way to Jerusalem and he does not expect to return (cf. v.25). The believers have met for the 'breaking of bread' and Paul talks on and on. Eutychus sinks into a deep sleep and falls from a third-floor window to the ground outside, being 'taken up dead'. Paul throws himself upon the lifeless figure and, embracing him, declares he is alive. After daybreak, when the gathering breaks up, the youth is taken away alive.

This story again comes from a 'we' passage, indicating Luke's presence. The implication in the account is that the youth really was killed by his fall.[20] Reflecting to some degree Elijah (1K.17:21) and Elisha (2K.4:34) in similar circumstances, Paul lies upon the prone figure and embraces him, then declares him alive. This is certainly a departure from the methods used in the gospel raisings perhaps due to the fact that Paul, unlike Peter, had not witnessed Jesus' approach.

Summaries of Healings

The six summaries in Acts attribute healings only to the apostles and to two of the Seven 'deacons' (6:5). This may be the result of Luke's general historiographical approach in writing Acts, i.e. focusing almost entirely on the activities of selected leading figures in the Church. Alternatively, healing may really have been left in the earliest days to those who most intimately observed Jesus' own miracles and a few others. Without further corroboration we cannot decide, though, judging by Paul's reference elsewhere to performing the 'signs of a true apostle'

---

[20]   Bruce, *Acts* (1990), 426; Haenchen, *Acts*, 585.

(2 Cor.12:12), it seems likely that apostles particularly *were* characterised by the performing of miracles.

It is the apostles alone to whom 'wonders and signs' are attributed after the conversion of about 3,000 in Jerusalem, following Peter's Pentecost sermon (2:43), and again after the demise of Ananias and Sapphira (5:12). Peter's activities resemble those of his Master. As Jesus attracted the sick from a wide area, and even touching the hem of his robe was enough to heal them (Mk.6:55-6) so, many from Jerusalem and the surrounding towns brought the sick, bed-ridden and those tormented by unclean spirits and laid them in the streets so that even Peter's shadow might fall on them, and they were healed (5:15-16). In the ancient world it was believed that a person's shadow conveyed his life-force.[21] Lampe recalls that 'overshadow' was used of Jesus in Lk.1:35, 9:34 and signifies divine presence and power,[22] but some see in the phenomenon a 'magical trace'.[23]

Stephen, the first of the Seven, described as 'a man full of faith and of the Holy Spirit' (Ac.6:5) and 'full of grace and power' (v.8) also performs great 'wonders and signs' among the people of Jerusalem.

After the persecution of the Church following the death of Stephen, when all but the apostles were driven from Jerusalem (8:1), Philip, the second of the Seven, went to Samaria and there, besides preaching, performed great 'signs'. Many unclean spirits came out of people, crying loudly, and many paralyzed and lame were healed. It made a great impression on the people of Samaria and many were baptized, including Simon Magus (8:4-13). But 'conversion' based on miracles proved inadequate, and the Holy Spirit was withheld until the subsequent ministry of the apostles Peter and John (8:14-24).

Later, like Peter in Jerusalem, Paul in Ephesus is seen to have a uniquely powerful healing ministry, so that sweat bands that had been tied round his head, and aprons[24] tied round his waist (whilst tent-making perhaps) were carried to the sick and to those with evil spirits and they were cured (19:11-12). In the ancient world a person's clothing

---

[21] Twelftree, *Name of Jesus*, 143.

[22] Lampe, 'Miracles', 175.

[23] Kee, *Miracle*, 215.

[24] Bruce, *Acts* (1990), 426. J.C. Thomas points out that 'apron' (σιμικίνθια) might be better rendered 'belt', *The Devil, Disease and Deliverance: Origins of Illness in New Testament Thought* (Sheffield: University Press, 1998), 281 nt. 234.

was believed to be imbued with its wearer's authority and power.[25] Paul, then, in his own way matches Peter (5:15-16), and follows in the steps of his Master (Mk.6:55-56). Here again some see magical traces.[26]

Miracles of Punishment

The deaths of Ananias and Sapphira (5:1-11) and the blinding of Saul (9:8) and the magician Elymas (13:11) are examples of judgement upon sin or misguided zeal. The battering of the Jewish exorcists (19:14-17) illustrates the danger of attempting to exorcise in the powerful name of Jesus without true faith in him. This apart, nowhere in Acts is sickness directly attributed to demonic activity.[27]

The Pauline Letters

Though Paul's references to his performing miracles are few, this does not mean miracles were insignificant in his ministry. In 2 Cor.12:12, declaring that he had performed the 'signs of a true apostle' during his missionary work at Corinth, he uses no less than three terms for miracle: 'signs', 'wonders' and '(works of) power'.[28] Again, summarizing his apostolic ministry *as a whole* in Rom.15:18-19, he declares that from Jerusalem as far round as Illyricum (now within the Balkan States) he has preached the Gospel of Christ, endeavouring to win obedience from the Gentiles by word and by signs and wonders in the power of the Holy Spirit.

It is evident too that his converts also performed miracles. "Does he who supplies the Spirit to you, and works (acts of) power among you do so by works of the law or by hearing with faith?" he demands of the Galatians (Gal.3:5). The present tenses imply this is a current phenomenon, or one that was so until the Galatians were led astray.

---

[25]   Cf. 1 Ki.19:19, 2 Ki.2:8, 14; Twelftree, *Name of Jesus*, 148-49.

[26]   Kee, *Miracle*, 215; Hull, *Hellenistic Magic*, 111.

[27]   Thomas makes the point that even 10:38 may not be an exception here, for 'doing good' may mean specifically healing the sick (cf. 4:9) and 'those oppressed by the devil' may be restricted to demonic activity. Luke uses 'heal' of exorcism elsewhere (Lk.6:18, 7:21, 9:42), *Devil*, 260-61.

[28]   Σημείοις καὶ τέρασιν καὶ δυνάμεσιν. Twelftree convincingly argues that references to 'power' as distinguished from 'word' or 'wisdom' in 1 Thess.1:5, 1 Cor.2:4-5, 4:20 also point to the performing of miracles (including exorcism), and that Paul's whole ministry can aptly be described as one of 'word and deed' (*Name of Jesus*, 69-71).

The performance of miracles by ordinary members of a Pauline church is made quite explicit in 1 Corinthians. Among the gifts of the Spirit conferred on members of the church are 'gifts of healings' (Gk. χαρίσματα ἰαμάτων) and 'workings of powers' (ἐνεργήματα δυνάμεων) – 1 Cor.12:9-10. Later, in the list of ministries in the Church, these two are mentioned again, in reverse order, just below the ranks of apostle, prophet and teacher (12:29-30), clearly showing that these supernatural abilities were not confined to the apostles. A *charisma* is that which is given by the grace (χάρις) of God. Ἐνέργημα here seems not to be of a different nature, but just a variant used to relieve stylistic monotony (cf.12:4-6) and stresses the practical outworking of miracles.

Robertson and Plummer comment on the phrase 'gifts of healings', 'The plur. seems to imply that different persons each had a disease or group of diseases that they could cure'.[29] But, as Thomas[30] points out, the singular 'to another' (v.9) suggests one person might cure various sicknesses. G.D. Fee comes to a different conclusion: the plural 'gifts' suggests not a permanent gift but that each healing occasion is a gift in its own right, and he quotes Bittlinger: 'Every healing is a special gift. In this way the spiritually gifted individual stands always in new dependence upon the divine Giver'.[31] If, however, prophecy and tongues were quasi-permanent gifts, why not also the ability to perform healings and other miracles? Such gifts would surely be exercised within the medium of prayer and faith. This is not to deny that other, perhaps lesser healings, might come as a result of any Christian's prayer. A.C. Thiselton suggests that 'the workings of powers' need not be confined to the miraculous, and he points to the belief of various Church Fathers that this category includes punishment miracles (cf. Ac.5:1-11) and the power to cast out demons.[32] Twelftree thinks exorcisms are not included because 1 Cor.12 is concerned with ministry

---

[29] A. Robertson and A. Plummer, *A Critical and Exegetical Commentary on the First Epistle of St. Paul to the Corinthians*, 2nd edn. (Edinburgh: T& T Clark, 1914), 266.

[30] *Devil,* 40. A.C. Thiselton thinks ἐνεργήματα δυνάμεων refers to 'various kinds of healing' embracing sudden or gradual cures of physical, psychosomatic and mental states, by the use of medical or more directly 'divine' healing – *1 Corinthians: A Commentary on the Greek Text* (Grand Rapids, MI: Eerdmans, 2000), 946-48.

[31] G.D. Fee, *The First Epistle to the Corinthians* (Grand Rapids, MI: Eerdmans, 1987), 594.

[32] Thiselton, *I Corinthians*, 952-53.

to those *within* the church, whilst the possessed are *outside* it.[33]
However, a further gift 'distinguishing between spirits' (διακρίσεις
πνευμάτων) referred to in v.10 is surely a preliminary to exorcism.[34]
Moreover there are a number of references in the patristic literature to
Christians being possessed by evil spirits.[35]

But signs and wonders are not the monopoly of true Christians. In the
last times, Paul says, the coming of the agent of Satan, the lawless one,
will be marked with deceptive (works of) power, signs and wonders (2
Thess.2:9).

Moreover, the Pauline letters reveal that Christians, even in apostolic
times, were not immune from sickness. We hear of Epaphroditus ill
almost to the point of death,[36] Trophimus left ill at Miletus[37] and
Timothy urged to take a little wine to settle his stomach and deal with
his frequent ailments.[38] Paul himself whom, to endure the rigours of his
missionary life, we might expect to have a tough constitution, reminds
the Galatians that it was because of a bodily ailment[39] that he first came
to them with the Gospel. Some have suggested he had some sort of eye
defect because he goes on to say that they would have been prepared to
take out their eyes and give them to him, but perhaps this means no
more than that their devotion would have stopped at nothing.[40] Of
particular interest is 2 Cor.12:7-9 where the apostle tells of a 'thorn in
the flesh'[41] which, linking the evil one with sickness, he also calls a
'messenger of Satan' sent to beat him lest he become arrogant from the
visions and revelations he has received (v.1). Three times he prayed for
deliverance from it, without success, instead he received the message
from the Lord (presumably Jesus): "My grace is sufficient for you, for
(my) power is made perfect in weakness." Some have suggested he

---

[33] Twelftree, *Name of Jesus*, 75.
[34] For an extended discussion of this phrase see Thiselton, *1 Corinthians*, 965-
      70.
[35] Perhaps most notably Tertullian's story of the Christian woman who went to
      the theatre and became possessed (*Shows* 26.1-2).
[36] Phil.2:25-30.
[37] 2 Tim.4:20.
[38] 1 Tim.5:23.
[39] Δι' ἀσθένειαν τῆς σαρκός (lit. 'through a weakness of the flesh'), Gal.4:13.
[40] Cf. R.Y.K. Fung, The Epistle to the Galatians (Grand Rapids, MI: Eerdmans,
      1988), 199.
[41] Σκόλοψ 'stake', then 'thorn, splinter', Bauer.

suffered from epilepsy, but in reality there is no indication of the nature of his affliction or even that it was physical.[42]

The epistles show Paul's firm belief in demons, which he mentions as closely involved in idolatry. To eat food that had been offered to idols he declares is to 'partake of the table of demons' (1 Cor.10:14-22). He does not mention demons in connection with sickness (apart from the 'messenger of Satan' we have considered), indeed he attributes weakness and death in the church of Corinth to the sin of eucharistic abuse (1 Cor.11:29-30). In Ephesians and Colossians he speaks of a whole range of malignant spiritual powers: 'chiefs', 'authorities', 'world rulers of darkness', 'wicked spiritual forces', which live in heavenly places (Eph.6:12).[43] To resist their attacks, he warns, the Christian must be clad in the whole armour of God (vv.13-18). These powers were once created through Christ (Col.1:16) and later, presumably since they had turned malevolent, were disarmed and defeated by Christ on the cross (Col.2:15), and will ultimately be destroyed (1 Cor.15:24).

The Epistle to the Hebrews

The author, whose identity remains uncertain,[44] was a second-generation Christian (2:3), apparently a Hellenistic Jew, perhaps writing from Rome.[45] As his argument so much involves Jewish religious institutions (though of the tabernacle rather than the temple), it would be surprising for him to omit all references to the national tragedy of AD 70 had he written after that date. In 2:4 he speaks of the Gospel's being declared to him and his contemporaries by those who had heard Jesus, and their message being confirmed by signs, wonders, a variety[46] of acts of power, and by distributions[47] of the Holy Spirit according to his will. Whilst the phraseology is different the thoughts are the same as Paul's:

---

[42] C.K. Barrett, *A Commentary on the Second Epistle to the Corinthians* (London: A & C Black, 1973), 315.

[43] The στοιχεῖα τοῦ κόσμου (lit. 'elements of the world') he mentions in Gal.4:3, 9 and Col.2:8, 20 may be further planetary spirit beings (see Bauer).

[44] Cf. C.K. Barrett, *A Commentary on the First Epistle to the Corinthians* (London: A & C Black, 1968), 10.

[45] F.F. Bruce, *The Epistle to the Hebrews* (Grand Rapids, MI: Eerdmans, 1964), 415.

[46] Ποικίλαις, 'various kinds' (Bauer).

[47] Μερισμός, 'distribution, apportionment' (Bauer).

the same three words relating to miracles as in 2 Cor.12:12 and the same message that Holy Spirit spreads around gifts (in the Church) as he wills (cf. 1 Cor.12:4, 7, 11). Clearly the author is much influenced by the apostle.

The Epistle of James

This letter is clearly a product of early Judaeo-Christianity.[48] It breathes an atmosphere far removed from charismatic Pauline Christianity; indeed it ignores the central matters of Christian doctrine: the death and resurrection of Christ, and the Holy Spirit, concentrating rather on the ethical matters of practical Christian living. While earlier scholarship[49] saw echoes of it in the writings of a number of early patristic writers, a more cautious evaluation suggests only Hermas (in Rome) in the second century knew it.[50] In the third century it is attested by Origen, who refers to it as 'the epistle of James which is current',[51] and it is quoted several times in the Pseudo-Clementine *First Epistle to Virgins,* once as 'Scripture'.[52] But, as the author of that work proceeds to ignore James 5:14-15 with its reference to the role of elders in healing, preferring to talk at length instead about lay gifts of healing, clearly he does not regard it as of over-riding authority.[53] Eusebius in *H.E.* 3.25.3[54] (c.AD 300) places it first among the 'disputed' books of the New Testament, along with Jude, 2 Peter and 2 and 3 John, because of its paucity of early citation. Later it won general acceptance.

Today it tends to be viewed as a pseudonymous work[55] or perhaps the work of a disciple of James editing his master's teaching.[56] To accept its traditional authorship one might surmise that its association with

---

[48] Jews who received Christian baptism and believed Jesus to be the promised Messiah, but who otherwise continued to live according to the Jewish Law and customs (cf. 1:1, 2:8-13, 4:11-12).

[49] J.B. Mayor, *The Epistle of St. James*, 2nd edn. (London: Macmillan, 1987).

[50] S. Laws, *Commentary on the Epistle of James* (London: A & C Black, 1980), 20-23.

[51] *Comm. Jn.* 19.152; cf. *Hom. Lev.* 2.4.5 qu. Jas.5:15.

[52] *Ep.* 1.11.

[53] The fact that he does not name the author is not significant. It is his usual practice to quote NT epistles without acknowledgement.

[54] Cf. 2.23.24-25.

[55] Laws, *James*, 41.

[56] R.P. Martin, *Word Biblical Commentary*, Volume 48: *James* (Waco, Texas: Word Books, 1988), lxxvii.

strongly Judaeo-Christianity long hindered its recognition by the Church as a whole.

James 5:14-16 lays down a procedure for helping the sick (v.14 ἀσθενεῖ 'is sick' suggests weakness of any kind). The sick person is to summon the elders of the church to pray over him and anoint him with oil in the Lord's name, and through this prayer of faith, the person will be raised up and find forgiveness for any sins he has committed. Let us examine the constituent parts of this statement.

(1) The *elders* (πρεσβυτέρους 'presbyters') of the church are to be summoned by the sick person. Presumably this means the elders of the *local* church, for the epistle is addressed to 'the twelve tribes in the Diaspora' (1:1), i.e. it seems all the dispersed Judaeo-Christian congregations. Elders had long been a feature of Jewish administration (e.g. Ex.24:9) and are quickly seen to hold authority in the Jerusalem church (Ac.11:30, 15:4, 6), but were also, according to Luke, appointed to lead newly formed predominantly Gentile churches (Ac.14:23).

(2) *Prayer.* One prayer or one session of prayer is suggested by the Gk. aorist imperative προσευξάσθωσαν ('let them pray').

(3) *Anointing with olive oil.* Olive oil was widely used in the ancient world as a medicament[57] (cf. Lk.10:34). The anointing here is symbolic, later 'sacramental' like the use of water in baptism. In the Old Testament oil was used in the ceremony for the cleansing of a leper (Lev.14:15-18). It was also used in the mission of the Twelve (Mk.6:13). In the present passage (v.14) the aorist participle ἀλείψαντες ('anointing') points to a single action. Presumably the prayer accompanied or immediately preceded this anointing. The fact that no instruction is given as to how to anoint suggests that the procedure is already a familiar.[58]

---

[57] Laws, *James*, 227 gives a variety of recorded uses.
[58] So C.L. Maconachie, 'Anointing with Healing' (Greenwich University Ph.D. Dissertation, 1990), 74.

(4) The phrase '*in the name of the Lord*' refers presumably to Jesus as in Acts 3:6, 9:34 (cf. Jn.14:13-14). In this epistle 'Lord' is used of Jesus in 1:1, though elsewhere of God.[59]

(5) '*The prayer of faith*'. Faith is frequently mentioned as a vital requirement in the healings of the gospels and Acts, but here the emphasis is on that of the elders. (The sick one displays faith by summoning them.) The phrase 'prayer of faith' is a little surprising as the common practice of the apostles, following the example of Jesus, was the *command* of faith (e.g. Ac.14:10). Perhaps there is a hint of that here because the Greek word used for 'prayer' is not the normal one προσευχή but εὐχή , translated elsewhere in the New Testament as 'vow' (cf. Ac.18:18, 21:23), though the meaning 'prayer' is found in classical Greek,[60] and that fits here as it surely refers back to the act of prayer and anointing in Jesus' name that has just been mentioned.

(6) *Will save the sick one* (Gk. κάμνοντα, 'worn out one'). 'Save' (σώζω) here may imply more than just a cure (cf. Mk.10:52), though 'heal' (ἰάομαι) is used for what is achieved by confession and prayer in v.16. C. Harris[61] comments that within the primitive Church there was a failure to draw any rigid distinction between spiritual and bodily healing.

(7) *Forgiveness of sins*. Jesus clearly accepted in some cases (Mk.2:5, Jn.5:14) the Jews' general assumption that sickness is caused by sin. This belief is reiterated here, even if it is mentioned almost as an afterthought, sin not being seen as invariably at the root of the trouble.

With v. 16 there is something of a change of tone. J. Wilkinson contrasts the present imperatives used here: 'confess' (ἐξομολογεῖσθε), 'pray' (προσεύχεσθε) with the aorists of v.14 and he believes the author has a different situation in mind – the day to day life of a local church, where mutual confession of sins and prayer for healing is expected to be

---

[59] 1:7, 3:9, 4:10, 15, 5:4, 10-11. Twelftree thinks there 'in the name of the Lord' here should be taken, following Jewish practice, as invoking the name of God (*Name of Jesus*, 181).

[60] See Thomas, *Devil*, 30, nt. 58.

[61] C. Harris, 'Visitation of the Sick' in *Liturgy and Worship*, ed. W.K. Lowther Clarke and C. Harris (London: SPCK, 1932), 510.

the normal response of church members to sickness.[62] If that were so perhaps we could surmise that it was for chronic cases only a sick person should resort to calling the elders for ministry, more minor ills being dealt with without bothering them. This seems an attractive idea. Against it is the fact that v.16 begins with 'then' or 'therefore' (οὖν) implying it is the consequence of what has just been said. There are various explanations:

(a) Dibelius[63] believes v.16 is the author's insertion into older material using the link word 'sin'.

(b) Laws[64] thinks there is one author of all these verses, but in v.16 his mind flits to a related subject – the ills (not necessarily physical sickness) that result from human sins.

(c) It is possible to view v.16 as merely a loose summary, reinforcing what has gone before and implying it should be a regular not occasional occurrence.

None of these solutions is totally conclusive but perhaps the third is the most straightforward.

The Apocalypse

The final book of the Bible does not speak of Christian miracles of healing. It does, however, speak of one of the great beasts, viewed as an agent of Satan, performing great signs and even making fire come down from heaven and deceiving many on earth (13:13-14). Significantly, in the New Jerusalem, the heavenly abode of the blessed, God will dry every tear of his servants, and there will be no more death, nor pain (21:4). Moreover the leaves of the tree of life will be for the healing of the nations (22:2).

Indirect Evidence from the Gospels

It is generally accepted today that the New Testament gospel writers, by the content and presentation of the material they use to tell us of Jesus

---

[62] J. Wilkinson, 'Healing in the Epistle of James', in *Scot.JT* 24(1971), 329.

[63] Dibelius, *James,* tr. M. A. Williams (Philadelphia: Fortress Press, 1975), 255.

[64] Laws, *James*, 232-33.

and those with whom he interacted, reveal also something of the nature and interests of the Christian community amongst which they lived. If this is so, how far does the material they give on healing, exorcism and raising the dead reflect what was actually happening in those first century communities and provide instruction for them?

M. Dibelius indeed suggested that details of Jesus' actions in miracle stories were set down

> to give guidance to Christians gifted with healing powers. This object may have arisen as a principal interest in cases where the healing is described in stages. When the epileptic falls into a death-like state or when the eyes of the blind man are only opened to see indistinctly, then Christian miracles workers would know what to do in similar circumstances.[65]

He thought that Aramaic words were sometimes placed on Jesus' lips for the same purpose, being the counterpart of foreign words used by a magician;[66] but this last point is surely wrong for ταλιθα κουμ ("little girl get up", Mk.5:41) and εφφαθα ("be opened", Mk.7:34) are not like the unintelligible foreign utterances of a magician[67] but rather direct commands in the language of the people addressed.

Let us now consider each of the four gospels in turn to see what other material might yield information.

Mark

The Gospel of Mark, generally recognized as the earliest of the four, is usually dated AD 65-70, and thought to have been written in Rome. Nearly one fifth of its entire contents (129 out of its 665 verses) is devoted to healing, exorcism or raising the dead. This may imply great interest in these matters in the Roman church of that time; but again it may just be a particular interest of the author.

In his recent study *In the Name of Jesus*, Graham Twelftree looks particularly at Mark's material on discipleship for information about exorcism.[68] He suggests that Mark, in relating that Jesus, as soon as he had chosen the Twelve, gave them authority to cast out demons (3:13-15), later reiterating this authority before sending them out on mission

---

[65] Dibelius, *Tradition to Gospel*, 86-87; cf. Twelftree, *Miracle Worker*, 97, 109, *Name of Jesus*, 117-18 *et passim*.

[66] Dibelius, *Tradition to Gospel*, 84.

[67] E.g. below ch. 6, 'Magical Practices', no. 19.

[68] Twelftree, *Name of Jesus*, 104-5.

(6:7), and finally, stating that the householder in the little parable about Jesus' second coming, gave 'authority' to each of his slaves to do their particular task while he was away (13:34), may be intending to convey the idea that 'the ministry of exorcism was the major work to occupy followers of Jesus while waiting for the return of the master of the house' (i.e. for Jesus).[69] But this may be reading much too much into the mere mention of authority in 13:34.

Twelftree calls the account of the exorcism of the mute spirit (9:14-29) 'A Lesson in Exorcism' in which would-be exorcists are informed that, in dealing with mute spirits, they are not to use commands, as in other exorcisms, but instead to turn to faith-filled prayer.[70] But surely, if Jesus was anything of a model to the later Church, this incident shows that a command (after prayer no doubt) will still be necessary to expel these spirits too. Twelftree may be on firmer ground when he sees the incident of the unknown exorcist (9:38-39) as teaching the use of the powerful name of Jesus in exorcism.[71]

It may be fair to deduce too that, in giving his audience four very different exorcism stories: one set in a place of worship (1:21-27), a case of multiple-spirit infestation (5:1-20), an exorcism at a distance (7:24-30), and the expulsion of the mute spirit (9:14-29), Mark may be desiring to impart to exorcists in the Church of his time a range of exorcistic skills. The same could be said of the stories of Christ's healings for they feature a wide range of ailments. C.D. Marshall may be right too when he says of Mark's gospel:

> The miracle-stories constitute one of the devices the author uses to issue and reissue the demand for faith.[72]

Luke

The Gospel of Luke is generally held to have been written c.AD 75-85 in Syrian Antioch by Luke, a native of that city.[73] Paul reveals Luke was a Gentile and calls him 'the beloved physician'.[74] It is evident that Luke uses Mark's Gospel as his primary source of material. He reproduces most of Mark's healing stories without substantially altering them,

---

[69] *Ibid.*, 112.
[70] *Ibid.*, 124-25.
[71] *Ibid.*, 125-27.
[72] Marshall, *Faith as a Theme*, 60.
[73] Eusebius, *H.E.* 3.4.7.
[74] Col.4:11-14.

though he enhances to some extent the seriousness of the complaints,[75] and he omits the whole of Mk.6:45-8:26 which includes the story of the Syrophoenician woman (Mk.7:24-30), which might have seemed offensive to Gentiles, and the two miracles in which Jesus uses spittle and manual acts (Mk.7:32-7, 8:22-6) which might have been too suggestive of a magician's practice;[76] the second story also tells of a two-stage healing of a blind man which might have detracted from Luke's portrayal of Jesus as a uniquely powerful healer. But he brings in five other healing miracles[77] and one raising of the dead.[78]

Such a strong interest in healings is consistent with Luke's being a doctor; but he appears intent on keeping Jesus' preaching and healing work in balance.[79] Instead of the sensational exorcism in the synagogue at Capernaum with which Mark introduces Jesus' ministry, Luke presents a synagogue scene in Nazareth in which Jesus reads from Isaiah 62:1-2 to announce his forthcoming ministry of preaching, healing and deliverance (Lk.4:16-21). Thereafter he preached the good news of the arrival of the kingdom of God (8:1) and demonstrated it through his exorcisms (11:20).[80] He pointed to his healing ministry as evidence of his messiahship (7:18-23).

Luke not only retains Mark's 'Mission of the Twelve', emphasizing healing and exorcism along with proclaiming the kingdom (9:1-6), but also introduces a 'Mission of the Seventy' who again heal, exorcise and announce the arrival of the kingdom (10:1-12, 17). The number seventy here may be intended to reflect the Jewish estimate of the number of nations in the world.[81] If so, Luke could be looking, in this passage, beyond Christ's time to the ministry of the Church in his own time when, amongst other things, demons are subject to the name of Jesus

---

[75] E.g. 4:33 where the demon cries out with a 'loud' voice (cf. Mk.1:23); 4:38 where he describes Peter's mother-in-law as having a 'high' fever (cf. Mk1:30).

[76] *Pace* Hull, who sees Luke's writings as 'penetrated by magic' (*Hellenistic Magic,* ch. 6).

[77] 7:10 (centurion's slave, from Q), 13:10-17 (bent over woman), 14:1-6 (man with dropsy), 17:11-19 (ten lepers), 22:50-51 (severed ear).

[78] 7:11-17 (widow of Nain's son).

[79] Cf. Twelftree, *Miracle Worker*, 145-46, 178-81, 188; *Name of Jesus*, 133.

[80] Mt. 12:28 has 'Spirit' for 'finger'. Luke generally loves to emphasize the Holy Spirit as the source of power (Lk.4:14, 18, 11:1, Ac.1:8) so it is likely that he would have retained it here if it were original – *pace* Twelftree, *Miracle Worker*, 169-70; *Name of Jesus,* 90-91.

[81] See Fitzmyer, *Luke*, 842 for a discussion of this passage.

(v.17).[82] The fact that Jesus dampens down these disciples' joy at their spectacular victories over evil spirits, may be a veiled caution to the contemporary Church not to overemphasize exorcism.[83]

Matthew

The Gospel of Matthew is clearly a product of Judaeo-Christianity.[84] Its author wishes to show the events of the life of Jesus fulfil the Jewish Scriptures, and he presents Jesus as the new and greater Moses giving his law (Mt.5-7) backed up by miracles (Mt.8-9). Showing evidence of being written after the fall of Jerusalem (AD 70)[85] and the wholesale exclusion of Christians from the synagogues (c.AD 85),[86] yet being quoted by Ignatius of Antioch (c.AD 107), this gospel surely comes from the period AD 85-100.

Matthew presents Jesus primarily as a teacher. As in Mark, his primary source, Jesus opens his ministry with a call to repentance in the face of God's approaching kingdom (Mt.4:17, cf. Mk.1:14-15). Like Luke he sees exorcisms as a powerful demonstration of that kingdom's arrival (12:28)[87] but, in general, he emphasizes miracles less than the other two evangelists. While Matthew retains most of Mark's healing stories, he abbreviates them, making small changes, and he adds only one of significance.[88] In the final Great Commission (28:18-20) healing is not even mentioned, though it may perhaps have been embraced in

---

[82] Twelftree, *Name of Jesus*, 140-41.

[83] *Ibid.* Here Twelftree makes a valuable point, but his subsequent distinction between the 'charismatic' exorcistic method of Jesus, viz. commanding evil spirits to leave by his own authority, and the 'magical' method of his disciples 'exorcising by some greater source of power-authority' than themselves, i.e. using the name of Jesus, is quite unwarranted. The disciples' method was the *same* as Jesus', merely substituting his name for his visible presence. It was most *unlike* that of magicians who endeavoured to manipulate gods to help them and to frighten the spirits they wished to expel by uttering sonorous gobbledygook (see below ch. 6, 'Magical Practices', no. 19).

[84] See nt. 48.

[85] Mt.22:7, cf.21:41.

[86] So the references to 'hypocrites' in Mt.6:2, 5, 16 and the woes to the scribes and Pharisees in Mt.23.

[87] See nt. 82.

[88] 8:5-13, the centurion's servant, from Q. The brief account of the healing of two blind men in Mt.9:27-31is presumably to compensate for the omission of Mark's blind man at Bethsaida (Mk.8:22-26) and the dumb demoniac of Mt.9:32-34 compensates for the loss of Mark's deaf mute (Mk.7:31-37).

the instruction to 'keep all that I have commanded you' (v.20). One reason why Matthew may have wished to focus less on the miracles was to avoid any suggestion that Jesus was a magician.[89]

Can we glean anything from this gospel about healing in the Church of its time? S. Légasse suggests references to the disciples' lack of faith (e.g. 17:16) may indicate that faith was flagging and miracle-workers were not plentiful among those for whom Mathew wrote.[90] E. Schweitzer sees the healing summaries of 4:23 and 9:35 as framing the picture of the Messiah in word (5-7) and deed (8-9), a teacher of the gospel of the kingdom and a healer of all sickness. 10:1, 7-8 follow when the disciples are sent out to heal and preach. He concludes that Matthew regards charismatic activity by Christ's followers as the continuation of that of Jesus. They too are to be stigmatized like their master with the name Beelzebul (10:24-5). In 9:8 Matthew has this shared ministry in mind when he speaks of the authority given to 'men' (not just to the Son of Man) after the healing of the paralytic and, in the healing of the epileptic (17:14-20), when he curtails the father's discussion with Jesus and instead brings in teaching for the disciples about the power of faith. Nothing will then be impossible to them (v.20). 'Thus it is charismatic healing,' Schweitzer concludes, 'in which the authenticity of genuine faith is proved'.[91] Twelftree too focuses on Matthew's account of the Mission of the Twelve, pointing out that, whilst vv.5-16 appear to be restricted to a Palestinian setting (the area of the original mission), vv.17-23 has a wider setting in mind both geographically (v.18) and chronologically (vv.22-3) and surely relate to the readers' time. This may find confirmation in that, at the end of the entire discourse (11:1) where, unlike in Mark and Luke (Mk.6:12-13, Lk.9:6), there is no reference to the disciples going out on their mission. He suggests then that the instructions about exorcism and healing (10:1, 8) relate to the church of his day and show what an important part these activities are intended to play in its evangelism.[92]

---

[89] Hull, *Hellenistic Magic*, ch. 7.

[90] Légasse 'Les Miracles de Jésus selon Matthieu' in *Les Miracles de Jésus selon le Nouveau Testament*, ed. X. Léon-Dufour (Paris: Édit du Seuil, 1977), 243-44.

[91] E. Schweitzer, 'Observance of the Law and Charismatic Activity in Matthew', *NTS* 16 (1969-70), 219-20. Twelftree broadly concurs with these points, *Miracle Worker*, 104.

[92] Twelftree, *Name of Jesus*, 164-67.

John

According to Irenaeus the Fourth Gospel was the last of our gospels to be written and was the work of the apostle John at Ephesus.[93] This latter claim has, in modern times, been widely disputed but still finds able defenders.[94] The gospel may be dated c.AD 100. Clearly the author is concerned that the claims and identity of Christ should be made intelligible to the Hellenistic world in which he lived.

The book relates seven astonishing feats of Jesus which include: the healing of a man paralysed for thirty-eight years (5:1-9), the giving of sight to a man born blind (9:1-7), and the raising of Lazarus who had been dead four days (11:38-44). Are we to conclude then that such miracles were characteristic of the church of the author's time? Jesus is indeed recorded in this gospel as saying that, after he has gone to the Father, his disciples would do 'greater works' than his (14:12). But such an achievement has seemed so improbable that, at least from the third century, the phrase has been interpreted as referring to the fruit of the Church's evangelistic activity rather than its miracles.[95] Jesus' astonishing miracles John sees as 'signs' (σημεῖα) pointing to the identity of Jesus as Messiah and Son of God (2:11, 4:4, 20:30-31).

No exorcisms are narrated in the Fourth Gospel. Does this imply that none were taking place in the church of that time? Again this is an unwarranted deduction. John was clearly aware of demons for he tells us some declared Jesus had one (7:20, 8:48-9, 52, 10:20-21). He also believed in Satan but, suggests X. Léon-Dufour,[96] John does not want us to think of Satan's activity as localized in the possessed for he is the ruler of this world, active in all whose hearts are not penetrated by the light (12:31, 35, 13:27, 14:30). Twelftree suggests John thought exorcisms too 'low grade' to reveal Christ's true identity. Jesus' whole ministry was a battle against Satan, and he achieved final victory over him on the cross.[97]

An important message of the Fourth Gospel is the repeated assertion of Jesus that prayer 'in my name' will be effective (14:13-14, 16:23-4,

---

[93] Irenaeus, *A.H.* 3.1.1.
[94] A case against apostolic authorship is stated by C.K. Barrett, *John*, 83-88, 105-7; L.L. Morris, *Studies in the Fourth Gospel*, ch. 4 states a case in favour.
[95] So Origen, *C.C.* 2.48.
[96] Léon-Dufour, *Miracles*, 282.
[97] Jn.12:27-33; Twelftree, *Miracle Worker*, 223, *Name of Jesus*, 192-93, 195-97.

cf.15:16). Here may indeed be a message, not just for the disciples, but for the Church at large; and it would seem a small step from using Jesus' name in prayer to employing it in commands to restore the sick and liberate the possessed (Ac.3:6, 16:18).

The Evidence of Papias

Two miraculous events, surely from the first century, reported by Papias, bishop of Hierapolis in Asia Minor (c.60-c.130), are quoted by Eusebius in *H.E.* 3.39. Papias claims to have received from the daughters of Philip the apostle, who lived at Hierapolis, a story of the raising of a dead person (the fifth-century historian, Philip of Side, claimed this was the mother of a certain Manaim[98]); also he reports that Justus Barsabbas (cf. Ac.1:23) once drank poison but 'by the Lord's grace, suffered no harm'.

General Conclusion

It appears from Acts that, in their healing ministry, the apostles patterned themselves quite closely on their master. They looked for faith in those to be healed. They issued commands sometimes in the name of Jesus to encourage this faith, and to the dead. Unlike Jesus they sometimes prayed before engaging in healing work. Paul appears to follow Old Testament examples in raising the dead. Healing ministry was, it seems, particularly characteristic of the apostles, though not entirely restricted to them. Healings often encouraged faith in spectators, though such spectators could draw wrong conclusions from them. As with Jesus, miracles were supplementary to the preaching of the word, not the primary focus.

From the epistles it may be fair to conclude that charismatic gifts of healing were more characteristic of the Gentile churches, whilst a more formal ('sacramental') anointing by presbyters (elders) in the name of the Lord Jesus developed faster in Judaeo-Christianity.

Finding evidence about healing and exorcism in the life of the late first-century Church from the four gospels is an exercise of 'reading between the lines'. Incidents and teaching purportedly relating to Jesus' first disciples *may* also communicate specific messages about contemporary church life. Interpretations of the evidence are subjective but it may be fair to deduce from Luke's Mission of the Seventy and

---

[98] But the reliability of his evidence has been seriously challenged by W. Lockton, 'The Martyrdom of St. John', *Theology*, 5 (1922), 80-83.

Matthew's account of the Mission of the Twelve that exorcism and healing are playing an important part in the mission of the contemporary Church. The tantalizing titbits given us by Papias encourage us to believe that more miraculous events were taking place in the first-century Church than those explicitly recorded in the pages of the New Testament.

CHAPTER 3

Encounter with the Hellenistic World:
The Second Century

In his *Counterfeit Miracles* B.B. Warfield provided the classic defence of the view of miraculous gifts that prevailed within Protestantism from the Reformation to the twentieth century:

> They were part of the credentials of the Apostles as the authoritative agents of God in founding the church. Their function thus confined them to distinctively the Apostolic Church, and they necessarily passed away with it.[1]

He makes great play of the fact that there is little or no evidence of miracle-working in the first fifty years of the Post-Apostolic Church.

The Apostolic Fathers

Of church life in the first half of the second century we have in fact a very inadequate record. The writers of this period, the 'Apostolic Fathers', leave us only a number of letters, a homily, a writing dealing with the relationship between Christianity and Judaism, a church order,[2] and a prophetic work. The earliest of these, the *First Epistle of Clement*, was written actually c.AD 96 to the church in Corinth. Clement, leader it seems of the church in Rome, is aware that various members of the Corinthian Church have received a spiritual gift (χάρισμα) and he urges that such be used with humility to ensure the health of the whole body (1 *Clem.* 38). The gifts then, such a prominent feature in the life of that church in its early years (1 Cor.12-14), are still in evidence at the end of the century. Does Clement's reference to 'health' hint perhaps that he is thinking particularly of gifts of healing? Later writers warn of the

---

[1] B.B Warfield, *Counterfeit Miracles*, (Edinburgh: Banner of Truth Trust, 1918 (1983)), 6.

[2] A form of early Christian literature that contains instructions on the ordering of church life. This one is the *Didache*.

danger of pride in those so gifted.[3] We cannot be sure. But clearly there are still sick people in the Corinthian Church for, in his lengthy prayer at the end of the letter, Clement asks God to 'raise up the sick' (59). When earlier he speaks of the missionary work of the apostles, he tells of their preaching and their appointment of bishops and deacons in the newly formed churches, but he makes no reference to their healing work (42). Clearly it was of no particular interest to him.

The Didache, which is generally thought to reflect church life in Syria c.AD 100, devotes three of its sixteen chapters to assessing the activities of itinerant 'apostles' and 'prophets' but makes no reference at all to healers. We can surely infer that there was no comparable order of itinerant healers within that church.

Bishop Ignatius of Antioch, travelling across Asia Minor, c.AD 107, to his martyrdom in Rome, addresses the members of the church at Smyrna as 'endowed with every gift (χάρισμα)', speaks of the eucharistic bread as 'the medicine of immortality',[4] and clearly shows himself positive towards medical science when he urges the young Polycarp to employ varied approaches to his work as a bishop and uses the medical metaphor, 'Not every hurt is healed by the same plaster. Allay fits of fever by means of poultices'.[5] But he does not elaborate further about healing. Curing pain would probably have been of no great concern to one who desired so urgently to be a martyr for Christ.[6]

Polycarp himself, when addressing the presbyters of the church at Philippi, tells them to be caring for all the sick,[7] but does not instruct them to cure them.

What should one deduce from this lack of any specific reference to healing ministry? That gifts of healing were not very numerous and that anointing with oil was not yet widely practised? Perhaps rather that healing was simply not the concern of the Apostolic Fathers when they wrote. For more explicit evidence we must look elsewhere.

The Odes of Solomon

The forty-two Odes of Solomon appear to constitute the earliest Christian hymnbook yet discovered. There have been debates about their date and provenance but, introducing his English translation of them, J.H. Charlesworth is confident enough to say that they were

---

[3]   Athanasius, *Life of Antony*, 38 (c.AD 360); Cassian, *Conferences* 15.1 (c.420).

[4]   *Ephes.* 20.

[5]   *Poly.* 2.

[6]   *Rom.* 4.

[7]   *Phil.* 6.

probably written in Antioch, c.AD 100. He calls them 'precious reminders of the first attempts to articulate the unparalleled experience of the advent of the Messiah'.[8] They are indeed alive with personal mystical faith. Strongly Jewish in tone, they have some kinship in thought with the Qumran documents.[9] Although known previously through quotations, the complete collection was found in 1907 in manuscripts containing also the Pharisaic Jewish *Psalms of Solomon* (first century BC), and may have developed the title 'Odes of Solomon' by association with them, or perhaps under the influence of 1 Kings 4:32, where it is stated that Solomon composed 1,005 odes. J.H. Bernard put forward the view that the Odes were composed as 'hymns of the baptised',[10] but while this is generally thought to be an exaggeration, it is recognised they were written for public worship (all end, for instance, with 'hallelujah'), and some contain clear allusions to baptism. Four speak of physical as well as spiritual renewal. Ode 6 is the first:

> 13. Blessed, therefore, are the ministers of that drink
>   who have been entrusted with his water.
> 14. They have pleased the parched lips
>   and have restored the paralyzed will.
> 15. Even lives who were about to expire,
>   they have seized from Death.
> 16. And members which had fallen,
>   they have restored and set up.
> 17. They gave power for their coming,
>   and light for their eyes.
> 18. Because everyone recognized them as the Lord's
>   and lived by the living water of eternity. Hallelujah.
>
> (tr. Charlesworth)

Commenting on our vv.15-16 (his vv.14-15) Bernard draws attention to the words of the fifth-century Syrian theologian Narsai: 'with feeble waters he was pleased to confirm feeble bodies' (*Hom.* 22) and other parallels.[11]

Next, Ode 18:

> 1. My heart was raised and enriched in the love of the Most High,
>   so that I might praise him with my name.

---

[8] J.H. Charlesworth (ed,) *The Old Testament Pseudepigrapha* I (London: DLT, 1985), 727.

[9] *Ibid.*, 728.

[10] J.H. Bernard, *The Odes of Solomon* (Cambridge: University Press, 1912), 42.

[11] *Ibid.*, 59.

    2. My members were strengthened,
        that they may not fall from his power.
    3. Infirmities fled from my body,
        and it stood firm for the Lord by his will.

Bernard explains the reference to 'my name' as the new name received by the Christian at baptism.[12] Physical healing and renewal are clearly referred to in vv.2-3.

Then, Ode 21:

    1. I raised my arms on high
        on account of the grace of the Lord.
    2. Because he cast off my chains from me.
        and my Helper raised me up according to his grace and his salvation.
    3. And I stripped off darkness
        and put on light.
    4. And even I myself acquired members.
        in them there was no sickness or affliction or suffering.

Commenting on v.1 Bernard draws attention to the baptismal ritual described by Cyril of Jerusalem, in which he tells of the catechumens' renunciation of the devil, and then with outstretched and uplifted hands facing eastward and professing their covenant with Christ.[13] Language of finding freedom and turning from darkness to light is well known from the New Testament in descriptions of salvation by Christ.[14] Physical renewal and health is evidently referred to in v.4.

Finally, Ode 25:

    7. A lamp you set for me both on my right and on my left,
        so that there might not be in me anything that is not light.
    8. And I was covered with the covering of your Spirit,
        and I removed from me my garments of skin.
    9. Because your right hand raised me,
        and caused sickness to pass from me.
    10. And I became mighty in your truth,
        and holy in your righteousness.

This is from one of the five Odes adopted by the Gnostic document *Pistis Sophia*, but its sentiments are not necessarily Gnostic; 'putting

---

[12] *Ibid.*, 85.
[13] *Ibid.*, 90.
[14] E.g. Col.1:12-13.

off' and 'putting on' are familiar Pauline phraseology for starting the Christian life.[15] V.9 speaks of healing resulting from the new life.

And so it is evident that in Syria, c.AD 100 renewed physical life was expected for the believer along with new spiritual life through the administration of baptism.

Rabbinic Material

That Palestinian Jewish Christians were quite numerous in the early second century is evident from Eusebius' statement (*H.E.* 3.35) that when Symeon, leader of the Jerusalem Church, was martyred in the time of Trajan (98-117) he was succeeded by Justus a Jew 'one of the vast number of the circumcision who by then believed in Christ'. If the five-volume work of Hegesippus, a second-century Jewish Christian greatly interested in the early history of the Church (*H.E.* 4.8.1-2, 4.22), had survived, we might have learnt whether healing was one of the continuing activities of such believers. That in fact it was is revealed by rabbinic sources, but from a very negative slant. Relationships between Jews and Christians had become hostile.

Seven times in his *Dialogue with Trypho* Justin Martyr declares that Jews curse believers in Christ in their synagogues.[16] In the second century the formula used seems to have varied, but later specified Christians as both heretics (*minim*) and Nazarenes.[17] Trypho retorts to Justin:

> Sir, it would have been well if we had been persuaded by our teachers who ordained that we should enter into discussion with none of you, not even to hold this conversation with you. (*Dial.* 38.1)

This ban included receiving any benefit from Christian healers, as the following rabbinic story shows:

> R. Eleazar b. Dama was bitten by a snake. And Jacob of Kefar Sama came to heal him in the name of Jesus son of Pantera. And R. Ishmael did not allow him [to accept the healing]. They said to him, "You are not permitted [to accept the healing from him], Ben Dama." He said to him, "I shall bring you proof that he may heal me." But he did not have time to bring the [promised] proof before he dropped dead. Said R. Ishmael, "Happy are you, Ben Dama. For you have expired in peace, but you did not break down the hedge erected by sages. For whoever breaks down the

---

[15] Gal.3:27, Eph.4:22, 24, Col.3:9-10.
[16] *Dial.* 16, 93, 95, 96, 108, 123, 133.
[17] W. Horbury, 'The Benediction of the Minim and Early Jewish Christian Controversy', *JTS* 33 (1982), 19-61.

hedge erected by sages eventually suffers punishment, as it is said, 'He who breaks down a hedge is bitten by a snake.'" [Eccles.10:8] (Tosephta,[18] *Hullin* ii, 22f, tr. Neusner)

The story is found again almost word for word in the Jerusalem Talmud *Shabbat* 14:4 IV and the Babylonian Talmud *Abodah Zarah* 27b. In the last case the story is prefaced by the rabbinic prohibition:

No man should have any dealings with the *Minim*, nor is it allowed to be healed by them even [in risking] an hour's life. (tr. Epstein)

In this account Jacob is called 'the Min of Kefar Sekaniah', but there is no reference to 'Jesus son of Pantera'; Ben Dama is not called a rabbi but is said to be R. Ishmael's nephew. Origen tells us that the title 'Jeshua ben Panthera' is used by Jews to malign Jesus' birth.[19] R.T. Herford[20] speaks of R. Ishmael as one of the most distinguished rabbis whose teaching is found in the Mishnah and Tosephta. He lived in the first half of the second century, spending the greater part of his life in Kefar Aziz, a village in the extreme south on the border of Idumea, but could well have met Jacob of Kefar Sama (or Sekaniah) of Galilee when he attended a rabbinic assembly at Usha in Galilee, c.AD 130. The reference to 'in the name of Jesus son of Pantera' surely refers to pronouncing the name of Jesus over the sufferer. Avoiding this 'catastrophe' Ben Dama is believed to have been saved from a fate worse than death by poison – punishment in the world to come. R. Kalmin[21] stresses that God's hand is seen in his death before he could reveal his Scriptural proof that might have led others astray.

Because of the long period of oral transmission before the Talmuds were written down[22] one cannot rely on the accuracy of the details of

---

[18] The Mishnah is a compilation of oral rabbinic laws written down c.AD 200. It was studied and interpreted by Jewish sages in the two centres Palestine and Babylon, their work being transmitted orally until the Jerusalem or Palestinian Talmud was written c.AD 400 and the Babylonian Talmud c.AD 500. The Tosephta ('addition') is another compilation of oral laws contemporary with and supplementary to the Mishnah, but lacking the latter's canonical authority. (See *ODJR*)

[19] Origen, *C.C.* 1.32. Jesus is said to have been, not the son of a virgin (Gk. *parthenos*), but of a soldier Pantheros (Panther).

[20] R.T. Herford, *Christianity in Talmud and Mishnah* (London: Williams & Norgate, 1903), 105.

[21] R. Kalmin, 'Christians and Heretics in Rabbinic Literature of Late Antiquity', HTR 87.2 (1994), 161.

[22] See nt. 18 above.

such stories.[23]   What does seem clear, however, is that Christians were known as healers in Palestine in the first half of the second century. In contrast, according to Origen, since their rejection of Jesus Christ the Jews no longer had any vestige of divine power among them.[24]

Other Pointers

The longer ending of Mark (Mk.16:9-20) is undoubtedly later than that gospel up to 16:8 and probably dates from the first half of the second century, written perhaps in Rome.[25] It contains a version of the risen Christ's Great Commission to his disciples to go into all the world and preach the good news about him. Those who believe will experience amazing signs: they will cast out demons in his name, speak in tongues, handle snakes (with impunity), drink poison without harm, and will lay hands on the sick who will then recover. If the content of the gospels reflects to some extent the concerns of the churches where they were written, this addition too may reflect the situation in Rome just then and perhaps in the rapidly expanding Western Church generally. These miraculous activities may well then have been much in evidence.[26]

Finally Tertullian, in his masterly *Prescription against the Heretics* written at the beginning of the third century, scoffs at Marcionites and Valentinians for claiming that people had to wait until their time to hear the truth:

> During the interval [from the founding of the Church to the mid-second century]
> the gospel was wrongly preached;

---

[23] Cf. Horbury's discussion of the reference to Jesus in *Sanh.* 43a ('Benediction', 56-58). Kalmin makes the interesting observation that as Minim (Christians) are referred to in six out of the eight occasions when names are used, by Yaakov (Jacob), the rabbinic story-tellers are using stereotype names. He thinks the content of the dialogues in the stories is also likely to be stereotyped not actual history ('Christians', 168-69). But this is obviously not so when the stories are far from identical. The story we have just considered is very different from two other 'Christian healer' stories we shall consider later (pp. 123-25 below).

[24] Origen, *C.C.* 2.8, *Hom. Lk.* Frag. 77.

[25] See D.C. Parker, The Living Text of the Gospels (Cambridge: University Press, 1997), ch. 8 for a discussion of the evidence.

[26] Exorcism is the first-mentioned sign to be performed by early believers (16:17); in v.9 there is also a reference to Mary Magdalene 'from whom (Jesus) had cast out seven demons'. Twelftree is quite confident from this that 'exorcisms not only provided evidence for their...faith, but also showed the veracity of their message' (*Name of Jesus*, 237).

men wrongly believed;
so many thousand thousands were wrongly baptized;
so many works of faith were wrongly wrought;
so many miraculous gifts (*virtutes*), so many spiritual endowments
(*charismata*) were wrongly set in operation... (29.3)

Clearly he had no doubt that miraculous activities were a part of Church life throughout the first half of the second century (and indeed continued in his own time[27]).

So, if the Apostolic Fathers supply no clear evidence for the continuance of the healing ministry within the Church of their time, these other sources we have considered indicate its reality.

For the second half of the second century the documentary evidence generally, and the information about the Church's healing ministry in particular, is considerably more plentiful.

The Greek Apologists

With the Greek Apologists Church literature directed itself for the first time towards the outside world. Most of the Apologists addressed their work to the emperors but also had a far wider audience in view. They used the philosophical terminology and rhetorical style normal to the Hellenistic world, and followed in the footsteps of the Jewish apologists Philo and Josephus. Their aims were:

1. to refute the charges being levelled against the Church and show that Christians lived exemplary lives and were a benefit to society;

2. to expose the absurdities of paganism, and

3. to present Christianity as the supreme truth.

They were therefore important theologians, though children of their age.

---

[27] He provides no support for Twelftree's view that exorcism (and presumably healing as well) had tailed off as the first century had drawn to a close and had only revived, first in Rome, in the mid-second century 'with the rediscovery of the Gospel of Mark with its recently produced new ending' (*Name of Jesus*, 291). Tertullian's further evidence we shall examine in ch. 4 below.

Justin Martyr

The greatest of these apologists was Justin. He was born c.AD 100 of pagan parents at Flavia Neapolis (Nablus) in Samaria. As a young man he undertook a serious quest for truth, which led him in turn to Stoic, Peripatetic (Aristotelian), Pythagorean and Platonic teachers. Then one day he fell into philosophical discussion with an elderly man, who directed him to read the Old Testament prophets, and, through doing so, he was in time converted to Christ.[28] From then on, wearing the robe of a philosopher, he devoted himself to teaching Christianity first at Ephesus and later, it seems, at Rome. He was martyred c.AD 165. Of his writings two *Apologies* survive; the first, addressed to the emperor Antoninus Pius, his son Marcus Aurelius and the philosopher Lucius, dates from c.155. The second is shorter and more impassioned. It is addressed to the Romans (Roman Senate). It is commonly seen as a sort of appendix to the first,[29] but may have been submitted to a different department of the imperial chancery; it was written apparently shortly after the accession of Marcus Aurelius (161).[30] Justin's only other extant writing is his *Dialogue with Trypho a Jew*, based on a real discussion which took place soon after the Bar Cochba revolt (132-5),[31] but, as it quotes the *First Apology*,[32] it must have been written up considerably later, perhaps c.155 or a year or two later.

In *2 Apology* 5 Justin shows he accepts the Jewish inter-testamental reworking of the story in Gen.6:1-4 though he simply says the offspring of the illicit union between the angels and women are called 'demons'. The angels then enslaved the human race by instructing them in magic, resulting in fears and punishments, and by teaching them to offer sacrifices, incense and libations which they needed since they had become enslaved by lustful passions.[33] But it is the demons who now

---

[28] *Dial*. 2-8.

[29] E.g. H. Chadwick, 'Justin Martyr's Defence of Christianity', *BJRL* 47 (1965), 277-78; L.W. Barnard, *Justin Martyr: His Life and Thought* (Cambridge: University Press, 1967), 18-19.

[30] Cf. *ODCC*, 3rd edn. ('Justin Martyr') for the dating, but see A. Ehrhardt, 'Justin Martyr's Two Apologies', *JEH* 4 (1953), 1-12, for a careful analysis of the terms used indicating the different destinations of the apologies.

[31] *Dial*. 1.

[32] *Dial*. 120.

[33] Justin then goes on to say the angels gave their own names to those now worshipped as gods. This was a novel view, see Annette Yoshiko Reed, 'The Trickery of the Fallen Angels and the Demonic Mimesis of the Divine: Aetiology, Demonology, and Polemics in the Writings of Justin Martyr' in *JECS* 12.2 (2004), 148, nt. 13.

pose as the gods.[34] When they came to know the prophecies concerning Christ, such as Is.35:6, they raised up pagan counterparts such as Asclepius.[35] They are responsible for pagan counterparts to Christian baptism and the eucharist.[36] They have raised up heretical sects to confuse people,[37] and brought about persecution of the Christians.[38]

As proof of Christ's divine origin Justin points to his fulfilment of Old Testament prophecy (to which he devotes a great deal of space) and to present-day miracles (δυνάμεις) happening in Jesus' name (*Dial.* 35.8). He never uses δυνάμεις for exorcisms and, as he frequently quotes the Synoptic Gospels and would have known Mt.7:22 which explicitly distinguishes performing δυνάμεις from casting out demons, it seems reasonable to assume the former term refers specifically to contemporary healings.[39]

Justin also speaks of those who have left the path of error and become disciples of Christ receiving gifts,[40] each as they are worthy, illumined through the name of Christ, and then lists a scrambled collection of them from Is.11:2, 1 Cor.12:7-10 and Rom.12:7:

> For one receives the spirit of understanding, another of counsel, another
> of strength, another of healing, another of foreknowledge, another of
> teaching, and another of the fear of God. (*Dial.* 39.2, cf. 4-5)

Clearly he has in mind what we know as the *charismata*, including the gift of healing. As elsewhere[41] he speaks of those who have been persuaded of the truth of Christ, instructed and then baptized, as 'illumined', it may well be that, like Tertullian[42] and Origen,[43] he sees these gifts as distributed at or after baptism. He is the first to speak of the need for 'worthiness' to receive these gifts.

---

[34] *1 Apol.* 5 *et passim.*
[35] *1 Apol.* 54, cf. *Dial.* 69.
[36] *1 Apol.* 62 (baptism), *1 Apol.* 66 (eucharist).
[37] *1 Apol.* 26, 56, 58 (Simon, Menander, Marcion).
[38] *1 Apol.* 57, *2 Apol.* 1.
[39] Cf. *1 Apol.* 30 where, in seeking to refute the charge that Jesus performed his mighty works by magic, Justin asserts, 'with our own eyes we behold things that have happened *and are happening* just as they were predicted'.
[40] Δόματα, but in Dial. 87-88 he uses the term interchangeably with χαρίσματα.
[40] *1 Apol.* 61.
[41] *Bapt.* 20.5,
[42] *Comm. Jn.* 6.166.

It is, however, exorcism in the name of Jesus Christ to which Justin devotes most attention. Of particular interest is his statement in 2 *Apol.* 6:

> For he (Jesus) was made man also…for the sake of believing man, and for the destruction of demons. And now you can learn this from what is your own observation. For numberless demoniacs[a] throughout the whole world, and in your own city (Rome), many of our Christian men exorcising them in the name of Jesus Christ, who was crucified under Pontius Pilate and have healed and do heal, rendering helpless and driving the possessing devils[b] out of men, though they could not be cured by all the other exorcists and those who used incantations and drugs. (6.5-6 ANCL)

a – δαιμονιολήπτος, 'demon grasped'[44]   b – 'demons'(δαίμονας)

Justin declares that destroying demons was a primary purpose of the Incarnation (cf. Mt.12:28, Lk.11:20). Elsewhere he interprets the visit of the Magi to the infant Christ as an act of revolt against demonic power (*Dial.* 78). Now clearly many Christians are performing exorcisms worldwide in the name of Jesus Christ, whom he identifies historically as having been crucified under Pontius Pilate.[45] At the end of this passage he points out the superiority of Christian exorcists to all others. Later he says this manifestation of Christ's power prefigures the final punishment of the demons, and those who serve them, in the eternal fire (*2 Apol.* 8).

In *Dial.* 30 Justin says that Christians' need to pray continually for protection from the demons, under whose thrall he himself once was. Another passage of great interest is *Dial.* 85: after interpreting Ps.24:7 as a reference to Jesus' reception into heaven as risen and ascended Lord of hosts, and he declares to Trypho:

> And of this you may, if you will, easily be persuaded by the occurrences which take place before your eyes. For every demon, when exorcised in the name of this very Son of God – who is the First-born of every creature, who became man by the virgin, who suffered and was crucified under Pontius Pilate by your nation, who died, who rose from the dead, and ascended into heaven – is overcome and subdued. But though you exorcise any demon in the name of any of those who were amongst you –

---

[44] So Lampe, PGL. In *1 Apol.* 18.4 he uses it of people possessed by the spirits of the dead.

[45] J.N.D. Kelly comments, 'In St. Justin we for the first time come across what can plausibly be taken to be quotations of semi-formal creeds', *Early Christian Creeds* (London: Longmans, 1950), 71.

either kings, or righteous men, or prophets, or patriarchs – it will not be subject to you. But if any of you exorcise it in [the name of] the God of Abraham and the God of Isaac, and the God of Jacob, it will perhaps be subject to you. Now assuredly your exorcists, I have said, make use of craft when they exorcise, even as the Gentiles do, and employ fumigations and incantations[a]. (85.1-3)

a - better 'spells', 'charms' (Lampe, PGL)

The extended credal statement in this passage, according to J.N.D. Kelly, 'bears every sign of being a fairly close replica of one which was actually used (in exorcisms)'.[46] But as this is the only time when speaking of exorcisms that Justin goes beyond saying that Jesus 'was crucified under Pontius Pilate', it may just be a confessional aside of his own. Justin then turns, it seems, to current Jewish exorcism. We know from the magical papyri that the formula 'God of Abraham, God of Isaac, God of Jacob' was deemed so powerful that it was adopted by Gentile exorcists,[47] and Josephus' account of the first-century exorcism by the Jew Eleazar (*Ant.* 8.47)[48] does indeed reveal a craft akin to pagan magic, but Justin seems unaware of the effective use of the name 'Solomon'.

There are further references to Christian exorcism in *Dial.* 30, 76 and 121, but the passages we have considered demonstrate clearly the prominence of Christians in exorcism, and at least the continuance of Christian healing in the mid-second century.

Tatian

Another interesting, though caustic, apologist was Tatian. He was a native of Mesopotamia (in modern Iraq) or Syria, born of pagan parents, and visited many lands, examining their religions. He studied rhetoric and clearly also some philosophy. He came to a Christian faith, it seems, at Rome after studying writings of the Old Testament.[49] There he was associated with Justin.[50] In about 172 he returned to the East where he is said to have founded the Encratites, a strongly ascetic sect, and to have

---

[46] *Creeds*, 75.

[47] PGM IV.1230-34 invokes the God of Abraham, Isaac and Jacob along with Jesus and the Holy Spirit for effective exorcism. See below ch. 6, 'Magical Practices', no. 19. While this papyrus dates from the fourth century it may well have been adapted from a second century non-Christian original (see Twelftree, *Name of Jesus*, 263).

[48] See above p. 12.

[49] Tatian, *Oration to the Greeks* 29-30, 35.

[50] *Orat.* 18-19.

propounded Gnostic and heretical views.[51] His *Oration to the Greeks* was published at some time between 160 and 180. A considerable part of this work is devoted to describing the nature and work of the demons (*Orat.* 7-20). The serpent in the Garden of Eden, he said, through choosing to act evilly, became a demon (7). The Greek gods too are demons (8-9, 12). Demons do not die as easily as men and will suffer a living death (14). They can only be easily detected by those 'whom the Spirit of God dwells in and fortifies' (15). Demons try to lead people astray, and would, if they had the power, even destroy the whole creation. Tatian continues:

> If anyone wishes to master them he must reject matter. Armed with the breastplate of heavenly spirit he will be able to protect everything it encompasses. Now there are diseases and disorders of the matter within us, but the demons take credit for these whenever they occur, and follow sickness wherever it strikes. Sometimes too they shake the body's system with a fit of their own madness; and then smitten by a word of God's power they go away in fear, and the sick man is healed. (16.2-3, tr. Whittaker)

Why should people reject matter? Tatian believed it to be part of God's creation and therefore not inherently evil,[52] but malleable[53] and, in man, subject to diseases and disorders. Tatian is sufficiently influenced by Hippocratic teaching though to declare that diseases can result also from a natural cause – a change of seasons.[54] But demons can use matter for their own devices.[55] In our passage he says only Christians can conquer demons, for they are protected by God's Spirit. Demons attach themselves to sick people, pretending to be the cause of their sickness, and sometimes add an element of their own. But the powerful word (of one exorcising) drives them out and cures the sickness, whatever its origin. In 11.1 he boldly declares, 'I scorn death, rise above every kind of disease, do not let grief consume my soul.'

Feeling he, as a Christian, has access to the power to conquer disease, he denounces magical remedies, almost universally employed by pharmacologists and physicians in Hellenistic times,[56] as the work of demons:

---

[51] Irenaeus, *A.H.* 1.28.1.
[52] *Orat.* 4-5, 11.
[53] *Orat.* 12.
[54] *Orat.* 20.
[55] *Orat.* 17.
[56] O. and C.L. Temkin (eds.), *Ancient Medicine: Selected Papers of Ludwig Edelstein*, 233-34.

A disease is not killed by antipathy[a], nor is a madman cured by wearing leather amulets. There are visitations of demons, and the sick man and the man who claims to be in love, the man who hates and the man who wants revenge, all take these as their helpers. This is how they contrive it...the varieties of roots and applications of sinews and bones are not efficacious in themselves; they are the elemental matter of the demons' wickedness, who produce effects in the areas where they have determined that each of these should be individually potent. Whenever they see that men have accepted service by these means they seduce them and make them their slaves...Their skill is to turn men away from God's service and contrive that they should rely on herbs and roots. (17.2-3)

a – Bolus of Mendes in Egypt (3rd C. BC) wrote a treatise based on the theory that 'sympathetic' means (drugs and magic) could foster, and 'antipathetic' destroy.

Tatian goes on to drive home the point that people should rely on the power of God to cure them not pharmacological means:

Pharmacy in all its forms is due to the same artificial devising. If anyone is healed by matter because he trusts it, all the more will he be healed if in himself he relies on the power of God...Why is the man who puts his faith in the material system unwilling to trust in God? For what reason do you not resort to the Lord of superior power, but choose rather to heal yourself like a dog with grass...? Follow the power of the Word...The most admirable Justin was right in pronouncing that demons are like bandits, for just as bandits are in the habit of taking men prisoner and then releasing them to their families on payment, so too those supposed gods visit men's bodies, and then in dreams create an impression of their presence and order their victims to come forward in sight of all. When they have enjoyed the eulogies they fly away from the sick, terminate the disease they have contrived, and restore men to their previous state.' (18.1-3)

So Tatian regards 'scientific' pharmacy as no better than unscientific magic; it has the same effect of drawing people away from relying on God for their good health. People should shun it and trust rather in the power of Jesus. And he castigates the healing cults, such as that of Asclepius, blaming them for first causing sickness then basking in the glory from removing it.

Tatian goes further than any other Church Father in opposing faith to scientific medicine. Recent studies[57] have pointed out that his

---

[57] Temkin, *Hippocrates*, 120-23; D.W. Amundsen, 'Tatian's 'rejection' of medicine in the second century' in *Ancient Medicine in its Socio-Cultural Context*, ed. Van der Eijk (Amsterdam: Rodopi, 1995), vol. 2.3.

denunciation is specifically of pharmacology, not of the other branches of medicine, surgery and dietetics. But since he scathingly denounces Greek philosophers in general,[58] is it likely he would have viewed these other branches of 'medical philosophy' any differently, especially as, like pharmacologists, Hellenistic physicians believed in treatment by 'sympathy' and 'antipathy'[59] and the use of amulets?[60]

Theophilus

Theophilus was, according to Eusebius,[61] the sixth bishop of Antioch in Syria. He tells us himself that he was from the region of the Tigris and Euphrates and was of pagan parents; he had been given a Greek education and was converted in adult life.[62] His work *To Autolycus*, addressed to a sceptical pagan friend, was written c.180.

He speaks much less than the other apologists about demons though he does declare that the Greek deities are not gods but idols, the work of men's hands, unclean demons (1.10). He also speaks of contemporary exorcisms in a chapter pointing out the contradictory statements made by historians, poets and philosophers about the gods:

> Inspired by demons and puffed up by them, they said what they said through them. For such poets as Homer and Hesiod, inspired as they say by the Muses, spoke out of imagination and error. This is clearly proved by the fact that up to the present day those who are possessed by demons are sometimes exorcised in the name of the real God, and the deceiving spirits themselves confess that they are the demons who were also at work at that time in the poets... (2.3, tr. Grant)

As elsewhere in his work, Theophilus refrains here from mentioning the name of Jesus (which presumably he felt would put people off reading his work), but by the phrase 'the real God' he is surely referring to him,[63] or perhaps more generally to the power behind Jewish and

---

[58] Tatian, *Orat.* 2-3, 25-26.

[59] Temkin, *Ancient Medicine*, 233-34.

[60] Galen included, Temkin, *Hippocrates*, 123-25.

[61] Eusebius, *H.E.* 4.20.

[62] Theophilus, *To Autolycus* 2.14, 2.24.

[63] Cf. Irenaeus, *Dem.* 96 (qu. below p. 60). Twelftree may well be wrong then when he takes this passage of Theophilus as clear evidence for Christian exorcism 'in the name of *God*' (*Name of Jesus*, 255). He rightly notes that Theophilus attests that exorcism has been practised by the Church up to his day, but again he may be wrong to infer from 'sometimes' that exorcisms were by then rare. Theophilus may rather be saying that only in *some* of the

Christian exorcism. Of healing in such a name he says nothing; indeed, in recommending that Autolycus commit himself to God to find out that he is real, he asks: 'What sick man can be cured unless he first entrusts himself to the physician?' Does he think there is any other way of being cured?

Justin, Tatian and Theophilus then provide evidence of active Christian ministry of exorcism and healing in the second half of the second century, but their comments also suggest there were differences of opinion within the Church as to whether one should seek healing simply by trusting God or by using medical means.

Other Theologians

We look now at two theologians of very different perspective: Irenaeus in Gaul and Clement in Alexandria.

Irenaeus

Irenaeus (c130-200) is generally considered the most important theologian of the second century. He was brought up, it seems, in Asia Minor for he tells us that when he was a youth he listened eagerly to the elderly Polycarp.[64] As bishop of Lyons he wrote in Greek his great work *Refutation and Overthrow of Falsely Named Knowledge,* which has come down to us in a literal Latin translation under the title *Against the Heresies.* This five-volume work was planned but written intermittently in the 180s. It is a principal source of information about various Gnostics but also tells us much about the Church of Irenaeus' time. A later work of his, *Demonstration of the Apostolic Teaching*, addressed to a certain Marcianus, has come down to us in an Armenian translation.

In book 5 of *Against the Heresies* Irenaeus is particularly concerned to rebut the Gnostic disparagement of the body and to show that it, like the human soul, is intended by God for eternal salvation. He lays great emphasis on the fact that Jesus restored blind eyes to the seeing state they had before, a withered hand to its original wholeness, and dead bodies to their original, living, state.[65] What was the point of healing the flesh if it had no permanent value?[66] One who talked in such terms

---

(perhaps many) present-day exorcisms do the possessing demons claim to have spoken through Homer and Hesiod.

[64] Bishop of Smyrna (modern Izmir) on the west coast of Asia Minor, Irenaeus *A.H.* 3.3.4; Eusebius, *H.E.* 5.20.5-7.

[65] 5.12.5, 13.1.

[66] *A.H.* 5.12.6.

would surely value the Church's continuing ministry of healing of the body, as in fact will become evident. Irenaeus also regarded the Holy Spirit as central to the life of the Church:

> For where the Church is there is the Spirit of God, and where the Spirit of God is there is the Church, and every kind of grace; but the Spirit is truth.[67]

It is scarcely surprising then to find him referring on a number of occasions to the Spirit's gifts to the Church. He mentions them in his extended reference to contemporary healings (2.32.4), to which we shall return later, using both the Greek terms δωρεά and χάρισμα (Eusebius in *H.E.* 5.7.3, 5 quotes the Greek of this passage). Δωρεά would seem to be taken from Eph.4:7, where it relates to the ministries Christ gave to the Church (v.11), while χάρισμα is undoubtedly echoing 1 Cor.12:4-11. He makes further allusions to the χαρίσματα of 1 Cor.12 in 2.28.7, 4.20.6-7, 4.26.5, 4.27.2 and 5.6.1. As Irenaeus was part of a church which nobly faced martyrdom,[68] A. Méhat is surely right in thinking Irenaeus sees these gifts not as luxuries but as a range of arms for Christians in the tough combat of life.[69] Irenaeus' interest in them clearly extends to the gift of healing as some remarkable passages in *A.H.* 2.31-32 reveal. By the end of 2.30 he feels he has successfully demolished the theoretical system of the Valentinians, and he turns to attack the Simonians, Carpocratians and any other Gnostics who employ magical feats to sustain their claims. Here he finds the healing works of the Church effective ammunition. But first he points out that, feeble though the Gnostics' efforts are, they are still dangerous. His argument in 2.31.2 deserves to be quoted in full:

> Moreover, those also will be thus confuted who belong to Simon and Carpocrates, and if there be any others who are said to perform miracles[a] - who do not perform what they do either through the power of God, or in connection with the truth, nor for the well-being of men, but for the sake of destroying and misleading mankind, by means of magical deceptions, and with universal deceit, thus entailing greater harm than good on those who believe them, with respect to the point on which they lead them astray[b]. For they neither confer sight on the blind, nor hearing on the deaf, nor chase away all sorts of demons – except those that are sent into others

---

[67]   *A.H.* 3.24.1 (ANCL).

[68]   The martyrs of Lyons and Vienne were heroic in the face of persecution in AD 177.

[69]   A. Méhat, 'Saint Irénée et les charismes', SP 17 (1982), 720, conclusion 1.

by themselves, if they can even do so much as this. Nor can they cure the weak, or the lame, or the paralytic, or those who are distressed in any other part of the body, as has often been done[c] in regard to bodily infirmity. Nor can they furnish effective remedies for those external accidents which may occur. And so far are they from being able to raise the dead, as the Lord raised them, and the apostles did by means of prayer, and as has been frequently done in the brotherhood on account of some necessity – the entire church in that particular locality entreating with much fasting and prayer[d], the spirit of the dead man has returned and has been bestowed in answer to the prayers of the saints – that they do not even believe this can possibly be done, [and hold] that the resurrection from the dead is simply an acquaintance with that truth which they proclaim[e]. (ANCL)

a - Lat. *virtutes* here is the equivalent of the Gk. δυνάμεις, 'powers'.
b - the results of magic are illusory, but dangerous in that they lead people astray.
c – i.e. by genuine Christians, the Lat. *evenit fieri* here does not make it clear whether the healings in the Church are in his own day; that is clarified in 2.31.3 and 2.32.4.
d – Gk. λιτανεία 'congregational prayer', later 'liturgical prayer' (Lampe, PGL).
e – or 'an acknowledgement of that which is said by them to be true'.

The raising of the dead Irenaeus mentions again in 2.32.4 adding that they 'remained among us for many years'. But these claims have been disputed. Warfield thought Irenaeus spoke about this matter as if he had past instances in mind.[70] In his more recent and detailed study Barrett-Lennard[71] points to the Greek past (aorist) tenses[72] as evidence of this, and thinks Irenaeus may be looking back to Hadrian's time (117-138) or even earlier. He suggests that Irenaeus' use of 'we' or 'among us' here and in 2.32.2-3 are references to the Church as a whole as against the Gnostics. Lampe,[73] however, is prepared to accept that Irenaeus is actually referring to contemporary raisings, and there are good reasons for thinking he is right:

1. Eusebius specifically quotes *A.H.* 2.31.2 and 2.32.4 (and 5.6.1) to show that such demonstrations of divine power were happening right up to Irenaeus' time (*H.E.* 5.7.1).

---

[70] Warfield, *Counterfeit Miracles*, 14.
[71] Barrett-Lennard, *Christian Healing*, 112, 126-27.
[72] 2.31.2: 'the spirit of the dead man has returned (ἐπέστρεψεν) and has been bestowed (ἐχαρίσθη).' 2.32.4: 'the dead even have been raised (ἠγέρθησαν) and remained (παρέμειναν) among us for many years.'
[73] In *Miracles,* ed. Moule, 215.

2. The whole purport of Irenaeus' argument is to contrast a whole
    range of miracles in Jesus' name *still occurring* in his time with the
    feeble performances of the Gnostic magicians. This point is
    emphasised further in 2.32.5.

3. In 2.31.2, while merely mentioning Jesus' own raisings and just
    adding that the apostles used prayer in theirs, he gives considerable
    detail as to how the local Christian communities performed their
    raisings: the entire church gathering, with fervent prayer, fasting and
    perhaps even liturgical formulations. The impression is that the
    whole procedure took a considerable time, but in the end the dead
    person's spirit returned. Such a description suggests familiarity with
    comparatively recent happenings. How then do we account for the
    past (aorist) tenses? By remembering that some lapse of time was
    necessary to show the power of the miracle. The longer people lived
    after being raised, the greater the miracle that accomplished it.[74]

In 2.31.3 Irenaeus contrasts the attitudes and motives of the Gnostics
with those within the Church who perform miracles:

> Since, therefore, there exist among them error and misleading influences,
> and magical illusions are impiously wrought in the sight of man; but in
> the Church, sympathy, and compassion, and steadfastness, and truth, for
> the aid and encouragement of mankind, are not only displayed without
> fear or reward, but we ourselves lay out for the benefit of others our own
> means, and inasmuch as those who are cured very frequently do not
> possess the things which they require, they have received from us; those
> men [the Gnostics] are in this way undoubtedly proved to be utter aliens
> from the divine nature, the beneficence of God, and all spiritual
> excellence...

While these Gnostics use magical tricks to deceive and, it seems, take
money from people, the Church, based on the truth, offers
compassionate help to the needy. Its health-giving miracles are free of
charge (cf. Mt.10:8) and followed by further charitable giving. Clearly,
many of those who came to the Church for healing were impoverished.

We may summarize 2.32.1-3: these Gnostics claim one should
experience every kind of activity, good and bad, but they do not attempt
all the arts, merely revel in lust. They claim to be followers of Jesus yet
really emulate Epicurus and the Cynics. They claim to be like, even
superior to, Jesus but the fact that they can but momentarily produce
phantasms shows that they are not like Jesus our Lord but Simon the

---

[74] This was Quadratus' point concerning those raised by Jesus, Eusebius *H.E.*
4.3.2.

magician (Ac.8:9-25). Moreover they die, but Jesus assuredly rose from the dead, showed himself to his disciples, and in their sight ascended to heaven. The next passage, 2.32.4, Eusebius found impressive enough to quote in full (*H.E.* 5.7.3-5):

> If, however, they maintain that the Lord, too, performed such works simply in appearance, we shall refer them to the prophetical writings, and prove from these both that all things were thus predicted regarding him and did take place undoubtedly, and that he is the only Son of God. Wherefore, also those who are in truth his disciples, receiving grace from him, do in his name perform [miracles] so as to promote the welfare of other men, according to the gift[a] which each one has received from him. For some do certainly and truly drive out[75] devils[b], so that those who have thus been cleansed from evil spirits frequently both believe [in Christ], and join themselves to the Church. Others have foreknowledge of things to come: they see visions and utter prophetic expressions. Others still, heal the sick[76] by laying their hands upon them, and they are made whole. Yea, moreover, as I have said, the dead even have been raised up and remained among us for many years. And what shall I more say? It is not possible to name the number of the gifts[c] which the Church, throughout the whole world, has received from God, in the name of Jesus Christ, who was crucified under Pontius Pilate[d], and which she exerts day by day for the benefit of the Gentiles, neither practising deception upon any, nor taking any reward from them. For as she has received freely from God, freely does she minister.

> a – δωρεά   b – demons   c – χαρίσματα   d – credal use as with Justin

There is much of interest in this passage. It is evident that Irenaeus is pointing to contemporary miracles here as evidence of the authenticity of Jesus' own miracles.[77] Then, the ability to exorcise is seen by him as a charismatic gift like prophecy and healing using the laying on of hands. His use of 'cleanse' for the work of exorcists is unusual but in keeping with the preferred Jewish term 'unclean spirit' (e.g. Mk.1:23)

---

[75] Irenaeus uses ἐλαύνω, 'I drive away', found only in the NT in Lk.8:29, rather than the normal term employed there ἐκβάλλω, lit. 'I throw out'.

[76] Barrett-Lennard draws attention to Irenaeus' use of ἰάομαι with κάμνοντας saying that, as κάμνω is rarely used of being sick in early patristic times, it implies the influence of Jas.5:13. He accounts for the absence of any reference to anointing with oil by the suggestion that baptismal use of oil had subsumed its healing use in some part of the Church by this time. But in fact Jas.5 does not mention the laying on of hands as found here. Moreover, κάμνω is used by Tatian (with θεραπεύω) in *Orat.* 16.3 regarding exorcism, clearly quite independently of the Jas.5.

[77] Cf. Justin, *Dial.* 35.8.

for a demon. Clearly also those delivered from evil spirits often joined the Church. He thinks innumerable gifts have been conferred on the Church. Finally he reiterates that they are used free of charge.

Irenaeus' last extended passage on contemporary healing is in the section that follows. He is contrasting the methods of Christians with those of the Gnostics:

> Nor does she [the universal Church] perform anything by means of angelical invocations, or by incantations, or by any other wicked curious art; but directing her prayers to the Lord, who made all things, in a pure, sincere and straightforward spirit, and calling upon the name of our Lord Jesus Christ, she has been accustomed to work miracles for the advantage of mankind, and not lead them into error. If therefore, the name of our Lord Jesus Christ even now confers benefits [upon men], and cures thoroughly and effectively all who anywhere believe on him, but not that of Simon, or Menander, or Carpocrates, or of any other man whatever, it is manifest that, when he was made man, he held fellowship with his own creation, and did all things truly through the power of God, according to the will of the Father of all as the prophets had foretold. (2.32.5)

Christians, in their healing, do not call on angels nor employ magic but simply pray to God in the name of the Lord Jesus and this brings effective and complete cures for those with faith. Invoking the names of a Gnostic leader or anyone else will not produce these results. Assuredly then Jesus when on earth performed the miracles attributed to him, by the power of God, as foretold by the prophets.

While Irenaeus shows considerably less interest in Christian exorcism than many Church Fathers (he never alludes to Jesus' own exorcisms, while he quite often alludes to his healings) he does mention them (and not the healings) in *Dem.* 96:

> And there is none other name of the Lord given under heaven whereby men are saved, save that of God, which is Jesus Christ the Son of God, to which also the demons are subject and evil spirits and all apostate energies. (tr. Armitage Robinson)

He is also aware of Jewish exorcisms, whose effectiveness, he says, is because 'all beings fear the invocation of him who created them' (*A.H.* 2.6.2). In common with other Church Fathers he regards the gods of the Gentiles as demons (3.6.3). Rather than attributing sickness to demons he stressed as a general principle the connection between sickness and sin (5.12.2).

CONCLUSION

Needless to say, Irenaeus is a key witness for the continuance of the healing ministry in the Church in the late second century. He speaks of a whole range of healing miracles: curing the blind, deaf, weak, lame and paralysed, exorcisms and indeed the raising of the dead. He implies that charismatic gifts are still plentiful in the Church, and includes among them exorcism in the name of Jesus Christ and healing using laying on of hands. All this is offered free of charge. He says those delivered from evil spirit generally join the church. Perhaps this was also true of others healed. But we might have heard of none of this had it not been for his desire to better the magical feats of the Gnostics, and to give grounds for accepting the miracles attributed to Jesus in his time on earth.

Clement of Alexandria

'Of all the Fathers', Jerome writes of Clement, 'he was the most learned'.[78] He knew Homer, also Plato whom he greatly admired, and was widely read in the secular authors, Hellenistic Jewish and the early Christian writings, including the apocryphal literature. Born c.150, perhaps in Athens, he later travelled widely studying philosophy and Christianity until he found in Alexandria an instructor, Pantaenus, who really satisfied him.[79] He became a Christian teacher there c.190, leaving in the persecution of Severus c.202. After that he stayed for a while with a friend in Cappadocia but by c.215 was dead.[80] The most notable of his surviving works are *Exhortation to the Greeks*, an earnest appeal to turn from the errors and immorality of Greek religion to the pure teaching of Christ; the *Teacher*, containing elementary instruction for new Christians; and *Miscellanies*, a compendium of further teaching on a wide range of subjects.

Clement seeks to portray Christianity as the middle way between intellectual Gnosticism and simple faith, fulfilling both the Old Testament which prepared the Jews, and Greek philosophy which prepared the Greeks, for Christ. His thought shows a considerable debt to Middle Platonism.[81] He thus sees the ultimate goal for the Christian as deification. He applies the term 'gnostic' to the Christian who has grasped the deeper teaching of the Logos. But, though he places great stress on the importance of knowledge, he remembers that faith is the foundation of true knowledge. He writes, in the main, in a pleasant, gracious style.

---

[78] Jerome, *Ep.* 70.4.
[79] Clement, *Miscellanies* 1.11.1-2 (ANCL 1.1).
[80] Eusebius, *H.E.* 6.14.9.
[81] S.R.C. Lilla, *Clement of Alexandria: a Study in Christian Platonism and Gnosticism* (Oxford: University Press, 1971), 41-51.

Like other Church Fathers he accepts that the demons are the outcome of illicit intercourse between angels and women.[82] They desire to make men fall,[83] and lead them into idolatry.[84] They are pagan gods who exult in men's insanity and enjoy human slaughter.[85] Before people believe in the Christian God their heart is 'full of idolatry, and…a house of demons'.[86] But Jesus heals both body and soul.[87] Clement does not elaborate on this statement, but elsewhere he testifies to baptismal healing.[88]

Now there were many wealthy people in Alexandria and Clement was concerned that they should have a legitimate place within the Church. In his extant sermon *Who is the Rich Man that is Saved?* he suggests they should enlist for their own benefit –

> an army of God-fearing old men, of God-beloved orphans, of widows armed with gentleness, of men adorned with love. Obtain with your wealth, as guards for your body and soul, such men as those whose commander is God. Through them the sinking ship rises, steered by the prayers of saints alone; and sickness at its height is subdued, put to flight by the laying on of hands; the attack of robbers is made harmless being stripped of its weapons by pious prayers; and the violence of demons is shattered, reduced to impotence by confident commands. (34.2-3, cf. 35.1-2)

No matter how unpalatable it may be to us today, Clement is clearly encouraging here donor/client relationships within the church. He is also saying that it is the poor, unencumbered by the things of the world, who are really effective in their prayers for healing. He is in fact reiterating a theme expressed earlier by Hermas in his prophetic book *The Shepherd* when he puts forward his allegory of the vine and the elm[89] to indicate that the rich in the Church are to maintain the poor, whilst the poor are to use their spiritual resources in prayer to bless the rich. A further example of this is found in the next century in the Syrian *Didascalia Apostolorum*'s instructions to widows.[90]

Clement thinks all good things in life come from God. He frequently applies that to philosophy (though with some caution), but also to

---

[82]   *Misc.* 4.96.1 (ANCL 4.14), from 1 Enoch 6 interpreting Gen.6:2.
[83]   *Ibid.* 2.56.2 (ANCL 2.13).
[84]   *Exhort.* 1.3.1.
[85]   *Ibid.* 3.42.1.
[86]   *Misc.* 2.116.4 (ANCL 2.20) qu. the *Epistle of Barnabas* 16.
[87]   *Teacher* 3.98.2 (ANCL 3.12).
[88]   *Ibid.* 1.6.4 (ANCL 1.2).
[89]   *Similitude* 2.
[90]   *Didasc.* 15.

health. For keeping fit he recommends a simple diet, the occasional bath and, better still for men and boys, moderate exercise in the gymnasium.[91] Medicine too he views positively and he frequently uses medical metaphors in explaining the way of salvation.[92]

But particularly in the incomplete *Miscellanies*, dating from late in his teaching career, he emphasizes there is also a positive value in suffering. In 4.5 he holds up for admiration the Stoic attitude to life, likewise the example of Job. He expects his gnostic to make 'excellent use of all circumstances'. As pain inflicted by a surgeon is beneficial (there being no anaesthetics) so discipline is beneficial for correcting manners (7.15.5 – ANCL 7.3). Indeed –

> Though disease and accident, and what is most terrible of all, death, come upon the Gnostic, he remains inflexible in soul, - knowing that all such things are a necessity of creation, and that, also by the power of God, they become the medicine of salvation benefiting by discipline those who are difficult to reform; allotted according to desert, by Providence which is truly good. (7.61.5 – ANCL 7.11)

Later he says poverty, disease and other such trials can have value as warnings, indicating wrong past action and the need for a change in direction in life (7.81.6-7 – ANCL 7.13). Espousing such Stoic attitudes it is not surprising that he spurns good health as the goal of the gnostic's quest:

> The Gnostic, who has reached the summit, will pray that contemplation may grow and abide, as the common man will for continual good health. (7.46.4 – ANCL 7.7)

The Middle Platonic quest for contemplation of God and enthusiastic development of the healing ministry seem scarcely compatible. Clement's attitude contrasts quite markedly with that of Irenaeus.

---

[91] *Teacher* 2.1 (diet), 2.2 (baths), 3.9 (exercise).
[92] *Misc.* 1.171.1-3 (ANCL 1.27), 6.157.1-2 (ANCL 6.17), *Exhort.* 1.8.2 *et passim*.

Early Apocryphal Acts

Alongside the historical and doctrinal writings of the apostles and their successors there grew up a popular, novelistic form of Christian literature. Of this genre were the Apocryphal Acts. They revel in adventurous journeys on which their heroes face all kinds of danger. Most abound in fanciful miracles stories with little or no historical basis. It appears they were designed as popular literature to replace erotic pagan narratives.[93] Their interest exceeds their entertainment value. In the words of M.R. James:

> They record the imaginations, hopes and fears of the men who wrote them; they show what was acceptable to the unlearned Christians of the first ages, what interested them, what they admired, what ideals of conduct they cherished for this life, what they thought they would find in the next.[94]

They are Encratite (ascetic) in tone and often mildly Gnostic. And they were soon rejected by the mainstream of the Church intent on proclaiming the historical basis of the Christian faith.

The *Acts of Andrew*, *Peter* and *Paul* all date from the later second century.[95] Tertullian tells us[96] the *Acts of Paul* was written by a presbyter in (the province of) Asia who, when his authorship became known, was removed from office. The authorship of the other two is unknown. The *Acts of Peter* may have been written in Asia Minor, or in Rome.[97] The *Acts of Andrew* may stem from Greece, where most of his miracles are said to occur, or perhaps Asia Minor, Syria or Egypt.[98]

Whereas in the four New Testament gospels raising the dead is infrequent, the subject of only three of the twenty-two healing miracle

---

[93] J. Quasten, *Patrology* I (Utrecht: Spectrum, 1950), 129.

[94] M.R. James, *The Apocryphal New Testament* (Oxford: University Press, 1924), xiii.

[95] Convenient English translations have been provided by E. Hennecke, *New Testament Apocrypha*, rev. edn. W. Schneemelcher, vol. 2, tr. R.McL. Wilson (Cambridge: J. Clarke, 1992), and J.K. Elliott (ed.) *The Apocryphal New Testament: A Collection of Apocryphal Christian Literature in an English Translation* (Oxford: University Press, 1993).

[96] Tertullian, *Bapt.* 17.

[97] Schneemelcher II, 104, 107.

[98] P.M. Peterson, *Andrew, Brother of Simon Peter: His History and His Legends* (Leiden: Brill, 1963) favours Greece or Asia Minor; J-M. Prieur, *Acta Andreae*, vol.1 (Turnhout: Brepols, 1989), 413-16, Syria, Asia Minor or Egypt.

stories of Jesus, in the Apocryphal Acts it is commonplace, occurring in eight of the twenty healing stories in the *Acts of Andrew*, four of the eight in the *Acts of Peter*, and in three of the four in the *Acts of Paul*. Let us look at some representative stories, not just those depicting the raising of the dead. I summarize from the documents concerned. The art of the story-teller is well illustrated by the following episode from the *Acts of Paul*, where two raisings and various healings are interwoven:

> At Myra Hermocrates, a man with dropsy, comes up to Paul and says, "Nothing is impossible for God but especially for him whom you preach, for when he came he healed many..." And he expresses a desire to believe in the living God. Paul promises that, through the name of Jesus Christ, without payment, he will become whole. His stomach opens, a large quantity of water comes out, he falls as dead, and is raised by the hand of Paul, given bread, and is made whole. He and his wife 'receive the grace of the seal' (baptism presumably). But their son Hermippus and his companions rise up against Paul. Hermippus had hoped his father would die and he would inherit his property. His younger brother Dion, however, hears Paul gladly. In the ensuing hostilities Dion dies. Following pleas from his mother Nympha, Paul raises him... As punishment for his hostility against Paul, Hermippus goes blind. He repents. Paul and the others pray for him, and he recovers his sight. Hermippus claims he has had a vision in which Paul came and laid his hands upon him. (4. *P.Held.* 28-34)

This story is clear enough though the manuscript from which it comes is much damaged and the details of how Paul healed are not related in full. The description of the physical dispersement of water from Hermocrates' stomach, bizarre though it is, only adds to the drama. The principle 'nothing is impossible with God (or Jesus)', enunciated here (as elsewhere in the Apocryphal Acts) allows free rein to the author's imagination. The story, however, depicts healing in the name of Jesus Christ, free of charge, and mentions the method of laying on of hands; repentance for sin is clearly important, and those healed become converts. All these points echo New Testament healings.

If the drama of that story is too bizarre to be real, a different sort of unreality pervades the following extract from the *Acts of Andrew*:

> Andrew meets a blind man who asks not for healing but for money for food and clothing. Andrew blames the devil for not allowing the man to receive his sight, then he touches his eyes and heals him. He also makes sure the man's filthy clothing is replaced with good clothes, and the man returns home thankful. (Gregory of Tours, *Epitome* 2)

It is strange that someone, knowing Andrew could heal him, comes to him asking for food and clothing. What a contrast to the desperate plea of Bartimaeus! (Mk.10:46-52) Unlike the accounts in the New Testament, blindness here is attributed to the presence of an evil spirit, yet no exorcism is performed. The simplicity of the cure follows that of Jesus' miracles (cf. Mt.9:27), but the reference to supplying clean clothes may reflect the charitable giving of the church with which the author was familiar.

Various motifs are evident in the next story, again from the *Acts of Andrew*:

> The son of Gratinus, having bathed in the women's bath is rendered senseless and tormented by a demon. Gratinus himself is in bed with a fever, and his wife afflicted with dropsy. Andrew orders the demon to depart from the tormented boy, which it does with much shouting. Gratinus Andrew reprimands for loose living, then tells him to rise and sin no more. His wife he rebukes for infidelity then heals her on condition it does not recur. Both are cured. In gratitude Gratinus sends the apostle presents, but they are declined and he is told to give them to the needy. (Gregory of Tours, *Epitome* 5)

Sickness and possession by a demon are both linked here with sin. That the public baths are a favourite abode of evil spirits is emphasized in *Epitome* 27 where it is related that the apostle himself, going for a bath in Corinth, is confronted by two possessed men. He delivers them but then cautions those with him:

> The enemy of mankind lies in wait everywhere, in baths and in rivers; therefore we ought always to invoke the Lord's name, that he may have no power over us.

Gifts are not accepted in payment for the apostle's services, rather they are to be given to the poor. Such attitudes and practices may well reflect those of the church which he knew. But the demon's noisy exit from the boy, the sicknesses fever and dropsy and perhaps some other details in the story, may be no more than reminiscences of New Testament stories (Mk.1:30, Lk.14:2, Mk.1:26…).

Finally, an example of Encratism from the *Acts of Peter*:

> Many people are healed by Peter on the Lord's Day. He is asked why he allows his beautiful virgin daughter to remain paralyzed, though a believer. He calls her to get up 'with the help of none except Jesus', to walk and then to lie down and be paralyzed again. She does all this. He then explains that once, because of her beauty, she was kidnapped by one,

Ptolemy, to be his wife. She became paralyzed and so retained her virginity and had remained so since. Ptolemy, through shedding many tears of remorse, had gone blind, but had come to Peter, received physical healing, and become a Christian. (Coptic papyrus fragment, Berlin 8502)

Clearly this story is designed to teach that moral rectitude, indeed chastity, is to be prized above good health and marriage.

These examples suffice to show the entertainment value of the Apocryphal Acts and their moralistic tone, yet also their desire to keep close to the principles of healing found in the New Testament. This may reflect contemporary practice or simply be a case of borrowing from the earlier narratives. One thing seems very likely: if this was Christian literature for the common people, its clientele was clearly interested healing miracles.

General Conclusion

The literature which tells us of the Church's healing activities in the second century is plentiful and varied. That the Apostolic Fathers pass over the subject virtually in silence may well be due to their not finding it relevant to the matters about which they were writing. More marginal sources do indicate, however, that healing miracles were taking place in the first half of the century both at baptism and through the exercise of gifts of healing. Justin is our primary witness for the powerful continuance of exorcism in the name of Christ, bettering both Jewish and pagan counterparts. Several other writers make passing, but no less confident, mention of this exorcism. For healing, our primary witnesses are Irenaeus and Tatian. The former tells of a great range of healing and confidently claims that even the dead have been raised, it seems within his memory; Tatian, whilst powerfully protesting the primacy of healing through faith over medical means, indicates that there are other Christians (surely including Clement and Theophilus) who are resorting to medical cures. Clement thinks the quest for good health should *not* be a primary concern of mature Christians. Justin and Irenaeus refer to healing and exorcism largely for apologetic reasons, to substantiate the divinity of Christ or reject heresy. But, if the educated Christian leaders of the second century are less than fervent in promoting the Church's healing ministry, statements of Clement and Irenaeus, and the stories of the Apocryphal Acts, indicate that the poor and less educated see it as a matter of vital concern.

CHAPTER 4

Consolidation and Complacency:
Early to Mid-Third Century

The writers of the Church in the first half of the third century continue to refer to healings, *charismata*, and particularly exorcisms performed by Christians. By the mid-century physical healings would seem to be less frequent. We shall explore the evidence and consider why this might be so, looking first at the evidence of the Western Fathers, who are in the main inter-related, and then at the more disparate evidence from the Eastern Church.

North Africa

Tertullian

Tertullian is rightly respected as the 'father of Latin theology'. Born perhaps c.AD 160, he was clearly brought up a pagan, educated in rhetoric, philosophy and law and became fluent in Greek as well as Latin. From c.207 he was influenced by Montanism, a prophetic movement from Phrygia in Asia Minor, and by about 213 appears to have been out of communion with the mainstream Church,[1] his last writings being virulently anti-Catholic. Jerome says that he was a presbyter.[2] He probably died c.225. For convenience we shall discuss all Tertullian's writings in this chapter even though his earliest date from the last years of the second century.

---

[1] This follows the revised dating of T.D. Barnes in the postscript (1985) to his *Tertullian: A Historical and Literary Study* (Oxford: University Press, 1971). Tertullian was probably not regarded as a heretic, rather he seems to have formed a 'church within a church' (D. Powell, 'Tertullianists and Cataphrygians', *VC* 29 (1975), 33-54. This would explain why Cyprian could call him 'master' (Jerome, *On Illustrious Men* 53), and Eusebius quote his work without embarrassment (*H.E.* 2.2.4-6 *et passim*).

[2] Though Tertullian himself twice speaks of himself as a layman (*Exhort. Chast.* 7.3, *Mon.* 12.2), see Barnes, *Tertullian*, 11.

Prior to his virulent stage his outlook had much in common with that of Irenaeus. Both were much concerned with refuting heretics; both lived in churches of the martyrs; both were strong believers in the resurrection of the body; both were strongly Pauline in much of their theology; both saw the Holy Spirit to be at the heart of the Church and the *charismata* to be important, though in time Tertullian developed a different stance. He, like Irenaeus, testifies to the Church's contemporary healing ministry. Indeed references to exorcism and healing are scattered through many of his writings.

Tertullian clearly believed in the devil, a fallen angel[3] and corruptor of the human race from the beginning,[4] who with his supporting angels are renounced by Christians at baptism.[5] Indeed Tertullian's references to angels are usually to these evil angels who once seduced human women (Gen.6:1-2). He accepts the Judaeo-Christian view that from this illicit union came the demons.[6] These demons inhabit the air,[7] attach themselves to pagan children from birth,[8] and are devoted to the deception of humans and hindering their faith.[9] They are the power behind idolatry, their special enterprise,[10] feeding on the odours and blood of its sacrifices[11] and revelling in the savagery of the amphitheatre.[12] They inspire the oracles of the pagan world, posing as gods.[13] They inspire the heretics.[14] They cause the persecutions of Christians and seek to get them to renounce their faith.[15] They can cause sicknesses of body and mind, which they can then cure if it suits their malicious purposes.[16] They can bring about premature death in what people commonly believe to be accidents.[17]

---

[3] *Marc.* 2.10.

[4] *Test. Soul* 3, *Shows* 2.

[5] *Shows* 4.1 *et passim*.

[6] *Apol.* 22.3.

[7] *Apol.* 22.8.

[8] Via the idolatrous practices to which new-born babies are subjected (*Soul* 39, 57).

[9] *Apol.* 22.4, 6, *Soul* 57.

[10] *Shows* 4 *et passim*.

[11] *Scap.* 2.

[12] 'It is the temple of all demons. There are as many unclean spirits gathered there as it can seat men' (*Shows* 12.7).

[13] *Apol.* 22.10, 23.5-11.

[14] *Presc. Her.* 40.

[15] *Apol.* 27.3-5, 28.1.

[16] *Apol.* 22.4, 6, 11 (a reference, it seems, to the healing cults).

[17] *Soul* 57.

EXORCISM

The name 'philosopher', he declares, is of no use in exorcism, indeed Socrates is often referred to as being guided by a demon.[18] Yet the name of Christ is highly effective:

> Yet all this sovereignty and power that we have over them [the demons] derives its force only from the naming of Christ, and this reminder of what they expect to come upon them from God at the judgement-seat of Christ. They are afraid of Christ in God, and of God in Christ; and that is why they are subject to the servants of God and Christ. Thus at a touch, a breath from us, they are seized by the thought, by the foretaste of that fire,[a] and they leave the bodies of men at our command, all against their will, in pain, blushing to have you witness it. (*Apol.* 23.15-16)

> a – cf. Justin, *2 Apol.* 8.

And he goes on to say that those who claim to be gods are forced during exorcism to reveal that they are merely deceitful demons (cf. 23.4-8). Clearly they are ordered to leave in the name of Christ and this may be accompanied by a touch or blowing.[19] Elsewhere he implies that fasting is another weapon against tenacious ones.[20] Tertullian does not refer to a class of exorcist but confidently declares that any Christian may exorcise.[21]

Christians, it seems, performed a frequent public service by their exorcisms, and that free of charge. He urges the magistrates of the empire to consider the dire consequences of Christians' withholding their services:

> But who would rescue you from those secret enemies that everywhere lay waste your minds and your bodily health? I mean, from the assaults of demons, whom we drive out of you, without reward, without pay. Why, this alone would have sufficed to avenge us – to leave you open and exposed to unclean spirits with immediate possession! (*Apol.* 37.9)

In 212 addressing Scapula, Proconsul of Africa, he names specific

---

[18] *Daimonium, Apol.* 22.1, 46.5, *Soul* 1, 15, 25 *et passim*.

[19] Cf. *Soul* 15: If Socrates' wisdom came from a demon how much greater is Christian wisdom 'before the very breath of which the whole host of demons is scattered'. Cf. PGM IV.3081-84. Even though blowing might appear to some a magical trait, it could well be rationalized as a Christian act since the breath or Spirit (πνεῦμα) of God or Christ indwells all Christians (1 Cor.6:19 *et passim*).

[20] *Fasting* 8.3.

[21] *Apol.* 23.4.

instances:

> The clerk of one of [the local advocates] who was liable to be thrown
> upon the ground by an evil spirit, was set free from his affliction; as was
> also the relative of another and the little boy of a third. (*Scap.* 4)

Christians generally, it seems clear, were protected from possession by
evil spirits but not if they were rash enough to enter enemy territory
such as the idolatrous theatre. In *On the Shows* Tertullian brings forward
a cautionary example:

> What is to save such people [Christians who attend shows] from demon-
> possession? For we have in fact the case (as the Lord is witness) of that
> woman, who went to the theatre and returned devil possessed. So, when
> the unclean spirit was being exorcised and was pressed with the
> accusation that it had dared to enter a woman who believed: "and I was
> quite right, too", said he boldly; "for I found her on my own ground".
> (26.1-2)

Here, as in other cases of exorcism, interrogation of the spirit took place
before any attempt at expulsion (cf. Mk.5:9).

HEALING

In response to faith, and following confession of sins, it is at baptism
that the Christian receives fundamental healing for, 'by washing away
the sins of our early blindness, we are set free into eternal life'.[22]
Thereafter he may expect to see God's healing power at work. Most of
Tertullian's references to healing occur in lists of Christian benefits.
Through *prayer*:

> Prayer is alone that which vanquishes God...It knows nothing save how to
> recall the souls of the departed from the very path of death, to transform
> the weak, to restore the sick, to purge the possessed, to open prison-bars,
> to loose the bonds of the innocent... (*On Prayer* 29.2)

Relying on *God's patience*:

> So amply sufficient a depository of patience is God...if pain, he is a
> healer, if death, he is a reviver. (*On Patience* 15.1)

As Christian *entertainment*, far better than secular shows:

> What greater pleasure is there...than to find yourself trampling underfoot

---

[22] *Bapt.* 1.

the gods of the Gentiles, expelling demons, effecting cures...? (*Shows* 29.3)

All these are from Tertullian's early writings. A little later, in his masterful work *Prescription against the Heretics* (29.3), as we have noted above[23] he speaks of 'so many works of faith...so many miraculous gifts...so many spiritual endowments (*charismata*)' in the life of the Church before the era of the Marcionites and Valentinians (mid-second century). In *On the Flesh of Christ,* another work from about the same time, he appears to give a catalogue of miracles currently taking place when he declares:

> Our birth he [God] reforms from death by a second birth from heaven;
> our flesh he restores from every harassing malady;
> when leprous, he cleanses it of the stain;
> when blind, he rekindles its light;
> when palsied, he renews its strength;
> when possessed with devils, he exorcises it;
> when dead, he reanimates it, -
> then shall we blush to own it? (4.4)

This could be a reference to Christ's own healing miracles when on earth, as a similar list of these is given in the *Apology* 21.17 (driving out devils, healing the blind, lepers and the paralysed, and raising the dead) but, on balance, it is probably not, for in the latter case he goes on to speak of the stilling of the storm and walking on water, and throughout employs in the Latin the imperfect (a past) tense, whereas here he always uses present tenses, and starts the sequence with a clear reference to Christian new birth. If this is then a reference to his own day it is the only passage in which Tertullian uses current healing miracles as a justification for belief in the resurrection of the flesh.

Tertullian appeals again to the large number of, it seems, recent miracles performed by the Church when in 212, between itemising known exorcisms and referring to a case of anointing, he ask Scapula:

> And how many men of rank, to say nothing of common people, have been delivered from devils and healed of diseases! (*Scap.* 4.5)

Occasionally Tertullian reveals some of the specific means used in contemporary Christian healing. The case of anointing just alluded to, the first reference to this means of healing in the post-apostolic literature, was particularly impressive in that it was the healing of the Septimius Severus, Roman Emperor 193-211. The anointing was, he

---

[23] Pp. 46-47.

says, by the Christian Proculus, surnamed Torpacion, steward of Euodus. In gratitude the emperor kept him in his palace until the day of his death – a form of medical insurance no doubt! It shows how a strategically placed Christian could influence even an emperor known for his hostility to the Church.[24] F.W. Puller comments on this incident:

> And we may be sure that, if Christians used oil to cure heathens supernaturally, much more did they use it for the supernatural cure of their own sick people in accordance with the apostolic direction.[25]

The first part of his assertion may well be correct; how far this was due to the influence of the epistle of James, to which he is alluding, is open to question. Jas.5:14-16 is not acknowledged in this respect in the patristic literature until the early fifth century.[26]

In his *On the Scorpion's Sting* (1) Tertullian, after listing various current pagan remedies for this catastrophe, says that in contrast Christians use faith (if they are not smitten by doubt), making the sign of the cross over the wounded part, commanding health [in the name of Jesus], and besmearing it with the crushed remains of the scorpion. This is the first reference to the use of the sign of the cross in healing (though in *Crowns* 3.4 Tertullian speaks of Christians' tracing the sign repeatedly upon their foreheads amidst the actions of daily life, and *Apostolic Tradition* 42A explains this is for protection against the devil). Here also a 'natural' cure appears to be mingled with explicitly Christian means of healing. But Tertullian adds that the successful combination has led to Christians often aiding even pagans in this way. Barnes suggests that Tertullian is merely using a 'stylized set piece'[27] to introduce his work against human 'scorpions' who are spreading heresies and trying to dissuade Christians from martyrdom; but this does not negate this passage as a source of information. Tertullian likes to draw practical examples from life to drive home his points.[28]

With regard to the *charismata* Tertullian's thought appears to show development. In his pre-Montanist work *On Baptism* (20.5) he urges all

---

24 Cf. Frend, *Rise*, 294.
25 F.W. Puller, *The Anointing of the Sick in Scripture and Tradition*, 2nd edn (London: SPCK, 1910), 151-52.
26 In Innocent I's *Epistle* 25 (to Decentius), see Woolley, *Exorcism*, 64, but it may have been influential in this respect in Rome (see below p. 85) and perhaps elsewhere.
27 Similar to those of Dio of Prusa, 'Tertullian's Scorpiace', *JTS* 20 (1969), 108 nt.
28 In *Scorp.* 5 he points out how painful is the treatment of a surgeon (there being no anaesthetics) that leads to blessing in the end; likewise martyrdom on the path to salvation.

the newly baptised to pray for 'distributions of *charismata*' without giving any limitation. In *Against Marcion*, a work from his early Montanist period, when discussing 1 Cor.12, 14, he quotes 'to another the gift of healings, to another miracles' but he does not discuss them. Instead he challenges Marcion to display some *prophetic* gift (5.8). In his virulently Montanist works he virtually identifies the *charismata* with the prophetic powers of Montanus, Priscilla and Maximilla;[29] at least, it appears theirs are the only *charismata* that really matter to him.[30] Nowhere does he suggest that healing works distinguished Montanists from the catholic Church.[31]

Whilst it is clear from the evidence above that Tertullian attests contemporary healings, it must be seriously doubted whether these included raising the dead, despite his mentioning this in two of his lists of the boons Christians enjoy (*Prayer* 29.2, *Flesh of Christ* 4.4) In *On the Soul* 57 he contrasts the feebleness of the heretic Simon Magus, who could only pretend to bring up the souls of prophets from Hades, with Old Testament prophets, Jesus and the apostles, who had performed palpable resurrections. Elsewhere he refers again to Jesus and the apostles raising the dead,[32] but his failure to mention any raisings in the post-apostolic Church suggests that, unlike Irenaeus, he has no personal knowledge of them. It is true, however, that he puts the apostles on a pedestal, for, on one occasion in a writing from his moderate Montanist period, he writes, 'For apostles have the Holy Spirit properly, who have him fully, in the operations of prophecy, and the efficacy of miracles, and the evidence of tongues; not partially as all others have.' He has just been claiming Paul's support for the chastity he is advocating. (*Exhort.*

---

[29] *Against Praxeas* 1.4-5: 'Whose [God's] very gifts (*charismata*) he [Praxeas] has resisted and destroyed. For after the Bishop of Rome had acknowledged the prophetic gifts (*prophetias*) of Montanus, Prisca and Maximilla…he…compelled him…to desist from his purpose of acknowledging the gifts (*charismata*).' Cf. *Mon.* 1.

[30] These points have been noted by D. Rankin in *Tertullian and the Church* (Cambridge: University Press, 1995), 124-25, 199.

[31] Though in *Soul* 9.4, from his earlier Montanist phase, he mentions 'a prophetic sister of ours' who, besides seeing and hearing mysterious communications and seeing into human minds, distributes remedies to those in need (rather different, it seems, from exercising gifts of healing). Further, is Proculus surnamed Torpacion the same as 'our own Proculus, the model of chaste old age and Christian eloquence' (*Against Valentinus* 5)? If so, he may well be none other than the Proclus to whom Eusebius refers as 'the leader of the Phrygian heretics' in Rome (*H.E.* 2.25.7). Barnes dismisses this idea but gives no reason (*Tertullian*, 316). It surely remains a possibility as both Proculi appear to have lived in Rome.

[32] *Flesh of Christ* 38 (Jesus); *ibid.* 39, *Presc. Her.* 30, *Chast.* 21 (the apostles).

Chast. 4.6)

MAGIC

Tertullian is aware that Jews dismissed Jesus' own miracles as magic but, he declares in reality they were evidence that he is the divine Logos.[33] Tertullian's eagerness to use miracles in Christian apologetic is tempered further by his knowledge that magicians and some heretics appealed to miracles too.[34] When the Marcionites pointed to Christ's miracles as evidence of the existence of their 'good' God (as against the vengeful 'just' god of the Old Testament) he replies that Christ warned that many would come performing signs to lead even the elect astray -

> He thus made it clear that the credit of signs and miracles is precarious, as these are quite easy for false Christs to perform. (*Marc.* 3.3.1)

And Tertullian envisages heretics on judgement day claiming that, because their own doctors of heresy raised the dead, healed the sick and foretold the future, they too should be regarded as apostles.[35]

MEDICINE

In a number of his works Tertullian displays a wealth of biological and medical knowledge unusual in a theologian. He quotes the second-century medical authority Soranus of Ephesus.[36] He castigates Hippocrates and other eminent physicians (including, more mildly, Soranus himself) for their use of the copper instrument, the 'embryo/foetus-slayer'[37] for abortions. But this hostility is exceptional, for he freely uses medical analogies, and without any hint of deprecation.[38] In *On the Soldier's Crown* he explains how it is that he can view pagan medicine positively. Medicine, he says, like letters, music, ships, clothing and household furniture, even if they have some connection with idolatry, are legitimately used by Christians for they are among those things which –

---

[33] *Apol.* 21.17, cf. *Marc.* 3.6, *Prax.* 27.
[34] Simon Magus (*On Idolatry* 9, cf. *Soul* 57); Philumene (*Presc. Her.* 6); heretical women (*ibid.* 41.5); magicians in general (*Apol.* 23.1). And he can quote the classes of spirits upon which magicians draw (*Soul* 28).
[35] *Presc. Her.* 44.
[36] *Soul* 6.
[37] Gk. ἐμβρυοσφάκτης (*Soul* 25.4).
[38] *Penitence* 10, *Scorp.* 5, *Marc.* 2.16 *et passim*.

to meet the necessities of human life supply what is simply useful and afford real assistance and honourable comfort so that they may be well believed to have come from God's own inspiration. (8)

How different is his attitude from that of Tatian with its scorn for pharmacology, and perhaps medicine as a whole, as coming from demons!

THE ORIGIN OF SICKNESS

Tertullian attempts no systematic explanation of the origin of sickness. While some illnesses he clearly attributes to demons,[39] he also alludes several times to the divine declaration in Deut.32:39: 'I will smite and heal, I will make alive and put to death'.[40] And he sees in plagues God's hand warning Christians and chastising pagans.[41]

CONCLUSION

The writings of Tertullian are then a very valuable source of information about the continuing ministry of the Church in exorcism and healing in the early third century, particularly in North Africa. Tertullian indicates that Christian exorcism is well-known in his time and indeed rendered as a public service, free of charge. He uses it to argue powerfully for the supremacy of Christ over the gods of the State. He gives no indication that there was by then any special order of exorcist, rather he declares any Christian can exorcise – perhaps he is thinking of the simplicity of the procedure – but how many would dare? He also refers to many physical healings. In connection with these he mentions variously the need for faith, commanding in the name of Jesus, making the sign of the cross, and the use of oil. He acknowledges the continuing *charismata* but, latterly at least, seems interested only in (Montanist) prophecy. He gives us no reason to believe that the dead are being raised in his time. Warfield alights upon this point, but the fact that he virtually ignores Tertullian's testimony to contemporary healings[42] seriously discredits his own case. Tertullian declares that Christians have the right to use secular medical science except when it leads to the termination of life, and he is not averse, it seems, to 'natural' remedies. God he views as the Lord of nature as well as grace.

---

[39]   *Apol.* 22.4, 6, 11.
[40]   *Flight in Persecution* 3, *Marc.* 2.14, *Mod.* 2.
[41]   *Apol.* 41.4.
[42]   B.B. Warfield, *Counterfeit Miracles*, 12-15.

Minucius Felix

Minucius Felix is known almost entirely from his one surviving work *Octavius*, a charming Latin dialogue in which legal advocates Caecilius and Octavius debate the relative merits of Christianity and paganism, with Minucius arbitrating. The setting is the seaside at Ostia, some twelve miles from Rome, where the three friends have resorted, taking advantage of a holiday from the law courts. It is possible that an actual event is recorded here, though written up long after (1.5), but the capitulation of Caecilius at the end seems too easy to be genuine (40).

Minucius practised as an advocate at Rome,[43] but there are indications that he came from Africa.[44] The date of *Octavius* has been long debated. The work's description of the activities of demons (26-27) bears considerable affinity to Tertullian's *Apology* 22-23. Most scholars today think this was due to Minucius' dependence on Tertullian, not the other way round.[45] We may date the work, which reflects a period of tranquility, between the persecutions of 212 and 250.

DEMONS AND EXORCISM

In *Octavius* 26.8-27.8 Minucius refers to the demons as 'unclean and wandering spirits, whose heavenly vigour has been overlaid by earthly soils and lusts'. Depraved themselves, they seek the degradation of humans and, by means of heathen superstitions, to separate them from God. They were known to the poets, discussed by the philosophers (Socrates having his own attendant demon), and used by the Magi to perform tricks. They lurk under statues, exercising the influence of a present god. They guide augury and inspire oracles. They disturb men, awake or asleep, creeping secretly into their bodies. They produce diseases, terrifying minds and distorting limbs, driving people to worship them, then, glutted with the sacrifices, they may relax their grip and seem to have effected a cure. They cause too the whirling dervishes and appear as gods in dreams.[46] Then he continues -

> All this, as most of your people know, the demons themselves admit to be true, when they are driven out of men's bodies (by us) by words of exorcism and the fire of prayer. Saturn himself, Sarapis, Jupiter or any other demon you worship, under stress of pain, confess openly what they are; and surely they would not lie to their own disgrace, particularly with

---

[43] Lactantius, *D.I.* 5.1.21-22, Jerome, *Ill. Men* 58.

[44] See S.A. Donaldson, *Church Life and Thought in North Africa AD 200* (Cambridge: University Press, 1909), 174-75.

[45] P. Siniscalco, 'Minucius Felix' in *EEC*.

[46] This is almost a précis of Tertullian's *Apol.* 22-23.

some of you standing by. When the witnesses themselves confess the truth about themselves: that they are demons, you cannot but believe them; when adjured in the name of the one true God, reluctantly, in misery, they quail and quake, and either suddenly leap forth at once, or vanish gradually, according to the faith exercised by the sufferer or the grace imparted by the healer. Challenged at close quarters they run away from Christians, though at a distance in mixed crowds they set you on to harry them (Christians)... (27.5-7)

Minucius tells us that a command 'in the name of the one true God' (like some of the Greek apologists he displays reluctance to mention the name of Jesus[47]) and prayer effect the exorcism. His reference to the supposed gods being forced unwillingly to confess they are really only demons finds a parallel in Tertullian's *Apol.* 23.16-17. The reluctance of the spirit to leave and the misery it expresses in doing so finds a parallel in *Apol.* 23.16 but are amplified here, suggesting that Minucius has had close acquaintance with exorcisms. These points find parallels even in Jesus' own exorcisms (Mk.1:24, 26, 5:7, 9:26). Jesus speaks of the need for faith for there to be a successful expulsion of a spirit (Mk.9:23), so here the faith of the one afflicted is said to affect the speed of the spirit's departure.   What is meant by 'the grace imparted by the healer'? A better translation of the Latin *gratia curantis* would seem to be 'the gift (ability or power) of the healer'.[48] Finally, the view that a demon, once expelled, in reprisal stirs up crowds to persecute Christians, is common among the Fathers.[49]

CONCLUSION

Again, in an apologetic work, exorcism is seen as a demonstration of the superiority of the Christian God (and Jesus Christ, albeit not named here) over the gods of the Greco-Roman Empire. How could one continue to worship those exposed and expelled as deceptive demons? The means of exorcism appear to have changed little since New Testament times: a word of command (in the name of Christ) assisted by faith, prayer, and, it seems, a *charisma* granted to the one exorcising.[50] Such sickness as a resident demon has afflicted upon its host's body or mind is healed, one might presume, when it departs (cf. Mk.5:15, 9:27).

---

[47] Theophilus, *Aut.* 2.8, Tatian, *Orat.* 18.1-3.

[48] In the Latin version of Irenaeus, *A.H.* 2.32.4 *gratia* renders the Greek χάρισμα found in Eusebius' extract from the passage (*H.E.* 5.7.5).

[49] Justin, *1 Apol.* 57, *2 Apol.* 1; Tertullian, *Apol.* 27.3-5; Origen, *C.C.* 8.43 *et passim.*

[50] Cf. Irenaeus, *A.H.* 2.32.4.

Cyprian

Cyprian came from a wealthy, land-owning family in North Africa and had been trained in rhetoric when he was converted c.246 through the ministry of the Carthaginian presbyter Caecilian. Soon after his baptism he was ordained presbyter and, in 249, elected bishop of Carthage. In developing his understanding of the faith he was clearly much influenced by the writings of Tertullian. Indeed Jerome says that he would daily call for them with the words, "Give me the master".[51] He also knew well Minucius' *Octavius*. Cyprian's own writings were largely brief and pastoral. His collected letters (sixty-five by himself and sixteen replies) give remarkable insight into the life of the African Church at that time of persecution, apostasy and plague in the mid-third century, and they also reveal the close relationship between the Church of Carthage and the Church of Rome, tested almost to breaking point by Cyprian's clash with Pope Stephen over the terms for admission of heretics and schismatics to the Church.[52] His writings are supplemented by a biography by his deacon Pontius, and an account of his martyrdom in September 258. Because of his close connection with the two previous Latin writers it seems best to consider his evidence in this chapter rather than delaying it to the next.

EXORCISM

Cyprian follows earlier Church Fathers in his beliefs about the demons. In *That the Idols are not Gods* he quotes almost verbatim *Octavius* 26.8-27 (adding some elements from Tertullian's *Apology* 22.4, 11). In his treatise to the elderly pagan magistrate Demetrianus in 252 he gives a dramatic account of Christian exorcisms. There are echoes of Tertullian[53] and Minucius[54] but Cyprian displays vivid descriptive powers of his own, suggesting perhaps that he has witnessed such scenes:

> Oh, would you but hear and see them when they are adjured by us and tortured with spiritual scourges, and are ejected from the possessed bodies with tortures of words, when howling and groaning at the voice of men and the power of God, feeling the stripes and blows, they confess the judgement to come! Come and acknowledge that what we say is true, and since you say that you thus worship gods, believe even those whom you worship...You will see that we are entreated by those whom you entreat, that we are feared by those whom you fear, whom you adore. You will

---

[51] Jerome, *Ill. Men* 53.
[52] Cf. *Ep.* 72.
[53] *Apol.* 23.8, 15-17.
[54] *Oct.* 27.5-7.

see that under our hands they stand bound, and tremble as captives, whom
you look up to and venerate as lords: assuredly even thus you might be
confounded in those errors of years, when you see and hear your gods, at
once upon our interrogation betraying what they are, and even in your
presence unable to conceal those deceits and trickeries of theirs. (*Dem.*
15; cf. his *To Donatus* 5)

How blatantly he uses Christian exorcism for apologetic purposes! But
how effective is brow-beating in winning true conversions?

In his letter to Magnus (*Ep.* 69.15-16), written in 255, Cyprian points
out that sometimes, despite being tortured by the commands of an
exorcist (by then a minor clerical office in the Church[55]) and repeatedly
professing it is departing, a demon may lie and remain. In such a case,
only through baptism, including clinical baptism of the sick by
sprinkling with water, can its expulsion assured:

> The facts of our own experience make us aware of this also: people
> baptized in extreme necessity on their sickbed and having thus gained
> grace are delivered from the unclean spirit which has previously been
> troubling them. They live on, held in honour and esteem in the Church
> and they daily advance and increase in heavenly grace as they continue to
> grow in faith. By contrast, however, we often find that of those who are
> baptized in good health, some upon falling into sin later are seized with
> trembling at the return of the unclean spirit. Hence we can plainly see that
> in baptism the devil is driven out by the faith of the believer and that he
> comes back again if that faith should subsequently falter. (16.1, tr. Clarke)

Cyprian is wishing to show that those who claim that clinical baptism of
the sick lacks the spiritual power of baptism by immersion are wrong.
Indeed he wishes to suggest that sometimes it is better. He declares also
that a demon may re-enter a Christian who backslides.

HEALING OR HOPE?

Evidence of healing miracles independent of baptism and exorcism is
notably absent in the writings of Cyprian. True, in a rhapsodic passage
in his early letter to Donatus (AD 246), he envisages that from baptism
onwards the Spirit can provide the Christian with power 'to quench the
virus of poisons for the healing of the sick, to purge out the stains of
foolish souls by restored health' and to exorcise; such powers being
granted according to the capacity of people's faith, their chastity and
integrity (*Don.* 5). He is thinking perhaps of *charismata* which his

---

[55] Cf. *Ep.* 23. J.D. Davies has shown this order was instituted in the period
c.215-250, 'Deacons, Deaconesses and the Minor Orders in the Patristic
Period', *JEH* 14 (1963), 1-15.

'master' said should be sought after baptism;[56] but (exorcism apart) he never tells us of anyone practising them. Any thoughts of such healing power received a sobering blow with the arrival of the plague, perhaps typhus or smallpox,[57] in 252. (Ten years later it would sweep away half the population of Alexandria.[58]) It is evident that Christians and pagans alike were struck down, which Cyprian had to justify both to pagans like Demetrianus, who no doubt scoffed, and to Christians, incredulous that they should be among the victims. To Demetrianus[59] he declared that Christians were not bowed down by such adversities but had the inner strength to bear them through God's Spirit; while pagans complained loudly at the plague, Christians accepted it calmly, rejoicing in God and awaiting the blessings of the next world. Yet, he assured him, we always pray for the well-being of the State.

In *On Mortality* Cyprian explained to the church that, as long as Christians are in this world they share the material lot of the human race: famine, invasion, drought, shipwreck, 'and the diseases of the eyes, and the attack of fevers, and the feebleness of all the limbs is common to us with others'(8). A Christian must be prepared to struggle more than others because of the attacks of the devil (9). Consider Job and Tobias (10). The apostles taught us not to murmur in adversity (11). Be prepared for all hardship (12). Our strength is to be made perfect in weakness - 2 Cor.12:7-9 (13). The trials of the plague are profitable for the proof of our faith (14). The plague tests devotion to sick relatives. Facing the threat of death from it, we are more willing to face martyrdom (16). The need for patient endurance, since bodily frailty is the lot of this mortal life, he stressed again in his later work *The Benefit of Patience* (17).

There was another factor too that might in part explain why Cyprian's church did not witness miracles. If faith issuing in virtue was a necessary prerequisite for healing gifts of the Spirit,[60] the Decian persecution (249-250) that preceded the plague revealed how low the faith and virtue of the North African Church had sunk after nearly forty years of relative tranquillity. The majority of the church in Carthage lapsed voluntarily, many before the persecution even began[61] and even some clergy apostatized.[62] Why? Cyprian pointed to the lack of

---

[56] Tertullian, *Bapt.* 20.
[57] See 'Plague', *OCD*, 3rd edn.
[58] E.W. Benson, *Cyprian: His Life, His Times, His Work* (London: MacMillan, 1897), 242.
[59] *Dem.* 18-21.
[60] Cf. *Don.* 5.
[61] *Laps.* 7-8.
[62] *Ep.* 14.

spirituality amongst the church membership. There was greed for commercial gain, vanity in adornment, marriage to pagans, malice, lying, quarrelling, hatred and pride,[63] and pride and even drunkenness, debauchery and promiscuity among the Carthaginian confessors.[64] If it was the zealous church of the martyrs in Gaul in the previous century that had witnessed an array of spiritual gifts, perhaps it is not surprising that the church of the lapsed in North Africa did not. What seems more surprising in a spiritual son of Tertullian is Cyprian's own lack of expectation of miracles. Commendably in the face of the ensuing plague he summoned the church to practical, compassionate action not only for themselves but also for their enemies,[65] but then merely rationalized the situation, declaring Christians must accept sickness as a price of being part of humanity.

If we have no accounts of healing we do in fact have several dramatic accounts in *On the Lapsed* 24-26 of physical and mental punishments: A man who had denied Christ became dumb. A woman who denied, and subsequently visited the baths, was possessed by an unclean spirit and bit off her tongue; later, experiencing stomach and bowel problems, she died. An infant girl too young to speak, who had been surrendered to the magistrates by her nurse and had eaten bread mingled with wine before an idol, when subsequently taken to eucharist by her mother, became emotionally volatile, refused the cup, and when made to drink sobbed and vomited. Others who received acted as if poisoned, or found the eucharistic bread was burnt, or went raging mad, and so on.

MEDICINE

Like other Fathers, Cyprian revealed a positive attitude to the medical profession, freely employing medical metaphors for spiritual matters.[66] He could both use Hippocratic theory, by speaking of the air as the carrier of the plague, and hold to Judaeo-Christian tradition by seeing it as provoked by human sin.[67]

---

[63] *Laps.* 6, cf. *Unit.* 26, *Ep.* 11.

[64] *Ep.* 13.

[65] Pontius, *Life of Cyprian*, 9.

[66] *Laps.* 14, *Ep.* 30.3, 31.7, 34.2, 36.3 *et passim*.

[67] *Dem.* 7. D. Grout-Gerletti, 'Le vocabulaire de la contagion chez l'évêque Cyprien' in *Maladie et Maladies*, Actes du Vᵉ Colloque International 'Textes médicaux latins', Bruxelles, 4-6 September 1995, (Bruxelles: Latomus, 1998), 244-45 discusses his medical terminology. But he is surely wrong to say that ultimately Cyprian attributes all sickness to demons (231ff, 244-46) for clearly in *Laps.* 24-26 he is attributing suffering to sin.

CONCLUSION

The evidence of Cyprian is a little surprising. He attests contemporary exorcism and the establishment of the order of exorcist. He speaks of baptism (even sprinkling) as even more effective in removing possessing demons and any sickness they may have caused. He does not tell us of any with gifts of healing, nor does he appear to expect healing. Rather he rationalises sickness.

Rome

Hippolytus

Hippolytus was the most important third-century theologian of the Roman Church, a man of wide-ranging interests to whom many diverse writings are attributed. In 1551 a stone statue of a headless, seated figure[68] was found in Rome, with the titles of a number of his works inscribed on the seat. Other writings are recorded by Eusebius[69] and Jerome.[70]

Hippolytus would not accept the teaching of Bishop Zephyrinus (198-217) because of the latter's support for the Sabellian heretic Noëtus and, it seems, allowed himself c.217 to be elected rival bishop to Callistus (217-222), a former convict. The schism continued throughout the two subsequent episcopates until Hippolytus and his rival Pontianus were in 235 both exiled to Sardinia where, it seems, they were reconciled before they died, and their bodies were subsequently brought back in 236 and honourably interred.

Amongst Hippolytus' works mentioned on the base of the statue is the church order the *Apostolic Tradition*. It appeared lost until, in the early twentieth century, it was identified with what had been known as the 'Egyptian Church Order' and dated c.215 by Dom Gregory Dix.[71] More recently scholars have focused on its clearly composite nature. In their commentary P.F. Bradshaw, M.E. Johnson and L.E. Phillips now state cautiously they believe it to be 'an aggregate of material from different sources, quite possibly arising from different geographical regions, and probably from different historical periods, from perhaps as early as the mid-second century to as late as the mid-fourth'.[72] Bradshaw

---

[68] See E. Prinzivalli, 'Hippolytus, Statue of' in *EEC*.
[69] *H.E.* 6.22.1.
[70] *Ill. Men* 61.
[71] G. Dix, *The Treatise on the Apostolic Tradition of St. Hippolytus of Rome*, rev. edn. H. Chadwick (London: SPCK, 1968), xxxv-vii.
[72] Bradshaw *et al*, *The Apostolic Tradition: A Commentary* (Minneapolis: Fortress Press, 2002), 14.

had pointed out earlier that all church orders were working documents, adapted by successive editors to suit their own situations.[73] It still remains quite possible, however, that Hippolytus was responsible for the original form of this work and, for this present study, we shall accept this as a working hypothesis.

Like Hippolytus' acknowledged works the *Apostolic Tradition* was written in Greek. The Greek is now only available for chapters 3, 11, 23 and 26. For the rest we rely on a literal Latin translation made from the Greek in Syria in the fourth/early fifth century, and later Sahidic, Arabic, Ethiopic and Bohairic versions which all come from a common strand of the text.

The document contains a number of interesting references to physical sickness and healing and to demon possession and exorcism. First, in the Prologue we find the following reference to an earlier work of the author:

> We have set down those things which were worthy of note about the gifts
> which God has bestowed on men from the beginning according to his
> own will, presenting to himself that image which had gone astray.[74]

As the base of the statue records amongst Hippolytus' writings one *On Charismata* (now lost) it is possible that that is being referred to here, especially as it is listed immediately above the *Apostolic Tradition*[75] but, if so, its scope was far wider than, say, a discussion of 1 Cor.12. The 'image' mentioned is surely God's own in man (Gen.1:26-7) which had 'gone astray' as a result of the fall.

The paragraphs of the rest of the *Apostolic Tradition* have been variously numbered. We shall follow the numbering and translation of G.J. Cuming in his English translation[76] unless otherwise indicated.

Of the Offering of the Oil

5. If anyone offers oil, (the bishop) shall render thanks in the same way as for the offering of bread and wine, not saying it word for word, but to similar effect, saying:
> O God, sanctifier of this oil, as you give health to those who are
> anointed and receive that with which you anointed kings, priests,

---

[73]   Bradshaw, *The Search for the Origins of Christian Worship* (London: SPCK, 1992), 71ff.

[74]   G.J. Cuming, *Hyppolytus: A Text for Students*, 2nd edn. (Nottingham: Grove Books, 1987), Grove Liturgical Study 8, text, 1.

[75]   Though see Bradshaw *et al*, *Apostolic Tradition*, 22.

[76]   See nt. 74. The reference subdivisions when given are from Bradshaw *et al*, *Apostolic Tradition*.

and prophets, so may it give strength to all those who taste it, and health to all those who are anointed with it.

This offering was made at the eucharist. Bradshaw *et al*[77] point out that neither the Latin nor the Ethiopic texts (our sources here) mention the bishop, so possibly the one offering oil is intended to say the prayer. But this is surely unlikely in a church order of this sort, particularly as later it is the bishop who gives thanks for the bread, wine and water (21.27, 29), even though section 5 may lack the fluency of the latter.

Tertullian refers to the practice of anointing priests in Old Testament times when speaking of baptismal anointing (*Bapt.* 7). That oil was used for healing by the church in Rome c.215 is probable in the light of Tertullian's reference to the contemporary case of Proculus' anointing the emperor Severus in 212.[78] These two references are the first in Christian literature since James 5:14-16. Since the epistle of James was almost certainly known in Rome in the first half of the second century[79] and probably encouraged the practice of anointing in the church in Rome, our present passage may well reveal what had long been going on there; but it does not specify that the anointing should be the prerogative of the clergy alone. Its reference to tasting the oil is unique in the pre-Nicene literature, and may possibly be the work of a later editor bringing it in line with a practice of the Post-Nicene Church,[80] though the fact that it is integrated into the prayer and not added as an afterthought suggests otherwise.

C. Harris[81] has drawn attention to several passages in the Babylonian and Jerusalem Talmuds indicating Jewish healers practiced a form of anointing the sick accompanied by a whispered prayer based on Ex.15:26. The rabbis disapproved of the whispering because of its magical associations.

Of the Gifts of Healing

14. If anyone says, 'I have received a gift of healing by a revelation', hands shall not be laid on him, for the facts themselves will show whether he has spoken the truth.[82]

---

[77]   *Ibid.*, 49.

[78]   Tertullian, *Scap.* 4.

[79]   See S. Laws, *James*, 2-23.

[80]   Cf. miracles of St Martin of Tours, ch. 6 below, 'Gifts of Healing'.

[81]   'Visitation of the Sick: Unction, Imposition of Hands and Exorcism' in *Liturgy and Worship: A Companion to the Prayer Books of the Anglican Communion*, ed. W.K. Lowther Clarke and C. Harris (London: SPCK, 1932), 510-11.

[82]   In the absence of the Latin, Cuming draws here on the other versions. The Ethiopic (cf. Arabic) have 'gift of healing', but the Sahidic has 'gifts of

In the absence of the Latin this form is taken principally from the Sahidic. This passage clearly testifies to the continuance of charismatic gifts of healing among the laity of the church in Rome in the early third century. Bradshaw *et al*[83] suggest it also indicates resistance to the creation of a special order of 'healers' within the church, parallel perhaps to that of 'prophets'. But in fact this passage is merely dealing with the authentication of claimed healing gifts. Results alone will settle the claim. It does perhaps indicate that by this time some thought healing should be the prerogative of the clergy alone.

Bishop's Ministry to the Sick

34. Each deacon, with the subdeacons, shall attend on the bishop. They shall inform him of those who are ill, so that, if he pleases, he may visit them. For a sick man is greatly comforted when the high-priest remembers him.

A.T. 20.1-2 specifies that all catechumens must have the testimony of witnesses that they have lived a life worthy of baptism. Amongst the considerations is 'whether they have visited the sick'. This is part of what one should expect of all Christians (cf. Mt.25:36). But care for the sick was also seen in the Early Church (as today) as a special responsibility of the clergy.[84] Here it is specified that the bishop, as senior cleric, should be kept informed of the sick, to visit those whom he chooses. One might suppose that he would give them prayer ministry and anointing. The term 'high priest' for a bishop is in line with Cyprian's referring to a presbyter as 'in priestly honour' (*Ep.* 61). Such terms reflect the beginning of a tendency to identify the Church's ministry with the priesthood of Israel under the old covenant.

Possession by a Demon

15. If anyone is possessed by [lit. 'has'] a demon, he shall not hear the word of teaching until he is pure. (15.8)

This is the last section of the scrutiny specified of those seeking to become catechumens. Having an 'impure spirit' (cf. Mk.1:26) renders a person impure. How to deal with this situation is not specified here but later in the document we hear of the following ritual exorcism:

---

healing'. *Apostolic Constitutions* 8.26.2 has, like 1 Cor.12:9, 'gifts of healings'. As *A.C.* 8 contains an augmented form of *A.T.* this may have been the original reading in *A.T.* 14.

[83]   *Apostolic Traditon*, 80.

[84]   See Polycarp, *Phil.* 6; Cyprian, *Ep.* 7.2; *Didascalia* 16.

Of Those Who Will Receive Baptism

20....From the time that they were set apart, let hands be laid on them daily while they are exorcised. And when the day of their baptism approaches, the bishop shall exorcise each one of them, in order that he may know whether he is pure. And if anyone is not good or not pure let him be put aside because he has not heard the word with faith, for it is impossible that the alien should hide himself for ever. (20.3-4)

If these candidates have passed the initial scrutiny for purity, why then this further exorcistic procedure? Bradshaw *et al*[85] point out that the Ethiopic version and the equivalent passage in the *Canons of Hippolytus* (Egypt, fourth century) make no mention of exorcism here and may be witnesses to an earlier form of the rite without exorcism. Why did baptismal exorcism develop? Perhaps because the Church viewed all pagans as contaminated by demons through their participation in idolatry.[86] The daily repetition of the exorcism would suggest the cleansing was believed to be gradual, perhaps imperceptible. The final assessment and exorcism were left to the bishop. Only failure to respond to the Gospel message in (repentance and) faith could inhibit the candidate's deliverance. The laying on of hands here for exorcism is a new feature. No doubt it was felt appropriate in what must have been generally a non-violent situation. During their period of preparation the catechumens were not allowed to partake of the eucharistic elements, but instead, it seems, were given special exorcised bread and their own cup of wine blessed by the bishop (26). Returning to *A.T.* 20:

On the Saturday those who are to receive baptism shall be gathered in one place at the bishop's decision. They shall all be told to pray and kneel. And he shall lay his hand on them and exorcise all alien spirits that they may flee out of them and never return into them. And when he has finished exorcising them, he shall breathe on their faces, and when he has signed their forehead, ears, and noses, he shall raise them up. (20.7-8)

---

[85] *Apostolic Traditon*, 109.

[86] This started with contamination from the idolatrous practices to which new-born babies were subjected, Tertullian, *Soul* 39. H.A. Kelly points to the 'sin demons' of the *Testaments of the Twelve Patriarchs* (of Jewish origin) which tempt each person from birth, to *Hermas'* good and bad angels trying to influence each person, and to the Gnostic Valentinus' teaching that evil spirits live in the human heart (*The Devil at Baptism: Ritual, Theology, and Drama* (New York: Cornell University Press, 1985), ch.3.

This is perhaps the bishop's final exorcism referred to in 20.3-4.[87] But again it may be that the rites described in this passage formed no part of the original *Apostolic Tradition* for, as Bradshaw *et al* point out,[88] they find no parallel in other Christian literature relating to baptism before the late fourth century.

Let us look at one more section of our church order:

> *Of the Conferring of Holy Baptism*
> **21.**....And at the time fixed for baptising, the bishop shall give thanks over the oil, which he puts in a vessel; one calls it 'oil of thanksgiving'. And he shall also take other oil and exorcise it; one calls it 'oil of exorcism'. And a deacon takes the oil of exorcism and stands on the priest's left; and another deacon takes the oil of thanksgiving and stands on the priest's right. And when the priest takes each one of those who are to receive baptism he shall bid him renounce, saying, 'I renounce you, Satan, and all your service and all your works.' And when each one has renounced all this, he shall anoint him with the oil of exorcism, saying to him: 'Let every spirit depart from you.' (21.6-10)

While Hippolytus' contemporary Tertullian tells of a public renunciation of the devil and his retinue before three-fold immersion in water[89] and of an anointing after it, he makes no reference to any pre-baptismal anointing.[90] This suggests this feature may not have been in the original version of the *Apostolic Tradition*. Indeed the use of oil as a further exorcistic practice may have derived ultimately from Gnosticism.[91]

CONCLUSION

The *Apostolic Tradition* clearly comes from a community concerned with the welfare of the sick. They must be visited and cared for by all, including the bishop. Part of the ministry to them must surely have been anointing with oil. There were in the church also lay people with gifts

---

[87] Though Kelly thinks not, as there appears no question of any of the candidates' being turned back. He sees this, like the later use of the 'oil of exorcism' as a 'dramatic recapitulation of what has gone before...to edify the congregation, strengthen the candidates, and warn the evil spirits not to return' (*Devil*, 87).

[88] *Apostolic Tradition*, 111.

[89] *Shows* 4, *Crown* 3.

[90] *Bapt.* 6-7, *Res. Flesh* 8.

[91] K. Thraede, 'Exorzismus', 85-86; Kelly, *Devil*, 74. Kelly devotes ch. 4 of his book to discussing the initiation rites of Theodotus, a disciple of the Gnostic Valentinus, which are preserved by Clement of Alexandria in his *Excerpts from Theodotus*.

of healing, and pressure to authorise their ministry by ordination is here firmly resisted. The complex baptismal procedure suggests we have here later elaborations of what was in the original form of this church order.

Cornelius

Cornelius was elected bishop of Rome in 251 following a fourteen-month vacancy of the see due to the martyrdom of his predecessor Fabian. Novatian, a presbyter who had played a prominent part in the Roman Church during the vacancy, feeling he had been unjustly passed over in the election, took up a rigoristic position on the treatment of those who had lapsed in the Decian persecution, and allowed himself to be elected as a rival bishop. Eusebius has preserved part of a vitriolic letter of Cornelius to Fabius of Antioch, attacking Novatian for this wicked presumption. In it he detailed the hierarchy of the Roman Church at that time:

> This vindicator, then, of the Gospel did not know that there should be *one* bishop to a catholic church, in which he was not ignorant (for how could he be?) that there are forty-six presbyters, seven deacons, seven sub-deacons, forty-two acolytes, fifty-two exorcists, readers and doorkeepers, above fifteen hundred widows and persons in distress...But not even did this great multitude...nor an immense and countless laity turn him from such a desperate failure and recall him to the Church. (*H.E.* 6.43.11-12)

In the Greek the 'fifty-two' comes after 'doorkeepers' showing it refers to the categories of exorcist, reader and doorkeeper in total but perhaps, as they are mentioned first, twenty or so were exorcists. The *Apostolic Tradition* does not mention the order of exorcist, but by the middle of the century it was clearly well-established in Rome. Indeed, since Firmilian[92] speaks of one active in Cappadocia c.235; c.240 Origen speaks of one in a sermon;[93] and in the 250s Cyprian alludes to them in his letters,[94] evidently the order had become widespread by then.

J.G. Davies has convincingly shown that the order came into existence to help the bishop and deacons control the insanely ill, and that they were not responsible for the more formalized pre-baptismal exorcisms.[95]

---

[92] In Cyprian, *Ep.* 75.

[93] *Hom. on Josh.* 24.1. Since the study of P. Nautin, *Origène: Sa Vie et Son Oeuvre* (Paris: Beauchnesne, 1977), 389-409, it has been generally accepted that Origen's homilies were delivered in the period 238-42.

[94] *Epp.* 23, 69.15.

[95] J.G. Davies, 'Deacons', 9-15.

Novatian

Of pagan parentage and well educated Novatian fell seriously ill, but on receiving clinical baptism he recovered.[96] He was ordained presbyter by Bishop Fabian (236-250) and, as we have already noted, played a leading part in the Church of Rome during the fourteen-month vacancy after the latter was martyred. His letters to Cyprian over the treatment the lapsed *(Epp.* 30, 36) have been preserved and are said to excel in style the other letters from Rome preserved in the corpus.[97] Disgruntled, it seems, when he was not elected Fabian's successor, he allowed himself to be consecrated 'anti-pope' by three Italian bishops. This act infuriated not only Cornelius, but also Cyprian[98] and much of the wider Church. Novatian died in the Valerian persecution (257-8), but his schism persisted much longer.

The third section of Novatian's fine doctrinal work on the Trinity contains the following passage about the work of the Holy Spirit:

> This is he who places prophets in the Church, instructs teachers, directs tongues, gives powers and healings, does wonderful works, counsels and orders and arranges whatever other gifts there are of *charismata*; and thus makes the Lord's Church everywhere, and in all, perfected and completed. (29)

R.A.N. Kydd,[99] noting the present tense of the verbs in this passage, thinks Novatian may be describing the current state of the Church in Rome. But how could anyone see in a Church afflicted by persecution, and torn by rivalry and enmity, anything 'perfect' and 'complete'? Novatian's fine cadences must not deceive us. He has just quoted Christ's promises of the Paraclete in Jn.14 -16, then briefly alluded to the Spirit's work in the apostles in Acts, and now he seems to be running through the list of *charismata* in 1 Cor.12:4-11, 28. Afterwards he moves on to the coming of the Spirit upon Christ at his baptism in the form of a dove. In other words he is making a tour of the New Testament's teaching about the work of the Spirit. Something more substantial than his dulcet tones is necessary to combat the impression given by Cyprian and by Dionysius of Alexandria[100] that supernatural healings were not generally in evidence at this time.

---

[96] Cornelius, *apud* Eusebius, *H.E.* 6.43.14.
[97] H.J. Vogt, 'Novatian' in *EEC.*
[98] Cyprian, *Epp.* 44-48, 52.
[99] Kydd, *Charismatic Gifts*, 61-62.
[100] Qu. by Eusebius, *H.E.* 7.22.

Syria

Didascalia Apostolorum

The *Didascalia Apostolorum* is the third of the church orders that have come down to us from the early Church after the *Didache* and the *Apostolic Tradition.* It represents Church life, it seems, in northern Syria and probably dates from the first half of the third century. Its atmosphere is Judaeo-Christian with many quotations from the Old Testament and its Apocrypha as well from a number of books of the New Testament. It takes the form of an address to the whole Church by the apostles and elders, a conscious imitation of the apostolic conference and letter in Acts 15. It presents quite a detailed picture of the life of the church it addresses.

Whilst amongst the duties of the bishop is the allocating of alms to the sick and needy (4, 9), and it is the deacons and deaconesses who are to visit, or arrange visits, to the same (16); rather surprisingly it is the order of widows which is entrusted with a ministry of prayer for them. These widows, aged not less than fifty, were supported by church charity and were expected to use their time beneficially:

> But a widow who wishes to please God sits at home and meditates upon the Lord day and night, and without ceasing at all times offers intercession and prays with purity before the lord. And she receives whatever she asks because her whole mind is set upon this. (tr. Connolly, 136)

Besides making woollen goods at home for the needy, she is expected to visit and minister to the sick, as directed by the ordained clergy. But there were some who fell far short of such expectations as the following reprimand reveals:

> But thou, 0 widow, who art without discipline, seest thy fellow widows or thy brethren in sickness, and hast no care to fast and pray over thy members, and to lay hand upon them and to visit them, but feignest thyself to be not in health, or not at leisure; but to others who are in sins or are gone forth from the Church, because they give much thou art ready and glad to go and visit them. You then who are such ought to be ashamed...Know then, sisters, that whatsoever the pastors with the deacons command you, and you obey them, you obey God. (Connolly, 140)

So it seems, in the Syrian churches represented by the *Didascalia,* effective prayer for healing was largely entrusted by the busy clergy to a class of the poor with time on their hands which might otherwise be misused![101]

The First Epistle to the Virgins

The two Pseudo-Clementine *Epistles to Virgins* in Syriac, found with a copy of the Syriac New Testament (the Peshitta) in 1732, are generally thought to have originated in the third-century Syrian Church. They were known to Jerome.[102] They breathe a very earnest spirit, well versed in both the Jewish Scriptures and many of the books of the New Testament including the Pauline epistles. They depict supreme devotion to the cause of Christ as requiring a life of chastity for both men and women. They place considerable emphasis on the Holy Spirit, who enables the Christian virgin to conquer the appetites of the flesh. But within the Church there are, too, shameless people, some of whom are openly worldly in their behaviour –

> Others gad about among the houses of virgin brethren or sisters, on pretence of visiting them or reading the Scriptures to them, or exorcising them. (1.10, ANF)

They desire to be teachers, and display their fine rhetoric, but do evil in the name of Christ. They appear to have claimed to speak 'the word of knowledge, or the word of instruction, or of prophecy' by the Spirit, but falsely (1.11). The following chapter contains an extended passage of great interest which deserves to be quoted in full:

> This also, again, is suitable and right and comely for those who are brethren in Christ, that they should visit those who are harassed by evil spirits, and pray and pronounce adjurations over them, intelligently, offering such prayer as is acceptable before God; not with a multitude of fine words, well prepared and arranged, so that they appear to men eloquent and of a good memory. Such men are "like a sounding pipe, or a tinkling cymbal;" and they bring no help to those over whom they make their adjurations; but they speak with terrible words, and affright people, but do not act with true faith, according to the teaching of our Lord, who hath said: "This kind goeth not out but by fasting and prayer", offered unceasingly and with earnest mind. And let them holily ask and beg of God, with cheerfulness and all circumspection and purity, without hatred and without malice. In this way let us approach a brother or a sister who is sick, and visit them in a way that is right, without guile, and without covetousness, and without noise, and without talkativeness, and without

---

[101] By the time the *Disascalia* was written up in the fourth-century *Apostolic Constitutions*, bk.7, this responsibility had been removed from the widows.

[102] *To Jovinus* 1.12.

such behaviour as is alien from the fear of God, and without haughtiness, but with the meek and lowly Spirit of Christ. Let them therefore, with fasting and with prayer make their adjurations, and not with the elegant and well-arranged and fitly ordered words of learning, but as men who have received the gift of healing from God, confidently, to the glory of God. By your fastings and prayers and perpetual watching, together with your other good works, mortify the works of the flesh by the power of the Holy Spirit. He who acts thus "is a temple of the Holy Spirit of God". Let this man cast out demons, and God will help him. For it is good that a man help those that are sick. Our Lord hath said: "Cast out demons", at the same time (commanding) many other acts of healing; and "Freely ye have received, freely give." For such persons as these a goodly recompense is laid up by God, because they serve their brethren with the gifts that have been given them by the Lord...

This passage gives a wealth of information. The 'gift of healing' and the reference to 'sounding pipe and tinkling cymbal' clearly echo 1 Cor.12-13. *Virg.* 1.11, 12 quote the epistle of James, referring to it as 'Scripture', but ignore Jas.5:14-16 with its reference to calling the elders of the church and anointing with oil. Exorcism appears as part, perhaps the primary work, of those exercising a gift of healing. It requires fasting, prayer (sometimes persistent prayer) and commands (presumably in the name of Jesus), all proceeding from an earnest and pure heart, and offered free of charge. Those who flaunt their education using verbose and polished words of exorcism but, lacking these qualities, clearly fail. Woolley suggests their speaking with 'terrible words' that 'affright people' may in fact refer to their use of magical charms containing terrifying names.[103] If so, they may be certain Gnostic teachers operating within the church. They may well have wished to charge for their services.

The Apocryphal Acts of John and Thomas

The *Apocryphal Acts of John* and *Thomas* are both believed to date from the first half of the third century, to have been written in Syriac, and to derive from East Syria though, since the location of most of John's activities is Ephesus, where the apostle is believed to have spent the last part of his life,[104] the *Acts of John* might have come from there and been written originally in Greek. These Apocryphal Acts, like those of the preceding century, were clearly designed for entertainment and depict the most bizarre happenings. In the *Acts of John* once more the most

---

[103] *Exorcism* 25 regarding the use of 'terrible words' by pagan exorcists see above p.10 ('sonorous nonsense syllables') and below p.147-48, no. 19.

[104] Cf. Eusebius, *H.E.* 3.23.

difficult form of miracle, the raising of the dead, is the most frequently performed. Nevertheless, the methods of performing the miracles still reflect those of the New Testament in their simplicity and directness. As with the *Acts of Peter*, Encratite[105] elements are present but, in addition, there are Gnostic[106] elements.

The most elaborate story in the *Acts of John*, the Drusiana saga (63-86), a full-scale novel in itself, gives the flavour of the document:

> Callimachus, a pagan, falls in love with the devout and continent Christian Drusiana, wife of Andronicus, John's host in Ephesus. She dies of grief that she should be the source of such temptation. Callimachus bribes Fortunatus, Andronicus' steward, to open her grave. While Callimachus is stripping the body of the dead Drusiana to violate it, a snake appears, gives Fortunatus a mortal bite, and wraps itself around Callimachus, preventing the foul deed. Andronicus and John, going to the grave, learn what has happened from an angel. Callimachus is then brought back to life from death's door and converted. Drusiana is next raised to life and wants Fortunatus raised too because Christians do not repay evil for evil. She takes him by the hand and commands, "Rise, Fortunatus, in the name of our Lord Jesus Christ!" He rises, but is clearly unrepentant and later dies again. Before the last act of the drama the believers break bread, celebrating the eucharist in Drusiana's tomb. (My summary)

Mildly Encratite elements are the continence of Drusiana and Andronicus' viewing her as his 'sister',[107] though such an attitude was scarcely sectarian.[108] The Christian motif of love of enemies is clear in the raising of Fortunatus, and in the means of raising - a direct command in the name of Jesus Christ.[109]

The *Acts of Thomas* is of interest to us, not only for its healing stories, but also because oil is used in Christian initiation (a Gnostic trait, it seems[110]) and is clearly expected to bring physical as well as spiritual healing. In *A.Th.* 120 a convert Mygdonia asks Thomas for 'the

---

[105]   See for instance *A.Th.* 51-52 with its stress on chastity.
[106]   See for instance *A.J.* 94-96.
[107]   Not stated in my brief summary but in the original.
[108]   Cf. Tertullian, *Wife* 1.6; Eusebius, *D.E.* 1.8.
[109]   Cf. Acts 9:34.
[110]   Thraede, 'Exorzismus', 85; Kelly, *Devil*, 74. The rationale is spelt out in the second-century Gospel of Philip, logion 95: 'The chrism is superior to baptism, for it is from the word 'chrism' that we have been called 'Christians', certainly not from the word 'baptism'.' See E. Segelberg, 'The Gospel of Philip and the New Testament' in *The New Testament and Gnosis*, ed. Logan and Wedderburn (Edinburgh: T & T Clark, 1983), 209.

seal of Jesus Christ' (i.e. initiation). He is willing to give it to her and, as he pours oil over her uncovered head, he says:

Holy oil, given us for sanctification; hidden mystery, in which the Cross was shown to us; you are the straightener of bent limbs; you are the humbler of hard works; you point out the hidden treasures; you are the sprout of goodness. Let your power come and rest on your servant Mygdonia, and heal her by this liberty. (121, from the Greek)

In the Syriac version the emphasis on healing is even more pronounced. It adds the invocation, as Thomas throws the oil on Mygdonia's head a second time: 'Heal her of her old wounds, and wash away from her sores, and strengthen her weakness.' (tr. Klijn) The link between the oil and the cross are said by Klijn[111] to be because an olive tree was believed to be growing in paradise, and the cross was identified with this tree of life.

In another story a beautiful woman requests Thomas to administer 'the seal' to her to give her protection from a demon that has been harassing her (42-50). In another, a Christian youth, who has murdered his lover because she would not adopt chastity as he had, attempted to receive the eucharist but found, as he did so, his hands withered and he could no longer put them to his mouth. Thomas perceives he has done something wrong and says:

The Eucharist of the Lord has convicted you. For this gift by entering many, brings healing, especially to those who come in faith and love; but you it has withered away, and what has happened has happened not without justification. (51)

The youth confesses what he has done, is cleansed and restored, and is invited to assist in raising the girl. There are no actual accounts in the pre-Nicene literature of healing through receiving the eucharist.

At the end of *A.Th.* a healing story is related in connection with Thomas' grave. King Misdaeus had been responsible for the apostle's death. Now, long after, one of his sons is possessed by a fierce demon that no-one can remove. Misdaeus is considering opening the grave and taking one of the apostle's bones to hang round his son's neck to effect a cure when Thomas appears to the king and asks how, if he had not believed in him whilst he was alive, could he believe in him now he is dead; yet, he continues, Jesus Christ has compassion on him. Opening the grave Misdaeus finds the bones gone (a believer had smuggled them

---

[111] *The Acts of Thomas: Introduction, Text, Commentary* (Leiden: Brill, 1962), 284.

to the West) so he takes dust from where they were and puts it on his son's neck saying, "I believe in you, Jesus Christ, now that he has left me who troubles men and opposes them lest they should see you." And the boy becomes whole.

This suggests perhaps that apostolic and martyr shrines were beginning to have a role in Christian healing even in pre-Nicene times. It is noteworthy, however, that, though dust associated with the apostle's relics takes the place of the living apostle, it is faith in Jesus Christ that is proclaimed to effect the cure.

CONCLUSION

As with the earlier Apocryphal Acts, the *Acts of John* is novelistic literature that may reflect an interest by its readership in current healing ministry and the straightforward methods being used, despite some Gnostic influence. The *Acts of Thomas* is of further interest in that it suggests anointing for healing has been subsumed under Gnostic-influenced initiation using oil. The administration of this 'seal' is seen both to bring healing and to provide protection against demons. *A.Th.*'s final story is the first intimation of martyrs' relics being used for (healing or) deliverance ministry.

Bardaisan

Bardaisan (154-222), philosopher and poet, was the first to produce Syriac Christian literature. Born of noble, pagan parents he was a refugee from Parthia, brought up at the court of Edessa with the future king Abgar IX, with whom he had an enduring friendship. He received a Hellenic education and gained a knowledge of cosmology. He became a Christian in the last quarter of the second century,[112] wrote against the Marcionites, and opposed the Valentinians to whom he once belonged. He thought of himself as orthodox, 'but', says Eusebius, 'in fact he did not completely clean off the filth of his ancient heresy'.[113] From what remains of his writings we find a Syrian Judaeo-Christian Gnosis similar to the Gospel of Thomas.[114]

While his own writings are known only from fragments, there is extant in Syriac *The Book of the Laws of the Lands* by his disciple Philip, which reproduces a dialogue between Bardaisan and the Marcionite Avida. Here we find a cosmology which fuses together the early chapters of Genesis and Babylonian astrology. Bardaisan has

---

[112] L.W. Barnard, 'The Origins and Emergence of the Church in Edessa during the First Two Centuries AD', *VC* 22 (1968), 173-75.

[113] *H.E.* 4.30-33.

[114] Barnard, 'Origins', 171.

wrestled with the issues of determinism and free-will and come to an understanding of their respective spheres. Nature causes life and growth, he says, but fate brings about diseases and blemishes in the body, deformed children and premature death.[115] I.e. nature is the power of life but fate is acting when the normal pattern is upset. Yet, as fate can crush nature, so freedom can crush fate. There are diverse laws among the nations and these cannot be put down to fate but are due to men's free decisions. Men freely change and abolish laws. Christians freely obey their own laws rather than the laws of the lands in which they happen to live. Nevertheless:

> Sickness and health, wealth and poverty, that which does not depend on their free-will, comes over them wherever they are.[116]

Yet when God wills anything it is possible; no-one can withstand it.

Since, within Bardaisan's world view, fate holds the key to sickness and health, he seems to allow little scope for a Christian healing ministry. Or could human freedom combine with the power of God to overturn the ravages of fate, even in this its stronghold? He certainly never mentions it.

CONCLUSION

If the intellectual Bardaisan has no confidence of changing such ill-health as befalls a person, the less educated, devout members of the Syrian churches in the first half of the third century: the devout widows and at least some of the readers of the Apocryphal Acts, as well as the celibate, would seem to have considerably more confidence in bringing healing to the sick, through prayer, anointing and other ministry in the name of Christ.

Asia Minor

The Montanists

In the late second century it was clearly the bishops of the Church who confronted the Montanist prophetess Maximilla[117] and would have exorcised Priscilla[118] but for the intervention of their supporters. Some half-century later (256) Firmilian, the long-serving bishop of Caesarea

---

[115] *The Book of the Laws of the Countries*, tr. H.J.W. Drijvers (Assen: Van Gorcum, 1965), 19.

[116] *Ibid.*, 61.

[117] Eusebius, *H.E.* 5.16.17.

[118] *Ibid.* 5.19.3.

in Cappadocia, relates in a letter to Cyprian[119] that c.235 a woman claiming to be a prophetess predicted an earthquake that happened, and performed 'astonishing feats', but was confronted by an exorcist, who interrogated her and revealed that the spirit within her was 'thoroughly evil'. It is interesting to note that the work of exorcism appears by then to have passed from the bishops to the order of exorcist, though neither bishop nor exorcist were able to expel what they took to be lying spirits in the mouths of those who claimed to be prophetesses.

Gregory Thaumaturgus

Gregory 'Thaumaturgus' ('Wonder-Worker') was born c.213 into a prosperous pagan family in Neocaesarea, Pontus. After studying rhetoric and law, he met Origen at Caesarea in Palestine, was converted through him, and remained his student for several years. Returning home in the 240s he became bishop of Neocaesarea. His episcopate appears to have been markedly successful, the pagan population of that district becoming Christian and greatly revering him. He died c.270. Neither his surviving writings nor Eusebius' references to him give any indication of his later reputation as a wonder-worker. The *Life of Gregory,* written about a century after his death by the theologian and bishop Gregory of Nyssa, whose grandmother had been taught by him, presents a different picture. Gregory drew on oral tradition. He appears to have been somewhat careless in establishing facts for he says Gregory was Origen's pupil in Alexandria and he never quotes Gregory's own writings. Some miracles he attributes to him seem clearly fabulous, as when he dries up a lake by prayer,[120] or when he plants his staff which grows into a tree and diverts a river.[121] Various exorcisms are attributed to him, including one at a local fair which impressed Telfer[122] enough to think that it was from an eye-witness account. But in fact Gregory's alleged method of exorcism: breathing on his shoulder cloth and then throwing it over the demonised youth, causing him great perturbation, before laying a hand on him which brings about the departure of the demon, seems to be making history a hostage to drama. The biblical and subsequent patristic pattern of exorcism is invariably to command a demon in the name of Jesus to depart, an approach notably absent here.

---

[119] *Ep.* 75 in the collection of Cyprian's letters.
[120] Slusser, FOC 98, para. 52-55.
[121] Slusser, para. 56-61.
[122] W. Telfer,'The Cultus of St. Gregory Thaumaturgus', in *HTR* 29 (1936), 230. The story is in MPG 941C-D (Slusser, para. 77).

Socrates the Church historian, writing in Constantinople in the 430s speaks of Gregory's healing the sick (as well as exorcising).[123] While Gregory of Nyssa's *Life* describes no individual healings it contains the summary statement: 'For his word amazed the hearing as his mighty deeds with the sick amazed the eyes'.[124] Furthermore at the end of the *Life* there comes a story relating to Gregory's ministry in Neocaesarea:[125]

There was a pagan festival in the city and so many flocked into the theatre that it overflowed with people. They cried out, "Zeus, give us space!" whereupon a plague was sent upon them and spread like wildfire. People resorted to pagan temples for healing and tried to cool themselves in springs, streams and cisterns, but to no avail. Many died. Then people turned to Gregory. When a house was threatened by the plague there was only one way of deliverance: 'that the great Gregory enter that house and by prayer drive out the disease which was invading (it)'. His success led to people abandoning oracles, sacrifices and idols, and finding salvation by faith in Christ. (My summary)

As this story is located early in Gregory's ministry in Neocaesarea, which started in the 240s, it might in fact have originated from an account of a local outbreak of the plague.

Gregory's reputation for miracles may have had some basis in fact,[126] but his biographer's overcredulous approach to the legends that had developed by his time regrettably leaves us without any means of recovering what really happened.

Egypt/Palestine

Origen

Born c.185 into a strongly Christian family in Alexandria, Origen received both a Hellenistic education and a good grounding in the Christian Scriptures. Eusebius says he received catechetical training from Clement.[127] Before Origen was seventeen his father was martyred

---

[123] Socrates, *H.E.* 4.27.

[124] Slusser, para.47.

[125] Slusser, para.99-103.

[126] See H. Crouzel, 'Gregory the Thaumaturge' in *EEC*.

[127] Eusebius, *H.E.* 6.6. J.W. Trigg *Origen* (London: Routledge, 1998), 9-11 thinks this likely; H. Crouzel, *Origen*, tr. A.S. Worrall (Edinburgh: T & T Clark, 1989), 7, is more cautious as Origen never mentions Clement by name and differs from him in various emphases, though he clearly knew his writings.

and his mother only deterred her son from following him by hiding his clothes. By eighteen he had been put in charge of the catechetical school in Alexandria. Perhaps as early as 212 he had begun his first literary venture. His life-style was strongly ascetic. By the 220s he had begun to write voluminously, perhaps shortly before 230 beginning his laborious *Commentary on John*, and about the same time the first work of Christian systematic theology, *On First Principles* (*Peri Archōn*), in the fourth book of which he propounded his approach to Scripture.[128] It was to be understood at three levels: the literal, the moral and the spiritual. The literal which was followed by 'simple' Christians, clearly posed some problems which were exploited by Jews and heretics.[129] The moral interpretation he rarely gave, but the spiritual or allegorical he constantly sought to express, believing this understanding came as a 'gift of wisdom' from the Holy Spirit[130] to those who sought it. This led him along paths of acute subjectivity.

Origen's fame spread far beyond Alexandria and he was invited to visit other churches. On one trip abroad c.230 he was ordained presbyter at Caesarea, an act which incurred the wrath of his bishop Demetrius, and soon Origen left Alexandria permanently. By 232[131] he had taken up residence in Caesarea, where he established another catechetical school. In Caesarea he wrote further commentaries and preached about 500 homilies, over half of which remain. His other surviving works include *On Prayer* (233-4), *Exhortation to Martyrdom* (235), and the weighty apology *Against Celsus*[132] (248) refuting Celsus' anti-Christian work *The True Doctrine* (c.180). In 250, during the Decian persecution, he was arrested and cruelly tortured, surviving only to c.254 when he died at Tyre.

DEMONS

Like other Church Fathers Origen believed demons are major players on the scene of life. He thought human souls are attended by them from birth,[133] which he viewed as a justification for infant baptism.[134] Conversion chastises them;[135] baptism brings freedom from them,[136] no

---

[128]   *P.A.* 4.2.4.
[129]   *P.A.* 4.2.1.
[130]   1 Cor.12:8; *P.A.* 1 Pref. 3, 8, 1.3.8 *et passim*.
[131]   Eusebius, *H.E.* 6.26. Crouzel, *Origen*, 2-3, and P. Nautin, *Origène*, 428-31, prefer a year or two later.
[132]   Generally known by its Latin title *Contra Celsum*.
[133]   *C.C.* 8.34.
[134]   *Hom. Lev.* 8.3.5.
[135]   *Hom. Num.* 27.8.
[136]   *Comm. Jn.* 20.340-41.

doubt by enabling the candidate to share in the triumph of Jesus over principalities and powers on the cross.[137] Yet particularly prominent in Origen's homilies on the books Exodus to Joshua is the concept of the Christian life as a constant battle with temptations posed by demons to the mind.[138] The Christian can be victorious by prayer, fasting, Bible reading, the eucharist and virtuous living.[139] Throughout these battles angels are at work in his heart drawing it towards good.[140]

EXORCISM

Origen was well aware of the reality of demon possession.[141] Indeed, in the midst of one of his homilies on 1 Samuel he provoked demonic cries of protest from one present when he declared in the words of Hannah, "My soul exults in the Lord", which he proceeded to repeat time and again to chastise the evil spirit.[142] We do not hear that he actually drove out the spirit, but he makes the point in his sermon that such situations often lead to a person's conversion. P. and M-T. Nautin, commenting on this incident, declare that Origen is here the first to enable us to relive the impact of the preaching of the patristic age.[143]

It is Origen's *Contra Celsum* that contains most of his references to actual exorcisms. Jewish exorcists and indeed almost all who deal in magic and spells, he says, use the formula 'the God of Abraham, the God of Isaac, and the God of Jacob', or again 'the God of Israel', 'the God of the Hebrews', and 'the God who drowned the King of Egypt and the Egyptians in the Red Sea'.[144] In Christian exorcism it is the name of Jesus that carries the power. In *C.C.* 1.6 he writes:

> After this, impelled by some unknown power, Celsus says: "Christians get the power which they seem to possess by pronouncing the names of certain daemons and incantations", hinting I suppose at those who subdue daemons by enchantments and drive them out. But he seems blatantly to misrepresent the gospel. For they do not "get the power which they seem to possess" by any "incantations" but by the name of Jesus with the recital of the histories about him. For when they are pronounced they have often made daemons to be driven out of men and especially when those who utter them speak with real sincerity and genuine faith. In fact the name of

---

[137] *Ibid.* 20.330.
[138] Kelly, *Devil*, finds Gnostic (ch.2) and Jewish influences (ch.3) here.
[139] *Hom. Ex.* 2, *Hom. Lev.* 6.2, 6.6.5, 16.6.5, *Hom. Josh.* 1.7, 8.7, 20.
[140] *Hom. Num.* 5.3, cf. *C.C.* 3.14, 8.35-36.
[141] *P.A.* 3.3.4.
[142] *Hom. Sam.* 1.10.
[143] Nautin, *Homélies sur Samuel* (SC 328), 67.
[144] *C.C.* 1.22, 4.33-34.

Jesus is so powerful against the daemons that sometimes it is effective even when pronounced by bad men. (1.6, tr. Chadwick)

Celsus is imagining that Christians exorcise using magical techniques. Clearly he has not actually witnessed them in action. Origen protests that they use just the name of Jesus, trusting sincerely in him and reciting 'histories' (ἱστορία) about him. Chadwick suggests that ἱστορία refers to a credal phrase such as 'crucified under Pontius Pilate'[145] or a gospel narrative such as found in the later magical papyri.[146] Origen is confident enough in the power of the name of Jesus to assert that, even on the lips of bad men, it has proved effective. Perhaps he is thinking of magical practitioners who venture to do this, as they invoke the 'the God of Abraham...' Origen returns to the power of the name of Jesus in exorcism in 1.25, where he is rebutting Celsus' claim that it is a matter of indifference by what name the Supreme Deity is called. Origen explains that only names in their original languages have special power; in so doing he reveals he has some knowledge of the techniques of magicians, but this is far from saying he endorses such practices.[147]

---

[145] Cf. Justin, *2 Apol.* 6; Irenaeus, *A.H.* 2.32.4.

[146] Cf. 'Holy, holy, holy Lord...who raised Lazarus from the dead even on the fourth day, who healed Peter's mother-in-law...Heal her, who wears this divine amulet of the disease afflicting her.' (Meyer, *Ancient Christian Magic,* no.13, fifth-sixth century.)

[147] Thraede goes so far as to say that Origen here and in *C.C.* 4.33-34, where he is speaking of the power of Jewish names for God derived from the Old Testament, is open to the charge of magic by encouraging confidence in 'depersonalised names and formulae, including the confession of Christ'. Such, Thraede thinks, is independent of true faith in Christ ('Exorzismus', 69-70). Twelftree, after a superficial look at *C.C.* 1.6 and 6.40 (where Celsus claims to have seen in the hands of Christian presbyters 'books containing barbarian names of demons and magical formulae'), declares, 'it is reasonable to conclude that, in the latter part of the second century, exorcism among "orthodox" Christians in that city [Alexandria] was indistinguishable from other exorcisms...' (*Name of Jesus,* 288, cf. 269-73). I believe such deductions are quite unwarranted. Thraede should attend to Origen's statements that Christian exorcism is particularly effective by those with 'real sincerity and genuine faith' (1.6) and involves 'prayer alone and simple adjurations' (7.4). Twelftree needs to look at the context of the quotations he is making. In 1.6 Origen is repudiating Celsus' assertion that Christians are using 'incantations' (spells) like magical exorcists. In 6.40 Origen declares Celsus' assertion to be as grossly wrong as the charges of cannibalism and sexual licence levelled against the Church, and he concludes, 'Would indeed, that all that is said by Celsus against the Christians was of such a nature as to be refuted by the multitude [of

In 7.4, speaking of the Pythian priestess at Delphi he asks what sort of spirit it could be that controls her and pours darkness on her mind, and he continues:

> Its character must be like that of the race of daemons which many Christians drive out of people who suffer from them, without any curious magical art or sorcerer's device, but with prayer alone and very simple adjurations and formulas[a] such as the simplest person could use. For generally speaking it is uneducated people who do this kind of work. The power of the word of Christ shows the worthlessness and weakness of the daemons; for it is not necessary to have a wise man who is competent in the rational proofs of the faith in order that they should be defeated and yield to expulsion from the soul and body of a man. (Chadwick)

a – lit. 'with prayer alone and more simple exorcisms'; Chadwick's interpretation here surely draws on 1.6.

The fact that Origen is again labouring here the methods Christians use implies how unusual, indeed unique, these were in the ancient world. It is quite a remarkable admission by Origen, who strove to lead people from simple faith to deeper wisdom, that it is generally uneducated Christians who performed most of the exorcisms. It explains why the order of exorcist, established by this time, was one of the *lower* orders of ministry. Such people needed just prayer and faith as they practised their uncomplicated, yet hazardous, art.

Origen makes a further reference to the power of the name of Jesus in *C.C.* 3.36. Later he tells us that Christians drive out demons, not only from people, but also from places and animals (7.67) and statues (8.43). In *Homily on Joshua* 24 he envisages that sometimes an exorcist, despite prolonged endeavour, might fail to evict a demon from someone possessed.

HEALING

In his statements on more general healing Origen declares emphatically that, because of their rejection of Jesus the Redeemer, God has withdrawn his favour from the Jews and bestowed it instead on the Christian Gentiles. No longer do the Jews experience signs, wonders, prophecy or other evidences of God's presence, whilst these are all to be found amongst Gentile Christians (*Hom. Lk.* Frag, 77, *C.C.* 2.8, cf. 7.8).

---

pagans], who have ascertained by experience that such things are untrue, seeing that most of them have lived as neighbours with the Christians...' (ANF).

Origen's longest passages on healing are *C.C.* 3.24 and 3.28. Let us look at them in turn. In 3.24 he says that evidence is lacking to support Celsus' assertion that untold numbers of men, both Greeks and barbarians, believe in Asclepius, but evidence is available to show that just such a number believe in Jesus; of these –

> Some display evidence of having received some miraculous power because of this faith, shown in the people whom they cure; upon those who need healing they use no other invocation than that of the Supreme God and of the name of Jesus together with the history about him. By these we also have seen many delivered from serious ailments and from mental distractions and madness and countless other diseases, which neither men nor daemons had cured.

The first line of this statement suggests that he is referring to those who have received a special *charisma* of healing. Clearly they deal with mental (demonic?) as well as physical disorders. Origen goes on to say that he has personally witnessed many such healings. Christians had succeeded where, it seems, physicians and healing cults had failed.

In 3.28 Origen is responding to Celsus' reference to a certain Aristeas, the Proconnesian, who had vanished (died) and reappeared to his people, and his comment that no-one had claimed he was a god. Assuming this actually happened, Origen points out, it is by no means evident why providence intended it; and he continues:

> But in our case, when we tell the stories about Jesus, we give a powerful defence to show why they happened. We argue that God wanted to establish the doctrine spoken by Jesus which brought salvation to men;[a] and it was strengthened by the apostles, who were, so to speak, foundations of the building of Christianity, which he was beginning to build, and it is increasing[b] even in recent[c] times, when many[d] cures are done in the name of Jesus and there are other manifestations of considerable significance.

> a – Origen seems to be saying that Jesus' miracles, in his time and subsequently, have validated his whole message.   b – ἐπιδιδόντα , better 'continuing'
> c – ἑξῆς 'subsequent'   d – οὐκ ὀλίγαι 'not a few'

Chadwick's translation here tends to exaggerate Origen's claim. Certainly healings had continued in the Church beyond the time of the apostles, and, as Origen says elsewhere, are happening in his time, but they are less numerous than before. Briefer references to such healing activity are found in 1.2, 46, 67, 2.8, 33, 3.33, 7.8, 8.58 and *Comm. Jn.* 20.315.

In some of these passages (*C.C.* 1.2, 46, 2.8, 7.8 and *Comm. Jn.* 20.315) Origen asserts that it is ἴχνη (*ichnē*) of miraculous power that remain in the Church to his day. Chadwick always translates this word 'traces', which gives the impression that such miraculous activity had become very slight; but the word does not necessarily mean that. Lampe in his *Patristic Greek Lexicon* says the singular ἴχνος (*ichnos*) in the patristic period means 'footstep' or 'foot'. In certain other statements of Origen unrelated to healing the best translation would seem to be 'evidence'.[148] In the first three of our present passages 'evidence' would fit well too. In *Comm. Jn.* 20.315, however, Origen reinforces ἴχνη with another word which does imply scarcity when he says: "ἴχνη and λείμματα ('remnants') of these signs (performed by Jesus) continue to occur in the name of Jesus up to the present in the churches'. Here the translation 'traces' is surely right. In *C.C.* 7.8 Origen is contrasting the state of affairs in his time with the plentiful miracles performed by Jesus and by others after his ascension: 'even to this day there are ἴχνη of him (the Holy Spirit) *in a few people* whose souls have been purified by the Logos...' Here 'traces' is a legitimate translation though the emphasis of the passage seems to be on the *few Christians* gifted with the Spirit's power rather than on the paucity of miracles they perform. Probably then we should accept Chadwick's translation 'traces' each time but, bearing in mind that in *C.C.* 1.46 and 2.8 prophecy is mentioned alongside miraculous powers, it may be legitimate to conclude with Kydd[149] that it is the small number of those who still exhibit *charismatic gifts* of healing rather than an overall paucity of miracles that Origen has in mind when he uses the word ἴχνη in these passages. Even those with healing gifts were not, it appears, always successful for in one brief reference he says, 'to this day people *whom God wills* are cured by his (Jesus') name. (*C.C.* 2.33)

CHARISMATA

It is interesting that Origen quite frequently specifically mentions the *charismata* of 1 Corinthians 12. He says the 'beginning and source' of them is baptism (*Comm. Jn.* 6). When he names any of them, however, it is almost invariably 'wisdom' and 'knowledge' that he specifies, believing these to be essential for a Christian's advance beyond mere simple faith to a spiritual (allegorical) understanding of Scripture (*P.A.* 1 Pref. 3, 8, 1.3.8). On the only occasion in *Contra Celsum* that he

---

[148] *P.A.* 4.1.6, *C.C.* 8.44, and perhaps *Comm. Jn.* 2.61.
[149] Kydd, *Charismata*, 367-69; *Charismatic Gifts*, 79.

mentions the miracle-working gifts it is to contrast them unfavourably with these 'higher gifts':

> And as (Paul) values reason above miraculous workings, on this account he puts 'workings of miracles' and 'gifts of healings' in a lower place than the intellectual gifts. (3.46)

He is clearly referring to 1 Corinthians 12:8-10. Consistent with this, when in one of his homilies (*Hom. Lev.* 2.4.5), he refers to Jas.5:14-15, his interest lies only in its reference to the confession of sins. He makes no mention of the oil or healing.

GREATER WORKS

Perhaps then it is not surprising to discover that Origen gives a spiritual interpretation of the 'greater works' Christ promised his disciples would do (Jn.14:12):

> And I might say that according to the promise of Jesus the disciples have done even greater works than the physical miracles which Jesus did. For the eyes of people blind in soul are always being opened and the ears of those who were deaf to any talk of virtue eagerly hear about God and the blessed life with him; and many too who were lame in the feet of the inner man, as the Bible calls it, but have now been healed by the Logos, do not just leap, but 'leap as a hart'[a], an animal hostile to serpents and superior to all the poison of vipers. In fact these same people who have been healed receive from Jesus power to walk on their feet, where before they were lame, over all the serpents and scorpions of evil, and in general over all the power of the enemy, and in their walk they do nothing wrong; for they have even become superior to all evil and the poison of daemons. (*C.C.* 2.48)

a– for the claims of the stag's power over snakes see Pliny *N.H.* 8.118, 28.149-51.

He is exulting over the effects of conversion.

Origen thought Jesus' miracles clear evidence of his divinity to those who witnessed them,[150] but admits that by his time they were viewed by some as myths; and he has to bring forward the argument of their fulfilling prophecy to buttress them.[151] He is often anyway far more interested in interpreting them allegorically of the spiritual enlightenment received by those who turned to Christ.[152] Celsus puts

---

[150] *Comm. Mt.* 12.2, *C.C.* 4.18, cf. *Philocalia* 26.8, *C.C.* 5.51.

[151] *Comm. Jn.* 2.204; J. Speigl, 'Die Rolle der Wunder im vorkonstantinischen Christentum', *ZKTh* 92 (1970), 309.

[152] *Comm. Mt.* 13.4-5, *Hom. Lk.* 32.4, *Philoc.* 26.8.

Jesus' miraculous powers down to magic which he learnt while in Egypt as a child,[153] but Origen retorts that Jesus would scarcely have worked his miracles by magic and then taught his hearers to obey God.[154] In his arguments with Celsus Origen shows himself well aware that miracles can be performed by the power of Satan, and that the Antichrist is expected to be one who will do just that.[155]

MEDICINE

Like Clement, Origen is generally positive towards the medical profession. In his *Homily on Numbers* 18.3 he sees in Eccles.1:1 ('all wisdom comes from God') warrant for a positive attitude to various branches of knowledge including medicine:

> And surely there can be no doubt about medical knowledge. For if there is any knowledge (that comes) from God – which will be more so than the knowledge of health, in which the virtues of herbs as well as the qualities of the humours are discerned?[156]

Elsewhere he describes the science of medicine as 'useful' and 'necessary' to the human race despite the disputes between the medical sects about the manner of curing bodies.[157] He frequently uses medical metaphors,[158] and once he describes the medical treatment of hydrophobia.[159] Moreover he realises the value of good diet such as honey, which strengthens the sick,[160] and dietary means of improving eyesight.[161] Yet he is adamant that physicians are wrong when they attribute lunacy to moist humours or the phases of the moon rather than to the presence of an evil spirit. The heavenly bodies were created by God and have no power to work evil among men, he says.[162]

When Celsus inclines towards the opinion of certain wise men that demons are absorbed with material concerns, including healing the body, Origen makes an interesting reply:

> I would affirm that it is not clear that these daemons, in whatever way they are worshipped, are even capable of healing bodies. A man ought to

---

[153] *C.C.* 1.28.
[154] *C.C.* 1.38, cf. 2.51.
[155] *C.C.* 2.49-50, 6.45.
[156] Qu. Temkin, *Hippocrates*, 130; cf. on the herbalist, *Hom. Lev.* 7.1, 8.1.
[157] *C.C.* 3.12, cf. 1.9.
[158] *P.A.* 2.10.6, *Hom. Lev.* 7.15, *Hom. Josh.* 7.6 *et passim*.
[159] *Philoc.* 27.
[160] *C.C.* 4.82.
[161] *Philoc.* 12.2 = *Hom. Josh.* 20.2.
[162] *Comm. Mt.* 13.6 discussing Mt.17:14-20.

use medical means to heal his body if he aims to live in the simple and
ordinary way. If he wishes to live in a way superior to the multitude, he
should do this by devotion to the Supreme God and by praying to him.
(*C.C.* 8.60)

He reveals here he is clearly sceptical about the efficacy of the healing
cults. He thinks the use of medical means legitimate, but that there is a
better way of life, that of devotion to God. (The context of this passage
shows that he is not thinking at all here of Christian prayer for healing.)

HEALTH AND SICKNESS

In two quite extensive passages, in works from early and late during his
residence at Caesarea, Origen shows that he does not regard health and
wealth as the proper focus for a Christian's endeavour in life. In
Concerning Prayer 17.1 he writes:

> For what comparison is there between bodily riches and the riches which
> consist in all utterance and in all knowledge? And who, unless he were
> mad, would compare health of flesh and bones with a healthy mind, a
> robust soul, and power of reasoning in accordance therewith? All of these
> things, if they are duly ordered by the Word of God, make bodily
> experience as it were an unimportant pinprick, or whatever we like to
> consider smaller than a pin-prick. (tr. Jay)

Origen's *Homily on Psalm 4* (*Philocalia* 26), which takes as its text
'Many say, who will show us the good things?' (Ps.4:6), reveals a
fascinating debate going on in the Church at that time as to what is
really 'good' and 'evil'. There are those who locate some good in
external conditions of life such as health, vigour and beauty. The
corollary is then that disease, sickness and deformity are bad. They
support their case by pointing to Old Testament verses that speak of
bodily health as a sign of God's blessing, and plagues as a sign of his
disfavour (Ex.15:26, Lev.26:16, Deut.28:58-61, 32:24). They refer also
to the fact that Christ healed many kinds of sickness and drove out
devils, and to the apostles exercising gifts of healing and working of
miracles. They point also to the next world and say, 'because pain is an
evil thing sinners are committed to age-long fire; and if pain is an evil
thing, pleasure must be a good one.' There are, says Origen, Christians
who are simple, yet profess themselves wise, who are taken in by these
arguments.

On the other hand, he points out, many good prophets suffered
hardship. The apostle Paul underwent trials in which he rejoiced (and he
surely did not rejoice in evil). What of the trials of Job? For him 'all
things work together ...' Moreover only ignorant people think fever is
inflicted on account of sins. The causes of such sickness often clearly lie

in the neighbourhood, the quality of water or the nature of the food.[163] And if health and wealth are rewards of the righteous, no ungodly man ought to have them. We must look for health rather in the constitution of a man's soul. Wounds, bruises and sickness often come as a result of lack of care. Moreover, if we keep certain commands just for the reward they entail, what becomes of virtue which is indifferent to rewards? What then is the 'good thing'? Man's determination to lead the good life, and God's power assisting him.

Then Origen reiterates what he says elsewhere: if Jesus healed people we must look chiefly for the spiritual meaning, namely that the Gospel heals disorders of the soul.[164] Besides which, Jesus' healings were intended to astonish people and to win over those unconvinced by argument and instruction – a point surely of continuing validity for miracles performed by Christians of subsequent ages, though Origen does not admit it.

In his early work *On First Principles* (2.9.3) Origen put forward the idea that sickness at birth is the result of sin in a previous life. We do not hear him reiterating that subsequently. Elsewhere he maintains God uses suffering to purify and reform people.[165]

CONCLUSION

Origen's evidence is wide-ranging and fascinating. Particularly in his apologetic work *Contra Celsum* he reveals that contemporary exorcism and healing are taking place. He contrasts this with the desolate state of the Jews who have lost God's favour and are spiritually enfeebled, and the dubious healing capability of the cults. He reveals that those who perform exorcisms are generally uneducated Christians. There are still a few in the Church, it seems, with charismatic gifts of healing, but Origen thinks the gifts of wisdom and knowledge far more important. It is legitimate for the mundane to resort to medical means to cure their bodies, but there is a much higher goal Christians should be aiming for: to live a good life drawing on the enabling power of God.

Dionysius

Dionysius 'the Great' was born c.200 into a pagan family. He became a pupil of Origen, was ordained, and c.232 took over headship of the catechetical school in Alexandria. In 248 he became bishop of Alexandria. During the Decian persecution (250-51) he was captured, escaped and went into hiding. He was banished in the Valerian

---

[163] A truly Hippocratic reply.
[164] *Hom. Lk.* 32.4, *Comm. Mt.* 13.6.
[165] *Comm. Mt.* 11.4.

persecution (257) and returned to face the onset of the plague and other problems. He died c.265. His festal letter, describing the effects of the plague that struck Egypt in 263, reveals the heroic efforts of the Christians. Eusebius quotes from it at length in *H.E.* 7.22. Dionysius says the plague was feared by the pagans more than any other calamity, and took away their hope, and he continues:

> Yet to us it was not so, but, no less than the other misfortunes, a source of discipline and testing. For indeed it did not leave us untouched, although it attacked the heathen with great strength. (22.6, Loeb)

While the pagans shunned their sick and left their dead unburied, the Christians devotedly nursed their sick and some recovered while those who had nursed them died. Even some presbyters and deacons so died.

The account given by Dionysius tallies closely with the earlier situation described by Cyprian in Carthage. Christians died, but without terror and the witness of their love in action must have had a considerable impact upon their heathen neighbours. But Dionysius makes no mention of healing in the name of Christ. Presumably the sheer size of the epidemic overwhelmed any such idea. It seems that, as in Carthage, the Church viewed such sickness as something Christians had to bear along with others as part of their common humanity.

General Conclusion

The healing ministry of the Church is very evident in the first few decades of the third century. There are those, including laity, with gifts of healing. In Rome oil is blessed at the eucharist and, it may well be, used to anoint the sick present. Some taste it. In Syria anointing for healing has evidently become merged with Christian initiation. In the Church at large exorcism in the name of Christ appears to have become a Christian service to the public and is free of charge. It proved too a useful apologetic weapon to the Fathers, a clear demonstration of the supremacy of Christ over the pagan gods. This remains true in the middle of the century by which time the minor clerical office of exorcist has arisen and become widespread within the Church. Healing gifts by then appear to have become few. It is chiefly the uneducated people, it seems, who are interested in healing and perform exorcisms. For the educated Fathers interest lies rather in other spiritual gifts and rationalizing sickness. The plague appears to have come as an overwhelming force which Christians (with the possible exception of Gregory Thaumaturgus) resisted only by heroic self-sacrifice in the interests of the sick and dead.

CHAPTER 5

In an Era of Persecution and Toleration:
Late Third – Early Fourth Centuries

For this period we have a smaller number of rather disparate sources. We shall start by looking at the two North African writers who have a certain amount in common.

North Africa

Arnobius

Arnobius was a Christian apologist in North Africa in the time of Diocletian (Roman Emperor, 284-305). Jerome writes of him:

> Arnobius is considered a distinguished rhetorician in Africa, who, engaged at Sicca in teaching young men rhetoric, was led by visions to the faith; and not being received by the bishop, as hitherto a persistent enemy of Christ, composed very excellent books against his former belief.[1]

It appears that he had formerly been swayed by the arguments of Porphyry's *Against the Christians* (c.290) which he then opposed in his own work *Against the Nations* (c.295-304). Arnobius displays considerable learning, but of the Christian writers he seems to know only Clement of Alexandria, Tertullian and Minucius Felix. He never quotes the Old Testament and has a limited grasp of Christian doctrine. Yet he speaks of his conversion from idolatry with some passion.[2]

Of great interest is Arnobius' emphasis on miracles. As Spiegl points out, before him no-one had so exclusively and forcefully constructed a

---

[1] *Chronicle* (for AD 326), qu. Brice and Campbell ANCL 19 (1882), introduction. In *Ep.* 5 Jerome is considerably less complimentary; cf. M.B. Simmons, 'In Arnobius we see the thought of a recent convert in transition: contradictory elements have not been worked out' – *Arnobius of Sicca: Religious Conflict and Competition in the Age of Diocletian* (Oxford: Clarendon Press, 1995), 18.

[2] *Against the Nations* 1.39.

proof of the divinity of Christ from miracles.[3] Arnobius was impressed that Christ had performed miracles without the aid of demons or magic, indeed without any external aids, just the power of his authority and entirely for people's good (1.43-4). If you draw a parallel, he says, with other gods who have given remedies and healed the sick, the tribute for those they cure must go to the remedy and not the god, while Christ healed merely by touch of hand and word of command (1.48). If you point to Aesculapius (Asclepius), how many who have petitioned that 'health giver' have failed to be healed? It is no good pointing to one or two cured when thousands are left unaided. Christ assisted all who came to him, good and bad alike and that was 'the mark of a true god and of a kingly power to deny his bounty to none' (1.49).

Furthermore, Arnobius continued, by his power he enabled his disciples, using his name, to perform miracles similar to his own (1.50). Jupiter could not do this (1.51). What magician could do it? (1.52) It shows he is God (1.53). The records of these events have been passed on to us by reliable witnesses. If not, how do you explain that so quickly the whole world has been filled with this religion? (1.54-5) Our (Christian) religious beliefs are based on witnesses, yours[4] on opinions (1.57). In 2.11 he gives a personal testimony:

> And we, indeed, have followed in him these things – his glorious works and most potent virtues which he manifested and displayed in diverse miracles, by which anyone might be led to the necessity of believing, and decide with confidence that they were not such as might be regarded as man's but of some divine and unknown power. (ANCL amended)

EXORCISM

In one passage Arnobius clearly speaks of contemporary exorcisms and the inhibiting of the activities of soothsayers, augurs and magicians:

> Was (Christ just) one of us…whose name, when heard, puts to flight evil spirits, imposes silence on soothsayers, prevents men from consulting augurs, causes the efforts of arrogant magicians to be frustrated, not by the dread of his name, as you allege, but by the free exercise of a greater power? (1.46)

Here it is evident that the name of Jesus is still being used with powerful effect in exorcisms. It is also clear that the power of Christ is coming into direct conflict with practitioners of the cults of the gods of the

---

[3] J. Speigl, 'Rolle', 311.
[4] Arnobius' work is an anti-pagan polemic.

Greco-Roman world. It was just such interference that Lactantius says finally triggered off the Great Persecution in 303.[5]

MEDICINE

Arnobius exhibits Roman scorn for Greek medicine when, in the course of derogatory remarks about gods who took the credit for healings that rightly belonged to the drugs they prescribed, he says:

> A similar mode of treatment is followed by physicians also, a creature earth-born and not relying on true science, but founding on a system of conjecture, and wavering in estimating probabilities. (1.48)

Again, in pointing out the weakness of the gods he has ceased to believe in, he writes:

> Aesculapius presides over the duties and arts of medicine; and why cannot (men in) more kinds of disease and sickness be restored to health and soundness of body? While, on the contrary, they become worse under the hands of the physician. (3.23)

Medicine, in Arnobius' estimate, suffers under the double disadvantage of being a young and experimental discipline which is under the patronage of pagan religion. He writes with the zeal of a recent Christian convert.[6]

ATTITUDE TO SUFFERING

On the origin of evil in the world Arnobius declares himself to a large extent agnostic but of one thing, he says, Christians are sure

> that nothing proceeds from God Supreme which is hurtful and pernicious. This we are assured of, this we know, on this one truth of knowledge and science we take our stand, - that nothing is made by him except that which is for the well-being of all, which is agreeable, which is very full of love and joy and gladness, which has unbounded and imperishable pleasures, which everyone may ask in all his prayers to befall him, and think that otherwise life is pernicious and fatal. (2.55)

This statement has the ring of exalted faith but scarcely of reality. The problem is that one cannot just be exempted from pain and conflict by prayer. That Arnobius is really asserting that *in the end* all will be well is made likely by another passage later in the same book: Christians and pagans are trading jibes that their gods are unable to prevent them from

---

[5] *Deaths of the Persecutors*, 10.2.
[6] Cf. Amundsen, 'Medicine and Faith', 348.

suffering disease and sickness, shipwrecks, fires, pestilences, wars, slavery and so on. Arnobius says of the Christians:

> No hope has been held out to us with respect to this life, nor has any help been promised or aid decreed us for what belongs to the husk of the flesh, - nay more, we have been taught to esteem and value lightly all the threats of fortune, whatever they be; and if ever any very grievous calamity has assailed (us), to count it as pleasant in (that) misfortune the end which must follow, and not to fear or flee from it, that we may be the more easily released from the bonds of the body, and escape from our darkness and blindness. (2.76)

In short, the future will rectify any deficiencies in the present.

The evidence of Arnobius seems to fit quite straightforwardly into the progression from Tertullian through Cyprian. While exorcism in the name of Jesus remains a part of the Church's work, rather than expect healing one must put up with present evils, looking forward to future joys. One feels that, if Arnobius had been aware of significant healing in the name of Jesus in his day, he would have gladly brought it, like contemporary exorcism, into his case for the divinity of Christ.

Lactantius

Lactantius was born c.250 probably in Numidia in North Africa. Jerome says he was a pupil of Arnobius, and appointed a teacher of rhetoric at Nicomedia in Bythynia (Asia Minor) by Diocletian.[7] He had read Minucius Felix, Tertullian and Cyprian and must have been converted some time before 300. When the Great Persecution of Christians broke out in 303 he lost his job[8] and had more time for writing. In extreme old age he was appointed tutor to Constantine's son Crispus in Gaul. He died perhaps c.325. Jerome tells us of a number of his writings but all that have come down to us are: *On the Workmanship of God* (c.304-5) which, as against the view of Epicurus, seeks to prove the existence of God from the wonders of the human body; *The Divine Institutes*, his magnum opus (c.305-13, revised later), written in eloquent style to rectify the deficiencies of previous Christian Latin writers,[9] which is an apologetic work for the educated classes consisting of seven books dealing successively with false religion, the origin of error, the false wisdom of the philosophers, true wisdom and religion, true worship, and the blessed life; An *Epitome* (c.315), which summarizes the foregoing

---

[7]   *Ill. Men* 80.
[8]   *Deaths* 13.1.
[9]   Particularly Tertullian and Cyprian (*D.I.* 5.1.4).

work in a single volume and adapts it a little to the new situation within the empire; *On the Anger of God* (c.315), which seeks to demonstrate, against the views of Stoics and Epicureans, that God is moved by anger against sinners as he is by benevolence to the just; and *On the Deaths of the Persecutors* (c.314-6), which describes in lurid detail the fates of Roman leaders who had persecuted the Church and, in the process, and provides a valuable account of the happenings of 303-313. Gregory of Tours attributes to him also the secular poem *On the Phoenix*.

Lactantius has been called the 'Christian Cicero' for his fine Latin style. To appeal to his intended readership, he often quotes Cicero and other classical authors, consciously starting in his magnum opus from their works rather than the inferior Latin of the Christian Scriptures. Jerome wished that he had been able to affirm the Christian faith as well as he destroyed paganism.[10] Let us consider what he has to say about demons and exorcism, then health and suffering.

DEMONS AND EXORCISM

An extended discussion of the origin and activities of the demons in *Divine Institutes* 2.14 reveals Lactantius' knowledge of Tertullian, *Apology* 22-23, and Minucius Felix, *Octavius* 26-27. His passage on the demons' activities deserves quoting in full:

> They fill all things with trickeries, frauds, deceits and errors. They cling to individual men and they seize all homes, indeed every last doorway. They take to themselves the name of *genii*, for thus they translate *daemones* into Latin. Men honour them in their inner chambers, and daily for them do they pour out wines. Knowing these demons, they venerate them as though they were terrestrial gods and dispellers of the evils which they themselves make and bring upon them. Since these spirits are light and incomprehensible, they insinuate themselves into the bodies of men and, secretly working upon the inner organs, they vitiate the health, incite sicknesses, terrify the thoughts by dreams, and disturb the minds with madness, so they force men through these evils to run for their help. (2.14.12-14, tr. McDonald)

In 2.16 he says they are the originators of astrology, divination, augury, oracle-giving, necromancy, magic and all other evil arts. They claim there is one king of all angelic spirits in heaven, Jupiter. Hidden in temples they often work prodigies. Elsewhere he says, while Apollo calls himself a demon (1.7), the gods were originally men (1.11-15). The demons have brought about the heresies, wishing to divide the people of God (4.30).

---

[10] *Ep.* 58.10.

Three times in the *Divine Institutes* Lactantius refers to exorcisms:

(a) 2.15.2-5 - This passage follows the quotation above. He says that people are just pleased when those possessing spirits do no harm and may think they deserve to be honoured, and he continues:

> They harm, indeed, but they harm those by whom they are feared, whom the powerful and high hand of God does not protect, and who are not initiated by the pledge of truth[a]. They fear the just, that is those who worship God; and adjured by his name[b] they depart from their bodies. At their words, as if beaten by rods, they not only confess that they are demons, but they also give out their names, those which are adored in the temples. Generally they do this in the presence of their worshippers, not, to be sure, for the opprobrium of religion, but for their honour, because neither to God by whom they are adjured, nor to the just by whose voice they are tortured are they able to lie. So often with mighty wailings do they proclaim that they are beaten and that they burn and that they are already going out: the knowledge of God and the justice of His power has so much hold over them. Whom, then can they harm if not those whom they have in their power?

a – at baptism   b – here Lactantius is summarizing (cf. 4.27 qu. below)

This is so heavily dependent on the earlier Latin writers (Tertullian, *Apol.* 23, Cyprian, *Dem.* 15) as to have little value as a testimony to contemporary exorcisms. But that is not the case with the next passage.

(b) 4.27.1-3 - Lactantius is seeking to answer the question why Jesus died the demeaning death of crucifixion. He gives a number of answers: to identify with the lowest humanity (i.e. criminals); to teach us we would be hated as Christians; he was lifted up for all the world to see; he opened his arms on the cross to embrace the world; and he continues:

> Now it is sufficient to explain how much the power of this sign[a] can accomplish. How much terror this causes demons he will know who has seen how far they flee from the bodies they have obsessed[b] when commanded in the name of Christ. For just as He Himself put all demons to flight by a word when He was living among men, and as He put back into their former sensibilities the disturbed minds of men and those raging from evil incursions, so now His followers by the name of their Master and by the sign of His Passion exclude those same defiled spirits from men. The proof of this is not difficult. For if someone is present having a signed forehead when they make sacrifices to their false gods, the sacred rites cannot be acceptable in any way.

a – the cross   b – Lat. *obsiderint* better 'inhabited'

Lactantius goes on to explain it is now a common occurrence for soothsayers to be unable to read the future from the entrails of a sacrificial victim when Christians present make the sign of the cross on their foreheads, and this enrages those in charge. He then asks why it is that the demons fear Christ but not Jupiter, unless it is because the latter is one of their own company! And he suggests that someone known to be demon-possessed and a seer of the Delphic oracle (believed to be inspired by Apollo) be put side by side in a public place and it will be quickly shown that the spirits inhabiting both will equally shudder and depart 'at the name of God' (cf. Tertullian, *Apol.* 23.4-6). He points out that the Greek poets and philosophers used the terms 'god' and 'demon' interchangeably, and Christians thus demonstrate this corresponds to reality (27.15-16). He seems to use the names 'God' and 'Christ' as virtually equivalent in these passages.

(c) 5.21-22 - In this passage Lactantius repeats points he has already made but adds that the demons Christians have expelled try to get their revenge by stirring up pagans to persecute them. He also says that it is only 'as long as there is peace among the people of God' that Christian exorcism is effective. Disunity clearly undermines it. He also tells us that those delivered from evil spirits join the Church.

SICKNESS AND HEALTH

Only once does Lactantius associate the Christian life specifically with health. In *Epitome* 42, speaking of Jesus' titles, he says:

> He is called Saviour on this account, because He is the health and safety[a] of all who believe in God through him. (ANCL)

a – Lat. *salus* better 'salvation'

What he means by 'health' he does not explain. If one were to infer that Christians are less prone to sickness than others, that is not supported by his other statements. Elsewhere he shows that, like Origen, he does not rate the healing of pain particularly highly. Bearing in mind he is writing at a time when Christians were suffering greatly through persecution, this is not so surprising. Considering the matter of the highest good in life he writes:

> To think that the highest good is the privation of pain is surely not characteristic of the Peripatetics or Stoics but of the clinical philosophers. For who would not understand that this is the part discussed by the sick

and those placed in some state of pain? What is so ridiculous as to consider that which a physician can give as the highest good? (*D.I.* 3.8)

Perhaps this is a display of Roman scorn for the medical profession. After further discussion he puts forward two answers that satisfy him: the highest good lies in the contemplation of God and serving him (3.9) and in the consequent immortality of man (3.12). Lactantius frequently poses the question: why does God allow evil? In his earliest work he answers that God allows sickness and affliction in this life as a preparation for man's inevitable death (*Workmanship* 4.7-8, 16):

> Since then, man was to be formed by God that he would die at some time the matter itself demanded that he be made an earthly and weak body...Thus it will be a consequence that man is subject also to diseases, for nature does not allow infirmity to be absent from that body which is at some time to be dissolved.

And a little later he adds another reason:

> If man were not able to get sick, and if he needed neither shelter nor clothing why should he fear wind or storm or cold, the power of which lies in the fact that they bring on sickness? It is on that account that he has received wisdom, to fortify his weakness against what might harm it.

His conclusion is that if man is no longer to be subject to sickness and untimely death then his reason and wisdom must also be withdrawn.

In his other writings Lactantius does not deal specifically with sickness but more generally with the difficulties of life. In an extended passage in *D.I.* 7.5 he asks, why did God not make man happy? He responds:

> (God) thought up this unspeakable[a] work: how to create an infinite multitude of souls, which He would place at first in frail and weak bodies, bound in the midst of good and evil, so that before those consisting by nature of both parts He might put virtue, lest they follow after immortality in a delicate and soft way, but that they might come upon that unspeakable[b] reward of eternal life with the greatest difficulty and great labours.

a – or 'indescribable' (Lat. *inenarrabile*)   b – or 'unutterable' (Lat. *ineloquibile*)

And he continues at length in the same vein. Several times elsewhere also he propounds this Stoic theme that evils and vice are necessary for the development of virtue.[11] Though such an attitude effectively discredits a ministry of healing, Lactantius does, however, stress the importance of caring for the sick:

> To take up also the work of caring for and cherishing the sick, who have no-one to assist them, is a great work of the highest sort of humaneness. Whoever will have done this will bring a living victory to God, and what he has given another in time, he will receive from God in eternity. (*D.I.* 6.12, cf. *Epit.* 60.7)

JESUS' MIRACLES

In *D.I.* 4.15 Lactantius tells of Jesus' baptism and subsequent miracles. He says the Jews attributed them to magic but in fact they were prophesied by the Jewish Scriptures (Is.35:3-6) and by the Sibylline Oracles;[12] the latter he has to defend against charges of falsification by Christians. He sees these miracles as demonstrating Jesus' power as the Son of God, though they aroused envy in the Jewish leaders which led to his death (4.16). He sees the miracles also as allegorical of the spiritual awakening Jesus brought to people's lives (4.26), and he says that the disciples were given power by Christ to work miracles in his name to confirm the new teaching they were spreading (4.21). But he fails to recognise that contemporary miracles could have the same value in his time.

He is aware that in the end times a false prophet will arise who will perform miracles (not of healing) and entice many away (7.17), but his victory will be short-lived and evil will be destroyed (7.19-20).

CONCLUSION

Lactantius' writings are most valuable for describing contemporary exorcism, but give us no evidence of healing, rather they contain an extensive rationale for why Christians should endure sickness.

Syria

The Pseudo-Clementine Literature

Chief among the Pseudo-Clementine literature are the *Homilies* and the

---

[11] *D.I.* 5.23, *Epit.* 29, *Anger of God* 20.

[12] The Sibylline Oracles consist of fourteen books of oracles, dating from the second century BC to perhaps the fourth century AD, and speak of world history and other matters. They are purportedly by Greek Sibyls (prophetesses), but many oracles are clearly the work of Jewish and Christian writers. (*ODCC*, 3rd edn.)

Chief among the Pseudo-Clementine literature are the *Homilies* and the *Recognitions*. Their supposed author Clement of Rome is depicted as a member of the Roman imperial family who is searching for the truth about life, immortality and the origin of the world. He tries the various philosophical schools before hearing of the Son of God in distant Judea. In response he travels there and, in Caesarea, meets Peter who instructs him in the teaching of the true prophet and invites him to accompany him on his missionary journeys. This he does, and listens to many addresses by Peter, witnessing his activities and his conflict with Simon Magus.[13] Ultimately, having become a convert, he is ready for baptism (*Hom.* 11.35). The *Homilies* and the *Recognitions* go over very largely the same ground but the *Recognitions,* in addition, depict Clement's reunion with long lost members of his family.

The twenty *Homilies* of Peter, which Clement is supposed to have sent from Rome to James at Jerusalem, are preceded by two letters to James, from Peter and Clement respectively, to explain the correct use of the work. The ten books of the *Recognitions* survive in the Latin translation of Rufinus, who, in an introductory letter, says he has made various curtailments. Judging by his other translations, and comparison with what appears in a Syriac version,[14] this means that he has toned down any unorthodox theology.

The literary and theological problems raised by the Clementines are by no means yet resolved but it is generally agreed that both main works depend on a common source (G), dating from perhaps the mid-third century. The *Homilies* represent a reworking of it, reflect mild Gnostic and Arian sympathies and come from, it seems, early fourth-century Coele-Syria[15]. The *Recognitions* appear to draw independently on G and date from probably c.350 Syria or Palestine.[16] Both the *Homilies* and the *Recognitions* display a strongly Judaeo-Christianity (almost Ebionism), though in the *Recognitions* it has been somewhat moderated. Quasten sums up admirably their affinity with the Apocryphal Acts:

> The narrative is in the last analysis merely an introduction to the missionary sermons of St. Peter and belongs properly to the class of apocryphal acts of the Apostles. It differs from other legends of the

---

[13]   Simon the magician of Ac.8:9-20 about whom much novelistic Christian literature was subsequently written.

[14]   Cf. F. Stanley Jones, 'The Pseudo-Clementines: A History of Research' in *The Second Century* 2 (1982), 4-6.

[15]   Literally 'hollow' Syria, the region of southern Syria disputed between the Seleucid and Ptolemaic dynasties.

[16]   G. Strecker in *New Testament Apocrypha* II, ed. Schneemelcher, 485.

Apostles in that its purpose is less to entertain than to furnish theological instruction and weapons for defending Christianity effectively.[17]

These writings do appear to provide some evidence of healing ministry in their communities in the third and fourth centuries.

In the introductory *Letter of Clement to James*, as in the *Didascalia*, one of the specified duties of the deacons is to find out who amongst the church membership are sick, and to bring them to the attention of the laity to visit and supply their needs, as directed by the bishop (12.3).

The Judaeo-Christian provenance of the *Homilies* is evident in its referring to Jesus generally as the 'true prophet' (Dt.18:15-18), its declaration that Moses provides salvation to believing Jews as Jesus does to believing Gentiles (8.5-6), its encouragement of marriage rather than abstinence (3.38), and its forthright attribution of sickness to sin. Peter says at one point:

> Give me the man who sins not and I will show you the man who suffers not; and you will find that he not only does not suffer himself but that he is able to heal others. (19.22, ANCL)

And he confidently declares that, for the sinless man, the poison of snakes, injurious plants, and the disturbance of demons would have no ill effect.

Evil deeds have brought mankind under the tyranny of the demons. They can cause sickness (8.9-11). To eat and drink in a pagan temple is to expose oneself to this (7.3, 9.9). *Homily* 9 is in fact an extended discourse on the way demons operate and how to restrict their activities. They are put to flight by abstinence, fasting and suffering affliction (9.10.3). Their hold over a person's life is inversely proportional to that person's faith (9.11). They operate through the healing cults, sometimes prescribing remedies, communicating through oracular utterances and dreams (9.14-15). They do not appear to Jews (= Christians?). 'Pythons prophesy,'[18] Peter says, 'yet they are cast out by us as demons and put to flight showing they are not gods' (9.16). Demons know what remedies are suited to various diseases. Why do they effect their cures only for some people? They prescribe for those they know will recover spontaneously, or who have recovered after prayer. How many only pretended to be ill in the first place? How many are cured by what was originally magical art, or by using charms? (9.16-18) Such a long diatribe against the healing cults suggests that, of Greco-Roman religions, these posed the greatest challenge to the Church.

---

[17] J. Quasten, *Patrology* I, 60.
[18] As in Ac.16:16.

Peter has referred to Christians' effectiveness as exorcists; he goes on to speak of the powerful cleansing and healing effect of baptism:

> But in the present life, washing in a flowing river, or fountain, or even in the sea, with the thrice blessed invocation, you shall not only be able to drive away the spirits which lurk in you; but yourselves no longer sinning, and undoubtedly believing God, you shall drive out evil spirits and dire demons, with terrible diseases from others. And sometimes they shall flee when you but look on them. For they know those who have given themselves up to God. (9.19.4-5)

Here we may have the distilled experience of the Judaeo-Christian communities.

In the *Homilies* Peter is always portrayed as a healer as well as a preacher and teacher, but seldom are his miracles described; usually they are referred to routinely following his preaching. For instance in Tripoli:

> Peter, only laying his hands upon them, and praying, healed them; so that those who were straightway cured were exceeding glad, and those who looked on exceedingly wondered, and blessed God, and believed with a firm hope... (8.24.1-2)

Clearly here his miracles are seen as engendering faith. Similar references are found also in 7.5, 8.12, 15.11, 16.21, 18.23 and 19.25 and give the impression of being a mere formula stating what one would expect of an apostle. Sometimes the healed are also baptised (e.g. 7.5). Occasionally it is said he healed or exorcised first and then preached (e.g. 8.8). It is stressed that, in contrast to Simon's tricks, Peter's miracles are philanthropic (2.34), and that he can heal conditions beyond the range of the medical profession and astrologers (14.5). This again may reflect the healing ministry of the Judaeo-Christian communities that gave birth to these writings.

The *Recognitions* state many of the same points as the *Homilies*. They also sharpen some and add a few more. Amongst their more interesting statements are:

Early mankind, obeying God's will, suffered no sickness and lived very long (4.9, 5.2, 8.46-52).
When a person with faith is baptised, the demon within is extinguished, but if that person proves unfaithful or gluttonous the demon retains a foothold (4.17-18).
When the righteous struggle with sickness and demons, they gain the palm of victory and the merit of rewards, so God is just (9.8).

CONCLUSION

The Pseudo-Clementines are pronounced in their Judaeo-Christian views, including attributing all sickness to sin. They accept that demons can be agents bringing sickness, and they speak of baptismal healing, and the conferring of gifts of healing and exorcism at baptism. Their emphasis on these things and Peter's healings may reflect to some extent a continuing practice of healing ministry in the communities from which they came.

Palestine

Rabbinic Material

As the rabbinic sources are hostile to Jesus so, as we saw in chapter three, they are likewise hostile to Christian healers. The two passages we shall consider, however, provide some interesting contrasts. The first is from the Jerusalem Talmud *Shabbat* 14:4 III (EE-HH):

> [Joshua b. Levi] had a grandson, who swallowed [something dangerous]. Someone came along and whispered over him in the name of [Jesus Panteri][a] and he recovered. When he (the magician) went out[b] [Joshua] said to him, "What did you say over him?" He said to him such and such a word. He said to him, "It would have been better for him if he had died and thus [had not been done for him]." It was "as an error that went out from before the ruler." [Eccles.10:5] (Neusner)

a – MS L contains a blank space later filled in with 'Jesus Panteri'.
b – MS L adds the words 'when…went out' between the lines.
Clearly this story caused the scribe some difficulties.

Herford[19] speaks of R. Joshua as one of the best known of the Talmudic rabbis who lived and taught mostly in Lud (Lydda) in the second half of the third century. He was clearly associated with rabbis in Tiberias where it is probable this incident took place. The grandson was probably the son of R. Joseph who had married into the family of Patriarch Judah II, who lived at Tiberias. In this story R. Joshua was not there in time to prevent the healing but deplored what had happened, viewing it as the command of a ruler given in error, which cannot be put right. Kalmin[20] takes this Scriptural quotation to be the editor's lament at R. Joshua's death-wish for his grandson, for the story goes on to report the grandson's death. Clearly healing by a Christian (thought to be as sinister as a magician) was deplored. One cannot judge how the healing

---

[19] R.T. Herford, *Christianity in Talmud and Mishnah*, 108-09.
[20] R. Kalmin, 'Christians and Heretics', 162.

was in fact effected but the name of Jesus was evidently the key to the cure.

The second passage is from the Babylonian Talmud *Abodah Zarah* 28a and follows an extended discussion of what sorts of illness may be healed on the Sabbath and by whom:

> Had not Rabba b. Bar Hanah said in the name of R. Johanan: Any sore for which the Sabbath may be profaned should not be healed by a heathen? - It is different with a distinguished man. What about R. Abbahu, who too was a distinguished man, yet Jacob the *Min* prepared for him a medicine for his leg, and were it not for R. Ammi and R. Asi who licked the leg, he would have cut off his leg? – The one [who attended] R. Johanan was an expert physician. – So too was that of R. Abbahu, an expert physician! – It was different in the case of R. Abbahu, for *Minim* adopt the attitude of 'let men die with Philistines'! (Epstein)

R. Johanan was being treated for scurvy by a female physician who was a Gentile. R. Abbahu lived in Caesarea at the end of the third and the beginning of the fourth century. He had frequent contact with Christians and not always unfriendly. The Gemara (commentary) within which this passage occurs seems to suppose that Jacob the *Min* intended to kill the patient by putting poison into the wound, and declares that, had not Rabbis Ammi and Asi licked it off (or sucked it out) Abbahu would have cut off his own leg rather than be saved by a Christian. The quotation of Jud.16:30 at the end is to show that a Christian would be willing to risk his own life, he was so determined to take Abbahu's. But this can hardly be the correct interpretation, Herford points out,[21] for Abbahu, as a distinguished man closely associated with the court of the Roman governor, would be attended by the physician of his own choice. Indeed the point of the story, illustrating R. Johanan's rule, implies Abbahu knowingly sent for Jacob the *Min* (the context shows him to be a Christian). Rabbis Ammi and Asi, however, would not tolerate Christian medical treatment for him, whether its intention was good or bad.

CONCLUSION

Because of the long period or oral transmission before the Talmuds were written down we cannot rely on the accuracy of these stories.[22] But, if we can deduce anything, it is that Christians were still known as healers in Palestine in the later third and early fourth centuries. Perhaps

---

[21] Herford, *Christianity*, 110-11.
[22] See ch. 3, nt. 18.

the fact that, in the earlier story, it is the name of Jesus that effects the cure, whereas in the later one pharmaceutical means are employed, reflects a development in their method.

Eusebius of Caesarea

Eusebius of Caesarea has deservedly been acclaimed the 'Father of Church History' for he was the first to treat ecclesiastical history as a subject in its own right, and he based his work as far as possible on the original documents. He was born c.260 and spent his youth in Palestine. He became a pupil of the scholar and martyr Pamphilus, upon whose impressive library he drew and who imbued him with a great love of Origen. When Pamphilus was martyred in 310 Eusebius fled to Tyre and then to Egypt where he was imprisoned for some months. By 315 he was Bishop of Caesarea. He became a supporter of Arius and was condemned by the Council of Antioch (324), but exonerated the next year at the Council of Nicea when he produced the baptismal creed of Caesarea. A great admirer of Constantine, he delivered the tricennial oration in 336 in honour of the thirtieth anniversary of the emperor's accession to power. He died c.339.

Eusebius wrote in all some forty-six works of which about a third survive in whole or significant part. It may be that he completed his *Chronicle*, giving an outline of world history in note form with dates, well before the end of the third century.[23] He drew on this, revising some of the dates, for his work of primary importance the *History of the Church*[24] which appeared first as books 1-7 before 303, to which three more books were subsequently added, and then the whole work was revised in 324/325.[25] Next most important are his massive *Preparation for the Gospel*[26] (15 books) and *Demonstration of the Gospel*[27] (20 books), conceived as two parts of a single work, intended to provide 'a definitive statement of the relationship between Greek culture, Judaism and Christianity'.[28] It is his answer to Porphyry's *Against the Christians*. The double work was written between 312 and 318. Amongst his lesser works is his *Against Hierocles* (perhaps c.315) which dissects and refutes the comparison between Christ and Apollonius of Tyana put

---

[23] Cf, *H.E.* 1.1.1.

[24] References to it are usually abbreviated '*H.E.*' from the Latin title *Historia ecclesiastica*.

[25] D.S. Wallace-Hadrill, *Eusebius of Caesarea* (London: Mowbray, 1960), 57.

[26] Lat. *Praeparatio evangelica* (*P.E.*).

[27] Lat. *Demonstratio evangelica* (*D.E.*).

[28] T.D. Barnes, *Constantine and Eusebius* (Harvard: University Press, 1981), 178.

forward by Hierocles, governor of Bithynia, in his work *Friend of Truth* (c.303).

References to demons are scattered through his works, but *P.E.* 5 he specifically devotes to considering the worship of demons. Here, as throughout the *Preparation,* he contents himself largely with quoting pagan authors. Near the outset he quotes Porphyry's lament:

> And now they wonder that for so many years the plague has attacked the city[a], Asclepius and the other gods being no longer resident among us. For since Jesus began to be honoured, no one ever heard of any public assistance from the gods. (5.1, tr. Gifford)

a – Rome

Eusebius comments triumphantly: 'the evil demons no longer have any power to prevail since our Saviour's advent among men.' Later, having quoted Plutarch, he notes that it was during the reign of Tiberius that the cry went up: "Great Pan is dead!" (5.17),[29] just at the time of our Saviour's sojourn among men. The demons and their rulers, Eusebius says, delight in the deification of dead men and sacrifices to their carved images. They have produced fictitious miracles, are responsible for sorcery, and have deceived people by curing bodies they themselves previously ravaged (5.2). Here he seems to be referring to the healing cults. He quotes Plutarch again for the assertion that it is demons not gods that presided over the oracles and bad demons that demanded human sacrifices, causing pestilence, barren soil, wars and seditions, until they received them (5.4).

In *Against Hierocles* he attributes the powers of Apollonius of Tyana, if he really had any, to demons.[30] In the *Demonstration* he attributes to demons not only idolatry but other false beliefs and the corruption of human morals,[31] and time and again, like Origen, he interprets Scripture passages allegorically to refer to the demons and their activities.[32]

EXORCISM

Compared with earlier Christian writers Eusebius is quite sparing in his references to exorcism. Only twice in these pre-Nicene works, it seems, does he clearly refer to contemporary practice. In *D.E.* 3.6 he is refuting Porphyry's charge that Jesus performed his miracles by sorcery:

[29]   Plutarch, *On the Cessation of the Oracles,* 17.
[30]   *Hier.* 35, cf. 39, 44.
[31]   *D.E.* 7.1.
[32]   *D.E.* 2.3, 6.13, 7.1 *et passim.*

I must again attack my opposer, and inquire if he has ever seen or heard of sorcerers and enchanters doing their sorcery without libations, incense, and the invocation and presence of daemons. But no one surely could venture to cast this aspersion on our Saviour, or on His teaching, or on those even now imitating His life. It must be clear even to the blind that we who follow Jesus are totally opposed to such agencies, and would sooner dare to sacrifice our soul to death than an offering to the daemons, yea, would sooner depart from life than remain alive under the tyranny of evil daemons. Who does not know how we love by the mere Name[a] of Jesus and the purest[b] prayers to drive away all the work of the daemons? The mere word of Jesus and His teaching has made us all far stronger than this invisible Power[c], and has trained us to be enemies and foes of daemons, not their friends or associates and certainly not their slaves and tributaries. And how could He Who has led us on to this, Himself be the slave of the daemons? How could He sacrifice to evil spirits? Or how could He have involved the daemons to aid Him in His miracles, when even today every daemon and unclean spirit shudders at the Name of Jesus as at something that is likely to punish and torment its own nature, and so departs and yields to the power of His Name alone? (3.6.34-6, Ferrar)

a – both ὄνομα 'name', and προσηγορία 'personal name' are used in this passage
b – suitable for expelling impure spirits   c – of the demons presumably

The power of the name of Jesus in Christian exorcism is very evident; at it demons shudder. It is used with sincere prayer.

In *Hierocles* 4 Eusebius is saying there is no comparison between Apollonius of Tyana and Jesus. At the end of a succession of points he writes:

Even now [Jesus] displays the virtues of his godlike might in the expulsion, by the mere invocation of his mysterious name[a], of sundry troublesome and evil demons which beset men's bodies and souls, as from our own experience we know it to be the case. To look for such results in the case of Apollonius, or even to ask about them, is absurd. (Loeb)

a – προσηγορία again

Eusebius is telling us he has witnessed such exorcisms, but he places this argument for the superiority of Jesus over Apollonius last of seven points, showing he is not one for sensationalism but prefers rational argument.

HEALING

In *D.E.* 3.4 Eusebius gives a brief review of Christ's miracles and raisings and concludes:

> Such were the far-famed wonders of [our Saviour's] power. Such were the proofs of his divinity. And we ourselves have marvelled at them with reverent reasoning, and received them after subjecting them to the tests and enquiries of a critical judgement. We have enquired into and tested them not only by other plain facts which make the whole subject clear, by which our Lord is still wont to show to those whom He thinks worthy, some slight evidence[a] of His power, but also by the more logical method which we are accustomed to use in arguing with those who do not accept what we have said, and either completely disbelieve it, and deny that such things were done by Him at all, or hold that if they were done, they were done by wizardry for the leading-astray of the spectators, as deceivers often do. (3.4.30-31, Ferrar)

a – μικρά τινα – smaller than the 'traces' of Origen's time.

It appears that there remain in the Church just a small number of those who have gifts of healing to demonstrate still the divine power of Jesus, but Eusebius would rather use rational argument because it is not susceptible to be dismissed as magic.

In *D.E.* 9.13 Eusebius first quotes Is.35:3 and then goes on to discuss the fulfilment of this verse and vv.5-6 in the miracles of Christ. Then he says:

> And the strongest confirmation of the Divine Power of the Saviour here foretold, by which He really used to cure the lame, the blind, the lepers and the palsied with a word according to that which is written concerning Him, is the power even now emerging through the whole world from His Godhead, by which is shown to them that can see what He was while on earth, since after so many years His proclamation of the word of God is seen to last on, invincible and true, overcoming all that have attempted from the beginning until now to withstand His teaching; He attracts to Himself great multitudes, from all the world, and releases them that come to Him from all kinds of evil[a] and diseases and troubles of the spirit. He summons to His holy school all races, Greek and Barbarian; He leads countless hosts to the knowledge of the one true God, and to a healthy and pure life, as befits those who promise to worship Almighty God.

a – ἁμαρτίας 'sin'

The chapter is concerned specifically to show Jesus' miracles fulfilled ancient prophecy and Eusebius finds in contemporary healings a useful confirmation of Jesus' divine power. But his reference here to 'great multitudes' being healed seems, at first sight, to be a direct contradiction to his statement in *D.E.* 3.4 that only 'slight evidence' of his power remains. However, by translating ἁμαρτία 'evil' rather than 'sin' Ferrar obscures the fact that Eusebius probably has baptism in mind here. This is surely confirmed when he says Christ 'summons to his holy school all races, Greek and Barbarian', reminiscent of the apostle Paul's words 'As many of you as were baptised in to Christ have put on Christ. There is neither Jew nor Greek...for you are all one in Christ Jesus' (Gal.3:27-28). If this interpretation is correct, Eusebius is testifying here specifically to widespread baptismal healing of afflictions of the body and soul in his time.

MEDICINE AND MAGIC

One might expect a man of Eusebius' sane rationality to be positive about secular medicine, but in fact he devotes very little space to the subject. In *P.E.* 8.14, in a long quotation from Philo, there is a reference to the value of venomous reptiles in supplying antidotes.[33] In *Hier.* 23 he does display a knowledge of Hippocratic medical theory about pestilence (the plague), saying it is 'a corruption and vitiation of the atmosphere, the circumambient air being changed into a morbid condition composed of noxious and evil exhalations'. (Loeb)

In *D.E.* 3.6 Eusebius tells us of the Church's proscription of amulets. He has been exonerating Christ of the charge of sorcery, and continues:

> And the disciples, who were with Him from the beginning with those who inherited their mode of life afterwards, are to such an incalculable extent removed from base and evil suspicion [of sorcery] that they will not allow their sick to do what is exceedingly common with non-Christians, to make use of charms written on leaves or amulets, or to pay attention to those promising to soothe them with songs of enchantment, or to procure ease for their pains by burning incense made of roots and herbs or anything else of the kind. All these things at any rate are forbidden by Christian teaching, neither is it ever possible to see a Christian using an amulet, or incantation, or charms written on curious leaves, or other things which the crowd consider quite permissible. What argument, then, can rank the disciple of such a Master with the disciple of a sorcerer or charlatan? (3.6.9-10)

Ferrar[34] comments that the 'charms written on leaves' were mystic figures or words such as the shield of David or the Hebrew Divine Name ('Tetragrammaton') written on metal discs, and he points to the

---

[33] Philo, *On Providence* 80.
[34] W.J. Ferrar, *Proof of the Gospel* I (London: SPCK, 1920), 146 nt.

catacombs for evidence of Christians using such tokens in contradiction
to Eusebius' claim here.

HEALTH AND SICKNESS

Again we must infer Eusebius' views from quotations he makes on this
subject. In *P.E.* 6.10.46 he seems to share Bardaisan's fatalistic
approach to sickness by quoting his statement that Christians 'submit to
sickness and poverty and sufferings and reputed infamies'.[35] In *P.E.*
8.14 Eusebius appears to favour a scientific rather than a religious
explanation of global phenomena when he quotes Philo:

> Earthquakes…and pestilences and thunderbolts, and all things of this
> kind, though said to be sent by God, are not so in truth (for God is not the
> cause of any evil at all), but these are produced by the change of the
> elementary atoms,[36] and are not primary works of nature, but follow
> necessary laws as consequences of the primary operations. (8.14.53,
> Gifford)

Shortly afterwards, Philo writes:

> In pestilential diseases some of the innocent perish with the rest, in order
> that the others may prudently keep aloof; apart from the fact that those
> who venture into a pestilential atmosphere must necessarily fall sick, just
> as those on board ship in a storm share equally in the danger. (8.14.55,
> Gifford)

Practical common sense is engendered here, informed by Hippocratic
teaching that the air is a carrier of disease. In *P.E.* 12.16 Eusebius
quotes Plato[37] who divides good things into two kinds: human and
divine, the former dependent on the latter. Of the human:

> The chief is health, and beauty second, and the third strength of body for
> running and all other movements, and wealth fourth, not blind but keen-
> sighted wealth, if it accompany wisdom. (12.16.3)

The divine are the familiar quartet of classical virtues: wisdom,
temperance, justice and courage, all of which rank above the bodily
goods. Tutored by Plato Eusebius must then have regarded pursuing
health as far from the primary object of life.

---

[35] *Book of the Laws of Countries* (tr. Drijvers), 61.
[36] The teaching of Democritus.
[37] *Laws* 631A.

CONCLUSION

Clearly Eusebius believes in the miraculous, but he is far more interested in rational argument. His statements about contemporary exorcism and healing are few and always in the apologetic cause of testifying to the divinity of Christ. He implies that gifts of healing are less numerous than in Origen's time but that baptismal healing is commonplace.

General Conclusion

It seems that by the late third and early fourth centuries gifts of healing are few and mentioned only by our Eastern sources. Perhaps some with such a gift are using medicine as well. Baptismal healing continues to be well attested. Our Western sources speak of contemporary exorcism but, far from attesting healings, rationalise the sufferings Christians are clearly facing.

CHAPTER 6

With the Empire at Our Feet: The Post-Nicene Church

One day in October 312 Constantine was with his army outside Rome wondering how, with fewer troops, he might capture the city from his rival Maxentius. Looking up at the sky he saw a portent, a cross of light. Subsequently, going into battle under that Christian emblem, he proved victorious.[1] From that time on he firmly believed the God of the Christians favoured him. In response, early in 313, he met with his eastern ally Licinius at Milan and issued an edict that, from then on, Christianity was to be a legal religion within the empire. Progressively he showered favours upon the Church. But concord between the two generals soon broke down and a protracted war ensued, terminating only in September 324 with Constantine's victory over Licinius at Chrysopolis on the eastern side of the Bosphorus. At last the whole empire was united under Constantine's rule. To his dismay, however, he found the Church torn apart by the Arian dispute. To bring this to an end he called the Council of Nicea (325), which gave birth to the first form of our Nicene Creed. The post-Nicene era was marked for the Church by freedom from persecution. This allowed its development in peace, but also led to a certain complacency and nominalism. Some pagans saw it opportune to adopt the new religion as a means of advancement.[2] This appears to have given a new impetus to monasticism, deeply dedicated Christians wishing to flee from the distractions of the world which were now invading the Church.

For the Post-Nicene Church the documentary material is far greater than in the pre-Nicene period. There are the histories of Socrates, Sozomen and others, biographies of various monks and church leaders, many sermons and letters, Bible commentaries, church orders and theological treatises. And consequently information about healing miracles is also more plentiful. In this final part of our study we shall select from it, working topically rather than by geographical region and

---

[1] Differing accounts of the incident are given by Eusebius in his *Life of Constantine* 1.28 and Lactantius in *Deaths of the Persecutors* 44.

[2] Cf. Eusebius, *Life of Con.* 4.54.

author. We shall consider in turn the attitude of leading theologians to miracles, the ministry and sacraments, gifts of healing, the role of the relics of the martyrs, the encroachment of magical practices, and medicine and suffering.

Theologians and the Miraculous

Theological leaders of the Church accepted that Christ's miracles established his divinity.[3] Chrysostom (c.347-407) says they show him to have been the world's creator and are a completion of the unfinished creation.[4] But Jerome (c.345-420) maintains Christ's greatest miracle was his prophetic act of the cleansing of the temple.[5] Athanasius (c.296-373) emphasizes that, while Asclepius could heal the body, Christ healed body and soul.[6] Like Origen, some of the post-Nicene Fathers were particularly fond of allegorizing Jesus' miracles, seeing them as illustrations of the new creation he wrought in people's lives.[7] How powerfully Augustine (354-430) uses the raising of Lazarus in this way!

> Rise in thy heart; go forth from thy tomb. For thou wast lying dead in thy heart as in a tomb, and pressed down by the weight of evil habits as by a stone. Rise and go forth. What is 'Rise and go forth?' Believe and confess. For he that has believed has risen: he that confesses is gone forth. (*Tract. Jn.* 22.7, NPNF)

These Fathers speak of the miracles as a means of convincing the 'grosser' sort of people, who would not be convinced by rational argument.[8] Chrysostom,[9] and Augustine, at first,[10] regarded miracles as simply a means of launching the Church, unnecessary once it was established.

But these same theologians also attest contemporary miracles in the Church of their time. Athanasius says that demons fear the sign of the cross[11] and, while non-Christians can drive them away from people, only Christians can totally banish them.[12] In writing about the Palestinian

---

[3]   Athanasius, *On the Incarnation* 38; Jerome, *Comm. Mt.* 20.34; Ambrose, *Hom. Lk.* 1.7.
[4]   *Hom. Mt.* 4.2, 56.2.
[5]   *Comm. Mt.* 21.15-16.
[6]   *Incarn.* 49.2.
[7]   Greer, *Fear of Freedom*, 38-39 (Ambrose), 57-59 (Cyril of Alexandria).
[8]   Jerome, *Comm. Mt.* 10.7-8; Chrysostom, *Hom. Mt.* 15.1, 27.3.
[9]   *Hom. Mt.* 4.2.
[10]   *True Religion* 25.47.
[11]   *Incarn.* 48.3.
[12]   See Barrett-Lennard, *Christian Healing,* ch. 6.

monk Hilary Jerome reveals his own interest in contemporary miracles. John Cassian (c.360-430+) speaks of many miracles in his *Institutes* and *Conferences*, written in Gaul in the early fifth century but using material he had collected earlier in the East. Even Chrysostom, who seems to be engaged in a polemic against miracles which people of his time are wanting, says that lack of faith can lead to lack of healing,[13] and he mentions that some of the faithful, when sick, are anointing themselves with oil taken from church lamps.[14] In the West Ambrose (c.339-397) recognises that healing can sometimes take place through the laying on of hands[15] and, according to his biographer Paulinus, he himself exorcised using this means.[16] He also attests the healing of a blind man during the translation of the bones of the martyrs Protasius and Gervasius to his new church in Milan in 386.[17] Augustine who in *Of True Religion* (390) had seen miracles as a temporary phenomenon for the founding of the Church, had by the 420s changed his mind. In *City of God* 22.8 he lists twenty-one miracles (healings and exorcisms) and says that, in the two years since the recording of miracles was started at Hippo (in 424), seventy had been noted and many more remained to be recorded. It was a similar situation elsewhere. But over sickness and health his belief in the sovereignty of God held sway. It is right, he says, to pray for relief from suffering but, pointing to the apostle Paul's 'thorn in the flesh', he affirms, God knows what is best for us.[18]

Ministry and Sacraments

Exorcist

The order of exorcist which had emerged by the middle of the third century continued in the Post-Nicene Church as a junior order of ministry. The Council of Antioch (330)[19] permitted rural bishops to appoint exorcists as well as readers and sub-deacons, but not to ordain the higher ranks of clergy. The Council of Laodicia (c.370) includes

---

[13] *Hom. Rom.* 8.6, where he speaks also of the use of the name of Jesus.

[14] Chrysostom, *Hom. Mt.* 32.9.

[15] Ambrose, *Penitence* 1.8.

[16] Paulinus, *Life of Ambrose* 28, 43.

[17] Ambrose, *Ep.* 22.2. And he mentions other miracles through touching the saints' robes or napkins that have been in contact with the relics (22.9).

[18] Augustine, *Tract. Jn.* 7.12. M. Jackson, in his article 'Miracles and 'Spiritual Correctness' in the Theology of St. Augustine', *SP* 38 (2001), 184-89, points out that, despite his awakened interest in contemporary miracles, Augustine did not wish to overemphasize them but rather stressed their continuity with the work of Christ.

[19] Council of Antioch (330), Canon 10.

exorcists among the clergy, enumerating them after readers and singers but before door-keepers and monks. The same council forbids them to exercise their function publicly in church or in private homes unless they have been 'promoted' to the office by the bishop. Woolley points out that in the old Roman rites there was no form of ordination, for an exorcist was 'given a commission' by the bishop. Only in the fifth/sixth century Gallican document *Statuta ecclesiae antiqua* did he find a form of ordination:

> Let an exorcist when he is ordained receive from the hand of the bishop a book in which are written exorcisms, the bishop saying to him, 'Receive and commit to memory (this), and have power to lay hands on him that is possessed, whether he is baptised or a catechumen'.[20]

By this time, clearly some of the spontaneity had gone from exorcising and yet the belief remained, as in the pre-Nicene period,[21] that a Christian could be possessed.

Gradually the office of exorcist appears to have been subsumed by the higher orders of ministry. The *Apostolic Constitutions* (almost certainly Syrian, c.350-80), while stating that an exorcist is not ordained, because his gift is one of God's grace which makes itself evident, goes on to stipulate that, if there is an occasion, he should be ordained bishop, presbyter or deacon (8.26). In the West, by the end of the fourth century, the office of exorcist had to some extent become a stepping stone to ordination to higher ministry. Both Martin of Tours and Felix of Nola temporarily occupied the office.[22]

Bishop, Presbyter and Deacon

The responsibility of the senior local clergy for the welfare of the sick within their churches, evident in the Pre-Nicene Church, is yet more obvious in post-Nicene times. *Apostolic Constitutions* 8.16 includes in its prayer for the ordination of presbyters the request that, endowed with God's Spirit, they may be 'filled with the gifts of healing'. Similarly Canon 3 of the *Canons of Hippolytus* (Northern Egypt, fourth century[23]) gives a consecration prayer for the bishop which includes the petition:

---

[20] Qu. Woolley, *Exorcism*, 43.

[21] Origen, *Hom. Ex.* 8; Cyprian, *Ep.* 69.16.1 *et passim*.

[22] Sulpicius Severus, *Life of Martin* 5; Paulinus of Nola, *Birthday 4 of Felix*.

[23] Barrett-Lennard, 'The Canons of Hippolytus and Christian Concern with Illness, Health, and Healing', *JECS* 13 (2005), 139-40. He notes R.G. Coquin's dating of the Canons 336-40, but believes the final form of the Canons may come from considerably later in the century.

'Give him, Lord...power to loosen every bond of the oppression of demons, to cure the sick and crush Satan under his feet quickly...' Canon 4 states that the same prayer is to be used in the ordination of presbyters. Clearly then, healing the sick was a task for which the ordained clergy were seen to be divinely equipped. Canon 24 speaks of the roles of the deacon and the bishop in this ministry:

> A deacon is to accompany the bishop at all times to inform him of everyone's condition. He is to inform him about each sick person, because it is important for the sick person that the high-priest visit him. He is relieved of his sickness when the bishop goes to him, especially when he prays over him, because the shadow of Peter healed the sick, unless his lifespan is over. The sick are not to sleep in the dormitory, but rather the poor. That is why he who has a home, if he is sick, is not to be moved to the house of God. Rather he is only to pray and then return home.[24]

The deacon notifies the bishop of the sick but the bishop performs the healing ministry. This canon is more explicit about the bishop's role than *Apostolic Tradition* 34. In both the bishop is designated 'high priest' but, whereas *A.T.* 34 merely says 'a sick man is greatly comforted' by the visit of the bishop, this canon specifies that he pray for the sick and his prayers are expected to bring healing, unless the person has clearly fulfilled the 'allotted span' of life. Barrett-Lennard comments that the bishop's role appears 'pivotal for the restoration of health'.[25] But in fact this canon may not show an enhancement of his role, rather attest continuity of healing ministry from the apostles, through the presbyter/elders as revealed in James 5:14-16, and down to this time.

This canon's further instructions indicate that some sick people want to sleep overnight in churches, as in temples of Asclepius, but this is not allowed. Those fit enough must visit the church to receive prayer ministry, though Canon 21 makes it clear that those seriously ill and close to death are to be visited daily at home by the clergy.

Canon 25 speaks of the appointment by the bishop of a 'steward of the sick' who, in his ministry, receives from the bishop a 'vessel of clay'. Barrett-Lennard deduces from the roughly contemporary canon 8 of the *Canons of Athanasius* that this vessel was a container holding

---

[24]   P.F.Bradshaw, *The Canons of Hippolytus* (Nottingham: Grove Books, 1987), 27.

[25]   Barrett-Lennard, 'The Canons of Hippolytus', 152. Bradshaw points out (*Canons of Hippolytus*, 12) this emphasis on the bishop as healer in eastern ordination prayers is not found in their western counterparts which merely follow the emphasis of *A.T.* 34.

food supplies for the sick. He thinks the steward was probably a priest (presbyter), but *Didascalia* 9, to which he also alludes, is specifically concerned with the work of the *bishop*, and appears to refer to him as the 'priest and steward of God'.[26] If he delegated the role to anyone else it would surely be to a deacon.

It seems then that, in the fourth century, those ordained were heavily involved in care for the sick, a ministry that ultimately can be traced back to the earliest days of the Church.

Healing Elements

The *Apostolic Tradition* (5) provided a prayer of blessing for oil for healing ministry. Canon 26 of the *Canons of Hippolytus* adds consecrated water:

> The sick also, it is healing for them to go to the church to receive the water of prayer and the oil of prayer, unless the sick person is seriously ill and close to death… (tr. Bradshaw)

Presumably the water was for drinking and the oil for anointing, for in the *Apostolic Constitutions* there is a prayer for consecrating just such water and oil, to be said by the bishop or, in his absence, the presbyter:

> O Lord of hosts, the God of powers, the creator of waters, and the supplier of oil, who art compassionate, and a lover of mankind, who has given water for drink and for cleansing, and oil to give man a cheerful and joyful countenance[a]; do Thou now also sanctify this water and this oil through Thy Christ, in the name of him or her that has offered them[b], and grant them a power to restore health, to drive away diseases, to banish demons and to disperse all snares through Christ our hope… (8.29, ANF)

a – cf. Ps.104.15   b – cf. *A.T.* 5: 'if anyone offers oil…'

---

[26] For a discussion of this matter see Barrett-Lennard, 'Canons of Hippolytus', 157-60. Connolly's translation of *Didascalia* 9 runs: 'For the bishop is well acquainted of those who are in distress, and dispenses and gives to each one as is fitting for him, so that one may not receive often in the same day or in the same week, and another receive not even a little. For whom the priest and steward of God knows to be the more in distress, him he succours as he requires.'

Woolley suggests that the person offering them took the consecrated elements away for home use.[27] Whilst this cannot be ruled out as the practice in the Syrian Church, it is perhaps more likely that, as specified in the Egyptian *Canons of Hippolytus* (21), the anointing was done in church, presumably at the eucharist, unless the sick person was chronically ill and unable to leave home. A similar prayer over water and oil in the *Sacramentary* of Serapion, Bishop of Thmuis in the Nile delta (c.339-360+), runs:

> We bless these created things through the name of your only-begotten Jesus Christ, we name the name of him who suffered, who was crucified and rose again and is seated at the right hand of the uncreated, upon this water and this oil. Grant healing power upon these created things, so that every fever and every demon and every illness may be cured through the drinking and the anointing, and may the partaking of these created things be a healing medicine and a medicine of wholeness in the name of your only-begotten Jesus Christ... (5, tr. Barrett-Lennard)

Here the power of the name of Jesus is twice brought to bear on the healing elements. In the same *Sacramentary* (17) there is another, longer prayer for the consecration of bread, water and oil, (perhaps originally just for oil), which contains the request that God's healing power in the elements may be a 'charm' (ἀλεξιφάρμακον) against every demon and illness. Barrett-Lennard thinks, because of the absence of other words with magical associations in the prayer, this word is better translated here 'remedy'.[28] But the prayer's verbosity, its piling up of phrases relating to spirits, diseases and cure, surely brings it close to being a magical text.[29]

---

[27] Woolley, *Exorcism*, 58. He mentions also the similar prayer of consecration of oil in *Testamentum Domini* 1.24, another church order from the 4th or 5th C. preserved in a 7th C. Syriac manuscript.

[28] Barrett-Lennard, *The Sacramentary of Serapion* (Nottingham: Grove Books, 1993), 48.

[29] Compare its 'Master let every satanic energy, every demon, ever plot of the adversary, every blow, every scourge, every suffering, every pain, or slap or shaking or evil phantom fear your holy name...' with 5th C. amulet: 'O lord Christ, son and Word of the living god, who heals every disease and infirmity, also heal and watch over your handmaid Joannia...and chase away and banish from her every fever and every sort of chill – quotidian, tertian, quartan – and every evil...' (no.16 in Meyer, *Ancient Christian Magic* - editor's capitalisation).

Barrett-Lennard's valuable study of the whole *Sacramentary*[30] shows that six others of its total of thirty prayers have some relevance to healing: prayer 15 is, it seems, to be made over the oil of exorcism used prior to baptism. Prayer 16 is a prayer of consecration for the oil of chrism used after the water baptism. Both prayers combat any satanic influence on the candidate, the second is to accompany signing with the cross. Prayers 22 and 30 are general prayers for the sick; the second is entitled 'the laying on of hands on the sick' and stresses the powerful name of Jesus. Prayer 27 includes a brief prayer for the sick alongside other categories of the needy. Furthermore prayer 1, the great eucharistic prayer, also contains a petition for healing of all who participate in communion:

> God of truth, let your holy Word come upon this bread that the bread may become the body of the Word, and upon this cup, that this cup may become the blood of truth. And make all who share it receive a medicine of life for the healing of every sickness and for a strengthening of all advancement and virtue, not for condemnation, God of truth, nor for reproof or reproach.

Barrett-Lennard comments that this is unique among the liturgies in focusing on healing at the central point of the eucharist.[31] Another reference towards the end of this prayer asks yet again for health of body and soul for all participating. Healing the sick then must have been an important part of Serapion's ministry, hardly surprising perhaps for one who was a friend of Antony and Athanasius.

For the Western Church we turn to Pope Innocent I's *Epistle* 25, to Decentius (early fifth century). Decentius has asked what James 5:13-16 really means. Innocent replies:

> There is no doubt that this should be interpreted and understood as referring to the faithful who are sick, who can be anointed with the holy oil of chrism when it has been consecrated by the bishop, and that it is lawful not only for priests but for all Christians to use it to anoint themselves in their own or their friends' necessity.

He goes on say it is of course lawful for bishops to visit the sick, or the presbyters when the bishop's time is occupied with other duties. It is fitting for the bishop to visit anyone he deems fit and to touch him with chrism. But the chrism may not be used on those undergoing penance, for it is a 'kind of sacrament', and how can it be granted to those to

---

30   Barrett-Lennard, *Christian Healing*, ch. 9; also his *Sacramentary of Serapion* from which we take the English translation of the prayers.
31   Barrett-Lennard, *Sacramentary* 27.

whom the rest of the sacraments are being denied? (*Ep.* 25.8) Woolley points out that this is the first known reference to James 5 in connection with healing the sick, and he thinks that 'chrism' here refers not to the mixture technically known by that name, but to simple olive oil.[32] It is interesting too that lay healing ministry using oil is clearly sanctioned.

Amongst the twenty-one cases of healing detailed by Augustine in his *City of God* 22.8 one mentions cattle disease and sickness among servants in the village of Zubedi, attributed to demons, cured after celebration of the eucharist and fervent prayer; others tell of a physician in Carthage with gout in his foot, an ex-showman from Curubis with paralysis and a hernia, and the elderly Martial with an unspecified sickness, all healed at the time of their baptism.

Gifts of Healing

From the fourth century various monks are known to have exercised gifts of healing, but their success posed a temptation to pride. John Cassian, in the preface to his *Institutes* which sets out the rules for monastic life, classifies those who perform miracles into three kinds:

1.   Those who by virtue of holiness are deemed worthy to receive the 'gift of signs'. (He quotes Mt.10:8.)
2.   Sinners who can heal when it is edifying for the church or because those bringing the sick, or coming sick for healing have faith. (He refers to Mt.7:22-23.) He comments that lack of such faith can prevent those with gifts of healing from exercising them.   (He quotes Mt.13:58.)
3.   Those who through the operation of demons, or puffed up with pride because of a gift of healing, attempt to exorcise, but the demons only pretend to be scorched or to flee.[33]

Speaking of Jesus' words 'Come and learn of me for I am meek and lowly of heart' he writes:

> Humility therefore is the mistress of all virtues…For he can perform all the miracles which Christ wrought, without danger of being puffed up, who follows the gentle Lord not in the grandeur of his miracles but in the virtues of patience and humility. But he who aims at commanding unclean spirits, or bestowing gifts of healing, or showing some wonderful miracle to the people, even though, when he is showing off, he invokes

---

[32]   Woolley, *Exorcism*, 64.
[33]   *Coll.* 15.1, NPNF (*Collatio = Conferences*).

the name of Christ, yet he is far from Christ, because in his pride of heart
he does not follow his humble teacher. (*Coll.* 15.7)

In Egypt Antony (d.356), the 'Father of Christian Monasticism', warns
similarly pointing out that any performance of signs is due not to the
person concerned but is the Saviour's work.[34] A similar warning against
pride is given in *Apostolic Constitutions* 8.1-2 to those exercising
supernatural gifts of the Spirit in the Syrian church.

Antony's own prayers for healing, we are told, were frequently
heard.[35] Fronto from Palatium who was in a bad state, biting his own
tongue and nearly blind came to Antony's mountain and was told by the
hermit, "Leave and you will be healed." He stayed and his condition
worsened. Eventually in faith the man obeyed and his health was
restored.[36] Again, a young woman suffering paralysis and a horrifying
discharge from her ears, came with her parents and waited outside as
others went in to Antony. Before being told what was wrong he
described her condition and then instructed that the girl should depart
and she would be healed. She was.[37] His prayers availed too for the
immediate healing at distance of Polycratia, described as a fine
Christian girl in Laodicea suffering from pains in her stomach and
side.[38] Antony's method was not to issue commands of healing but to
pray and call on the name of Christ. He deplored the popularity his
success brought.[39] Not all he prayed for were in fact healed and he
encouraged petitioners to be patient, realising that it is God's
prerogative to heal whoever and whenever he wishes. To the Lord alone
they should give thanks.[40]

Pachomius (c.290-346), the former soldier who took up the life of a
hermit in Egypt, is said to have sent consecrated oil to a father to anoint
his daughter to drive out a demon. He did so and she was restored to her
former health.[41]

In his *Lausiac History* (c.419) Palladius tells of Benjamin, an ascetic
in Egypt's Nitrian desert, who, through the laying on of hands and the
use of oil he had blessed, healed all the sick brought to him.[42] Macarius
of Alexandria (d.394) is said to have cured 'countless demon-ridden

---

[34] Athanasius, *Life of Antony* 38.
[35] *Ibid.* 56.
[36] *Ibid.* 57.
[37] *Ibid.* 58.
[38] *Ibid.* 61.
[39] *Ibid.* 84.
[40] *Ibid.* 56.
[41] *Life of Pachomius* 43, cf. 44.
[42] Palladius, *Lausiac History* 12.1. A similar claim is made for Stephen the
Libyan, but his methods are not revealed (24.1).

people',[43] and in one instance laid hands on, anointed with oil, and poured water over a possessed boy, but legendary elements seem evident in the story.[44] He is also credited with healing a paralysed virgin by anointing with oil and praying for her for a period of twenty days.[45] Palladius claims to have witnessed the healing of a possessed and paralysed young man in Palestine through six hours of continuous prayer by Innocent, his own first monastic instructor.[46]

Hilary (291-371) is said by Jerome to have blessed bread and oil for individual use,[47] to have sent blessed oil to heal shepherds and husbandmen bitten during a plague of poisonous reptiles,[48] to have cured a woman of blindness by anointing with saliva,[49] and to have saved a dying couple by anointing.[50]

In his *History of the Monks of Syria* (*Historia religiosa*, c.428) Theodoret of Cyrrhus speaks of miracles as of central importance to the lives of monks, yet he stresses they are the work of the Holy Spirit. Hermit Maro healed fevers, all manner of diseases, and cast out devils.[51] Hermit James healed by giving water he had blessed to be taken, it seems, as a draught.[52] Hermit Peter healed a woman's eyes by the laying on of hands and making the sign of the cross.[53]

In the West, outstanding for his healing power was Martin of Tours (c.330-97). His biographer Sulpicius Severus tells how he healed a possessed boy by laying on of hands.[54] He also gives a detailed account of how Martin healed a paralysed girl: first he prostrated himself and prayed, then he blessed oil and poured some of it into her mouth and immediately her voice was restored, then, as he touched them little by little, all her limbs were restored and she stood up before all the people.[55] He used consecrated oil orally also to restore a dumb girl, holding her tongue in his fingers while he administered it.[56] Even the touch of his clothes is said to have had healing power.[57]

---

[43]   *Ibid.* 18.11.
[44]   *Ibid.* 18.22 – the boy levitates, swells up...
[45]   *Ibid.* 18.11.
[46]   *Ibid.* 44.2-3.
[47]   Jerome, *Life of Hilary* 30.
[48]   *Ibid.* 32.
[49]   *Ibid.* 15.
[50]   *Ibid.* 44.
[51]   Theodoret, *Hist. rel.* 16.
[52]   *Ibid.* 21.14.
[53]   *Ibid.* 9.7.
[54]   Sulpicius Severus, *Life of Martin* 17.
[55]   *Ibid.* 16.
[56]   Sulpicius Severus, *Dial.* 3.2.
[57]   Sulpicius Severus, *Life* 18.

Remarkable though these miracle stories are, in quite a few the methods of healing are complex and the time protracted, contrasting with the simplicity of earlier years. It is moreover paradoxical that those who sought to mortify their flesh for spiritual gain, and viewed their own physical sickness as beneficial in this quest, should practise the healing of others.[58]

The Relics of the Martyrs

Reverence for those who had died for their faith led, by the mid-fifth century, to the organization of the cult of the martyrs throughout the Church. The martyrs' examples became less important, but the presence of a relic of a martyr was believed to make available for people the powerful prayers of that martyr.[59] Huge shrines were built around martyrs' graves in the cemeteries and became centres of pilgrimage. Sometimes martyrs' remains were transferred elsewhere. It became customary, indeed obligatory, for new churches to contain some relics within their walls,[60] and pilgrimages to the various shrines became popular. In the late fourth century Pope Damasus sought his martyred predecessor Cornelius' relics to benefit him, and Ambrose's transfer of the remains of Protasius and Gervasius to his new church was for a similar purpose.

The practice of incubation (sleeping in a church), no doubt derived from pagan healing cults, was particularly linked with certain saints deemed to have healing power, such as Cosmos and Damian at Constantinople, Cyrus and John at Alexandria, and Thecla at Seleucia. The cult of St. Michael the Archangel, venerated as a healer and protector against the power of the devil, became widespread.[61]

Augustine includes amongst the twenty-one miracles he lists in *City of God* 22.8: the healing of the blind man which he and Ambrose had witnessed, through contact with the remains of Protasius and Gervasius; a demon-possessed boy with a damaged eye cured at a shrine on a country estate dedicated to the same saints; and a blind woman, a bishop with fistula, a Spanish priest, three gout victims, a child near death, and

---

[58] See Peregrine Horden, 'The Death of Ascetics: sickness and monasticism in the early Byzantine Middle East' in *Studies in Church History*, ed. W.J. Shiels, vol. 22 (1985), 41-52.

[59] See P. Brown, *The Cult of the Saints* (London: SCM, 1981), ch. 1; Greer, *Fear of Freedom*, ch. 5.

[60] S.L. Rayner, 'The Early Church and the Healing of the Sick' (Durham University M.A. Dissertation, 1973), 114.

[61] *Ibid.*, ch. 4 (end) summarises the evidence.

a convulsive brother and sister all healed, and three recently dead people restored to life through some contact with the relics of St. Stephen.

How does one explain such phenomena? Hilary of Poitiers declares the working of wonders at the tombs of the apostles and martyrs bears witness to the power of Jesus.[62] Augustine attributes it to the faith that Christ rose from the dead and ascended into heaven, to which the martyrs were witnesses.[63] But while living healers could point out to those who came to them the need for repentance and amendment of life, and speak of the wholeness Christ came to bring, the relics of martyrs, however noble, were but mute witnesses and could lead to superstitious awe little removed from that associated with magic.

Magical Practices

Statements of late fourth and fifth-century Fathers, canons of various councils, and the discovery of magical papyri in Egypt with extensive Christian elements, all testify to the fact that Church members of this period, perhaps a considerable number, were crossing the boundary between acceptable Christian practice and illegitimate magical means in their quest for good luck, health and safety.

Cyril of Jerusalem (c.315-387) warns the newly converted against using amulets in times of sickness, burning incense by fountains or rivers, writing charms on leaves or making deductions from the behaviour of birds.[64] Chrysostom warns women against superstitious practices at childbirth and when faced with sickness, and he advocates just the sign of the cross.[65] Augustine, who is horrified that Christians should use amulets,[66] is happy to allow them to put a gospel on the head of a sick person as a Christian alternative.[67]

Woolley points to Canon 35 of the 'Canons of Basil' (c. AD 400):

> If a Christian resorts to any astrologer, magician or wizard, no priest shall pray over him, none anoint him with oil from the church in his sickness, since it stands written, Ye cannot serve God and mammon. The holy oil of the altar has no communion with the oil of uncleanness of wizardry, and the prayer of the priest none with the phylacteries of wizardry.[68]

---

[62]   Hilary of Poitiers, *Trin.* 11.3.
[63]   Augustine, *City of God* 22.9.
[64]   Cyril of Jerusalem, *Cat.* 19.8.
[65]   Chrysostom, *Hom. Col.* 8.5.
[66]   Augustine, *Tract. Jn.* 7.6.
[67]   *Ibid.* 7.12.
[68]   Qu. Woolley, *Exorcism*, 60-61.

It also tells of a sort of 'white magic' being proffered:

> If a Christian goes to a magician and is told in answer to his question, 'Wait till the sun rises, and then do so and so', or 'When the sun is at its zenith set water before you and anoint the sick with it', or, 'When the sun sets, say over oil so and so and anoint him with it', or, 'Tie phylacteries on yourself', or, 'Lay heavy iron on yourself, for devils are driven out thereby, for devils are afraid of iron'...[69]

sounding no doubt deceptively innocent to some.

As early as the Council of Ancyra (Ankara) in 314, its canon 24 declares that those who follow pagan customs and seek magical remedies must be sentenced to five years' penance and other penalties. Canon 36 of the Council of Laodicea (sometime between 343 and 381) lays down:

> Those of the order of the priesthood, and clergy generally, must not be magicians or soothsayers, or computers or astrologers, or make what are called phylacteries, which are fetters to their souls; and those who wear such we order to be cast out of the Church.[70]

Woolley refers to a homily of Isaac of Antioch (c.450) showing that the abuse by both clergy and laity could be quite blatant:

> Instead of the blessings of the saints, lo, they carry about the incantations of magicians; and instead of the holy cross, lo, they carry the books of devils...one carries it on his head, another round his neck, and a child carries about the devil's names, and comes (to Church).[71]

An indication of what is being referred to is provided by the Greek and Coptic magical papyri. M. Meyer's *Ancient Christian Magic* gives numerous examples and he writes with some justification: 'the more closely these texts are actually read, the harder it is to maintain any distinction between piety and sorcery'.[72] Let us consider four of the earlier Greek texts:

No. 12   4th/5th C. amulet (text: Amsterdam 173)

> A✝O By Jesus Christ heal Megas whom
> D.... bore [of] every disease, and pain

---

[69] *Ibid.*, 67.
[70] Qu. Greer, *Fear of Freedom*, 120.
[71] Woolley, *Exorcism*, 67.
[72] M. Meyer, *Ancient Christian Magic,* 2.

of the head and of the temples, and fever,
and shivering fever A+O.

This seems a perfectly unobjectionable prayer presumably for a sick child. The only objectionable aspect is that it is not prayed once but stored as a charm in constant contact with the child, so the method is magical, the content Christian.

No. 15   4th C. amulet (text: Oxyrhynchus 924)

Truly guard and protect Aria from the one-day chill and from the daily chill and from the nightly chill and from the mild fever of [the top of the head]. You shall do these things [graciously] and completely, first on account of your will and also on account of her faith because she is a handmaid of the
    living God, and that your name may be glorified continually.

[Power]	A of Jesus	father, son, mother	Christ	O
E		holy A O spirit		U
I		Abrasax		O

This is clearly of Gnostic provenance and based on standard magic amulet formats. The danger is stated and the divine power commanded to provide protection, the reasons why it must do so are stated: God's will is for healing, the person has faith and is God's servant, and for glory to God's name. The names of the persons of the Christian Godhead are arranged symmetrically at the bottom together with the six vowels of the Greek alphabet and alpha and omega (AΩ). Besides this magical format, Gnostic traits are evident in the introduction of 'mother' into the Godhead, representing possibly a promotion of the Virgin Mary, and the mention of Abraxas (=Abrasax), a Gnostic term from Basilides who saw the numerical value of its Greek letters amounted to 365.[73] Clearly this amulet would have crossed the boundary of what was acceptable to orthodox Christianity, but the one wearing it would no doubt protest that the words and sentiments were very largely Christian.

No. 16   5th C. amulet (text: Oxyrhynchus 1151)

+ Flee hateful spirit! Christ pursues you: the son of god[a] and the holy spirit have overtaken you. O god of the sheep-pool, deliver from all evil your handmaid Joannia whom Anastasia, also called Euphemia, bore. + In the beginning was the Word, and the Word was with god, and the Word was god. All things were made through him, and without him was not anything made that was made. O lord + Christ, son and Word of the

---

[73]   Irenaeus, *A.H.* 1.24.7.

living god, who heals every disease and every infirmity, also heal and watch over your handmaid Joannia whom Anastasia, also called Euphemia, bore, and chase away and banish from her every fever and every sort of chill – quotidian, tertian, quartan – and every evil. Pray through the intercession of our lady, the mother of god, and the glorious...

a – lack of capitalisation here and throughout these texts is due to the editor

Again this is clearly modelled on pagan magical texts, though using Christian 'ammunition'. It envisages sickness and especially fevers and chills are caused by evil spirits. It is for the protection of Johannia, perhaps the new-born baby of a Christian, or sectarian, Anastasia (from Gk. *anastasis*, 'resurrection'). Presumably Euphemia was her pre-Christian name, which some still called her. 'God of the sheep-pool' would seem to be an invocation of the one who healed at the pool by the Sheep Gate in Jerusalem (Jn.5:2). The quotation of Jn.1:1-3 suggests perhaps a Gnostic provenance of the amulet as the Gnostics especially liked the Fourth Gospel. At the end the prayers of saints and archangels are invoked for good measure. Again, a 'simple' believer would no doubt find nothing wrong in such a Christian-sounding text.

No. 19 4th C. spell and amulet (Great Magical Papyrus of Paris, PGM IV.1227-64)

Excellent spell for driving out demons:

Formula to be spoken over his head. Place olive branches before him and stand behind him and say, "Greetings, god of Abraham; greetings god of Isaac; greetings, god of Jacob; Jesus the upright, the holy spirit, the son of the father, who is below the seven, who is within the seven. Bring Yao Sabaoth; may your power issue forth from N., until you drive away this unclean demon Satan, who is in him. I adjure you, demon, whoever you are, by this god Sabarbarbathioth Sabarbarbathiouth Sabarbarbathioneth Sabarbarbaphai. Come out demon, whoever you are, and stay away from N., hurry, hurry, now, now! Come out, demon, since I bind you with unbreakable adamantine fetters, and I deliver you into the black chaos in perdition."

Procedure: Take seven olive branches. For six of them tie together the two ends of each one, but for the remaining one use it as a whip as you utter the adjuration. Keep it secret: it is proven.

After driving out (the demon), hang around N. an amulet, which the patient puts on after the expulsion of the demon, with these things written

on a tin metal leaf: "BOR PHOR PHORBA PHOR PHORBA BES
CHARIN BAUBO TE PHOR... protect N."

Twelftree[74] points out that, though this papyrus is generally agreed to
date from the fourth century, its contents probably come from the
second century and are not of Christian origin. An indication of this is
the use of χρηστός (*chrēstos*, here translated 'upright'), a Greek word
frequently substituted by non-Christians for the less well-known χριστός
(*christos*). Moreover 'Jesus the upright, the holy spirit, the son of the
father' is part of a Coptic insertion into the Greek text interrupting the
flow of the spell, and its phrases are, from a Christian perspective, out of
order.

Meyer explains that the reference to 'the seven' must indicate the
seven spheres of the sky. The sonorous nonsense words added are
standard practice in a magical spell and are intended to terrify the
demon.[75] The treatment, using an olive branch as a whip, sounds violent
indeed. Meyer thinks the initial words on the amulet may be a verbal
transformation of the name of the Egyptian god Horus, and subsequent
words may invoke the Egyptian god Bes, the Greek for 'favour'
(*charis*), and the Greek woman of Eleusian legends, Baubo.

This papyrus shows clearly how Jewish and Christian names for God
could be absorbed into Egyptian magic. Whilst totally at variance with
the practice of Christian exorcism indicated in the pre-Nicene literature,
in the light of the statements of fourth-century Fathers and Councils
quoted above, it is possible that some Christians were by then using it.[76]

Medicine and Suffering

In the Pre-Nicene Church most of the Fathers appear to have adopted a
generally positive attitude to the practice of medicine. In the Post-
Nicene Church this attitude continued. Chrysostom declares that God
gave us both physicians and medicine.[77] Augustine speaks well of one
Vindicianus whom he describes as one of the most eminent physicians
of his day,[78] though the ultimate success of medical cures, he says,

---

[74] Twelftree, *Name of Jesus*, 263.
[75] Cf. Kee, *Medicine* ch. 4.
[76] But Twelftree (*Name of Jesus*, 264) has no sure grounds either here or in the
      statement of Celsus for saying that it is highly likely that even prior to AD
      200 Christians were involved in magical exorcisms. See above ch. 4, nt.
      147.
[77] Chrysostom, *Hom. Col.* 8.
[78] Augustine, *Ep.* 138.3.

comes from God.[79] Likewise Jerome urges medical care for sick monks,[80] but declares that physicians labour in vain without God's aid.[81] Basil (c.330-379) writes to a Christian archiatrus (senior physician) Eustathius:

> In my opinion, to put your science at the head and front of life's pursuits is to decide reasonably and rightly. This at all events seems to be the case if man's most precious possession, life, is painful and not worth living, unless it be lived in health, and, if for health, we are dependent on your skill. In your case medicine is seen, as it were, with two right hands; you enlarge the accepted limits of philanthropy by not confining the application of your skill to men's bodies, but by attending also to the cure of the diseases of their souls. (*Ep.* 189.3, Loeb)

Here he appears to see medicine as *the* means by which physical health can be maintained, though he stresses also the importance of spiritual health. In his *Longer Rule* 55, in dealing with the question 'whether recourse to the medical art is in keeping with the practice of piety' he declares that the medical art should not be viewed as wholly responsible for our health, rather its success should be seen as redounding to the glory of God.

Like the pre-Nicene Fathers the Fathers of this period maintain also that there is some positive benefit in suffering. Augustine gives a number of benefits, saying that God allows Christians to endure physical ills because they heal pride, test and prove patience, punish and eradicate sins,[82] they remind Christians of their mortality and cause them to rely on God.[83] Chrysostom, in a sermon on 1 Timothy 5:23,[84] gives no less than twelve explanations of why Christians should suffer, including that it is to keep them humble, to enable them to show endurance, to demonstrate their belief in resurrection and eternal life, to be a means of consoling others who are suffering, and, by giving thanks to God in the midst of suffering, to deliver a blow to the devil. He adds that God would not permit suffering were it not for Christians' good. In short one might summarize their position: a healthy body is good, but a healthy soul is even more important and sometimes sickness assists in attaining it.

Nevertheless, the Church's positive attitude to the medical art led to monks copying and preserving the medical writings of the ancient

---

[79] Augustine, *Tract. Jn.* 3.30.
[80] Jerome, *Ep.* 125.16.
[81] Jerome, *Hom. Is.* 8.
[82] Augustine, *Ep.* 130.
[83] Augustine, *Hom. Ps.* 39.18.
[84] Chrysostom, *Hom. on the Statues* 1.

world, especially those of Galen, and showing practical care for the sick. In his monograph[85] A.T. Crislip argues that the early monastic movements' provision for its sick evolved into the hospital system, of which Basil of Caesarea in Cappadocia in the late fourth century was the first representative. Crislip refers to the *Life of Pachomius* (c.324) which says that, after Pachomius had established the administrative structure of his first monastery at Tabennisi on the east bank of the river Nile in Upper Egypt, he appointed a house of stewards for the care of the sick. Archeological evidence from the monastery of Apa Jeremias at Seqqara, south-west of Cairo, in the late fifth century reveals an infirmary near the refectory, away from the other buildings.[86] Crislip speaks of doctors who became monks as the 'mainstay' of fourth-century monastic communities, of nursing ministries developing then, and of stewards of the sick who were responsible for assessing whether or not monks were sick enough to be admitted to the infirmary and who provided clothing, instruments and food to those who remained in their own quarters. He distinguishes between non-medical ministry offered by those with gifts of healing and through prayer and anointing,[87] and the medical means of special diets, the provision of bedclothes, bathing, pharmacology and surgery.[88]

Whilst most of Crislip's information relates to monasteries established after Basil founded his hospital, his reference to Pachomius' provision for the sick of his communities lends credibility to his case. Pachomius, who before adopting a monastic lifestyle, had been a soldier in the army of Licinius, must have been influenced to some extent by the military provision for sick and wounded soldiers in *valetudinaria*, though Crislip will scarcely allow that such provision was a precursor of the hospital.

Basil established a complex of buildings at Caesarea: a hospital for the sick, a hospice for lepers, a poor house and a hostel for travellers.[89] His institution was copied elsewhere in the eastern Church, though not in the West, where monks simply continued to provide for their own sick.

---

[85] A.T. Crislip, *From Monastery to Hospital: Christian Monasticism and the Transformation of Health Care in Late Antiquity* (Ann Arbor: Michigan University Press, 2005).

[86] *Ibid.*, 12.

[87] *Ibid.*, 21-28.

[88] *Ibid.*, 28-38.

[89] *Ibid.*, 103-20.

General Conclusion

In the post-Nicene period the mantle of healer fell to quite a large extent, it seems, on the bishops and other parochial clergy. They were responsible for praying for the sick and consecrating oil for anointing them and water for them to drink in church or, if they were chronically ill, at home. Some laity clearly anointed themselves. The sacraments of baptism and the eucharist were also viewed as means for promoting health of the body as well as the soul. Exorcists were minor clerics but their importance, it would seem, diminished and their office became a stepping stone to higher offices within the Church.

Some of the more dramatic healings were performed by monks renowned for their holiness. They prayed for the sick and made full use of consecrated elements. We do not hear of them commanding healing in the name of Jesus, and sometimes their healing procedure was protracted. In the flush of their success the temptation to pride was great.

The cult of the martyrs quickly became a focus for sometimes spectacular healings. Whilst Church leaders were happy to encourage this, they deplored the use of magic. But, it seems, the clear distinction between the 'right' touching of a sacred bone and the 'wrong' use of an amulet or even an exorcistic spell containing Christian elements, escaped some of the less educated Christians. Whilst suffering could be viewed as beneficial, the Church's positive attitude to the medical profession continued to develop, and Christian social and medical institutions emerged.

Conclusion

The Paths of Healing

Reviewing her pioneering study of healing in the Early Church Evelyn Frost wrote:

> For the Ante-Nicene Church, at any rate in its earlier years, post-baptismal disease was as false a situation as post-baptismal sin, and, although there were examples of both, neither was normal in the regenerate life and both were ideally impossible.[1]

This was always an overstatement. In New Testament times not only do we hear of Paul's 'thorn in the flesh', resistant even to persistent prayer (2 Cor.12:7-9), but also of the sicknesses of Epaphroditus (Phil.2:27), Timothy (1 Tim.5:23) and Trophimus (2 Tim.4:20). There never was a golden age when Christians were exempt from sickness, or indeed from sin. Some sicknesses do appear to be connected with sin.[2] Might these perhaps be removed, in response to a candidate's repentance and faith, in the waters of baptism? Such baptismal healing is indeed testified in the Early Church, as we have seen, from the *Odes of Solomon* (c. AD 100) to Augustine's *City of God* 22 (AD 422). It may well have occurred throughout Church history, though it seems to have been little publicised.

Miracles of healing unrelated to baptism were also widely attested in the Early Church. The canonical Acts depicts the apostles as carrying on Christ's healing ministry (using his powerful name); and this is confirmed for Paul himself by his own statements (Rom.15:18-19, 2 Cor.12:12). That others besides the apostles were involved in healing activity is indicated not only by Acts but also by the references to charismatic 'gifts of healings' in 1 Cor.12:9, cf. 28-30, and the 'prayer of faith' with anointing by church presbyter/elders in James 5:14-16. The virtual silence of the Apostolic Fathers on the subject does not mean that healing had ceased, only that their concerns in writing lay elsewhere. Justin's reference to gifts of healing.[3] Irenaeus' catalogue of conditions healed (including even raising the dead[4]), and healings

---

[1] E. Frost, *Christian Healing*, 226.
[2] Cf. Mk.2:5-12, Jn.5:14.
[3] Justin, *Dial.* 39.2.
[4] Irenaeus, *A.H.* 2.31.2.

referred to by Tertullian, most prominently the anointing of the Roman Emperor Septimius Severus,[5] and a few earlier straws in the wind,[6] give us confidence to believe that the Church's healing ministry continued vigorously throughout the second and early third centuries.

It is clear though that the pre-Nicene Fathers were primarily interested in healing miracles because of their apologetic value. Contemporary miracles in Jesus' name gave credibility to those claimed to have been performed by Jesus himself on earth, and were further evidence of his divinity.[7] They showed his superiority over Gnostic leaders[8] and, as there were no longer, it seems, Jewish healers, they were claimed as an indication that God's favour had now moved from the Jewish race to the, predominantly Gentile, Church.[9] That these Fathers were little interested in the miracles themselves is indicated by their failure to describe any individual cases. It was the less educated 'common people' who were interested in the miracles *per se*. This is evident from the prominence of miracle stories in the Apocryphal Acts which appear to have been written for just such a readership, from Clement's advice to the affluent Christians of Alexandria to use their wealth to enlist the support of the devout poor who will, when required, pray for their healing[10] and from the healing role entrusted to widows dependent on the charity of the churches of Syria in the early third-century.[11] Of relevance too is Origen's statement that it was often uneducated people who performed the exorcisms.[12] It is legitimate then to ask whether it was particularly the devout poor who received *gifts* of healing. Justin says such gifts were given to 'each as he is worthy'[13] and Origen to those 'whose souls have been purified by the Logos and by the actions which follow his teaching'.[14] They were given, it appears, at least to some of those who prayed for them at the time of their baptism.[15] In the early fourth century Eusebius declares that the Church consisted then of two classes of Christian: those who were celibate, possessed no property and devoted themselves to the service of God, and those who married and had children, took secular jobs and played a full part in

---

5   Tertullian, *Scap.* 4.
6   See above pp. 41-47.
7   Justin, *Dial.* 11.4; Origen, *C.C.* 3.33.
8   Irenaeus, *A.H.* 2.32.5.
9   Origen, *C.C.* 2.8, 7.8, *Hom. Lk.* Frag. 77 (on Lk.11:24).
10   Clement of Alexandria, *Rich Man* 34.2-3, 35.1-2.
11   *Didascalia*, tr. Connolly, 136, 140.
12   Origen, *C.C.* 7.8.
13   Justin, *Dial.* 39.2, cf. Eusebius, *D.E.* 3.4.30-3 *et passim*.
14   Origen, *C.C.* 7.8.
15   Tertullian, *Bapt.* 20, Origen, *Comm. Jn.* 6.166.

society.[16] It was amongst devout celibates in Syria in the previous century that gifts of healing (or at least exorcism) were displayed.[17] Perhaps then it is likely that such gifts *were* chiefly characteristic of the devout poor, whether their poverty came through choice or the misfortunes of life. They were precursors of the monks.

Alongside baptismal healing and the ministry of those with special gifts there seems to have been from early times in many local churches a ministry of healing by ordained clergy, involving prayer and anointing with oil. Though the authenticity of the epistle of James was long disputed, and the influence of the epistle is uncertain, the brevity of James 5:14-16 suggests that the procedure for anointing may already have been well-known, though perhaps not reserved for the clergy (cf. Mk.6:13). When in the early third century we next hear of oil for anointing it is in the cure of the emperor Septimius Severus[18] for whom surely only a tried and tested means would do, and as an apparently normal part of the eucharistic proceedings in the Church at Rome.[19]

Did the number of miraculous healings within the Church lessen with the passing of time? Frost certainly thought that to be the case.[20] She noted hints of spiritual decline in the time of Cyprian and believed that such decline was accelerated by Constantine's endorsement of the Church - prophecy dying out and healing being thereafter performed by the 'saint', exceptional not normal (by then often nominal) Christians. Then syncretism arose connected with the relics of the martyrs, charlatan healers appeared, and all were eventually swept aside by medical science. The idea had crept in that it was not God's will to heal as pain assisted the salvation of the soul.

Can such a case be substantiated? In the West indeed in the mid-third century Cyprian mentions no healings apart from those at baptism,[21] and Arnobius and Lactantius some half-century later are also silent on the subject. In the East Origen speaks, it seems, of only a few charismatic healers continuing in his time,[22] and Eusebius of even fewer by the early fourth century[23] though, it appears, baptismal healing remained common.[24] Bearing in mind also that Cyprian complains bitterly of

---

[16]   Eusebius, *D.E.* 1.8, and see Ferrar's notes on this interesting passage.
[17]   Ps-Clementine *Virg.* 1.12.
[18]   Tertullian, *Scap.* 4.
[19]   *A.T.* 5
[20]   Frost, *Christian Healing*, ch. 9.
[21]   Cyprian, *Ep.* 69.16.1, after the removal of an unclean spirit.
[22]   Origen, *C.C.* 7.8 in the light of my discussion of *ichne* above p. 105.
[23]   Eusebius, *D.E.* 3.4.30-31.
[24]   Eusebius, *D.E.* 9.13, discussed above pp. 128-29.

worldliness in the North African church of his time,[25] that the
Didascalia chastises widows for falling well short of the pious
dedication to service expected of them,[26] and that Eusebius says
Constantine's patronage of the Church led some to pose as Christians
just to benefit from the new climate,[27] there may well have been a
decline in the healing activity of the Church.

Other factors would no doubt have contributed to it. The Jews
attributed Jesus' miracles to magic[28] making apologists emphasise rather
his fulfilment of Old Testament prophecies.[29] His followers would not
have enjoyed being tarred with the same brush, though the entirely
benevolent nature of their cures and the fact that they were free of
charge must have helped to blunt such an accusation.[30]

The development of medicine and its acceptance by most of the
Fathers undoubtedly undercut the need to some extent for miraculous
cures. In the Pre-Nicene Church, despite Tatian's protests[31] and
Arnobius' scorn,[32] Tertullian,[33] Clement[34] and Origen[35] all saw it as a
benefit, and Cyprian[36] and Eusebius[37] echoed Hippocratic teaching. In
addition, Clement advocated attention to a healthy lifestyle,[38] and others
natural remedies.[39] A Montanist woman to whom Tertullian refers[40] is
said, not to have laid hands on the sick or anointed them, but to have
'distributed remedies'. But no Father stated the case for using medical
means better than had Ben Sirach[41] in the second century BC, when he
declared that the physician should be honoured as God's agent; he prays
that he may make a correct diagnosis, and God blesses his work. God
also made the natural products used by the pharmacist. But the sick who

---

[25] Cyprian, *Laps.* 6, *Ep.* 13.
[26] *Didasc.,* tr. Connolly, 140.
[27] Eusebius, *Life of Constantine* 4.54, cf. 4.31.
[28] Justin, *Dial.* 69.6-7, Lactantius, *D.I.* 4.15, Eusebius, *D.E.* 3.4.
[29] Spiegl, 'Rolle', 304-05, stresses this.
[30] Irenaeus stresses such points, *A.H.* 2.31.3, 2.32.5.
[31] Tatian, *Orat.* 18.1-3.
[32] Arnobius, *Ag. Nat.* 1.48, 3.23.
[33] Tertullian, *Crowns* 8.
[34] Clement of Alexandria, *Misc.* 6.157.1-2 (ANCL 6.17).
[35] Origen, *Hom. Num.* 18.3, *C.C.* 3.12.
[36] Cyprian, *Dem.* 7.
[37] Eusebius, *P.E.* 8.14.55 quoting Philo.
[38] Clement, *Teacher* 2.1, 3.9.16-18.
[39] Cf. Origen, *C.C.* 4.82, Tertullian, *Scorp.* 1.3 - crushed scorpion!
[40] Tertullian, *Soul* 9.4.
[41] Ecclus. 38.4, 14.

resort to these medical people must also be careful to repent of their sins and pray, an emphasis perpetuated in the Church.[42]

Greer[43] maintains it was the Platonism of the third-century Fathers that led them to rely on a rational presentation of the Gospel and to disparage the miraculous. Clement indeed, at the end of the previous century, sets before his Christian 'gnostic' the task of praying that he may contemplate God rather than, like the common man, pray for continual good health,[44] and Origen thinks anyone who could compare health of body with 'a healthy mind, a robust soul, and power of reasoning' quite mad.[45] Eusebius moreover readily declares his preference for reasoned defence of the faith over pointing to the miraculous[46] and is happy to accept Plato's verdict in elevating the cardinal virtues of wisdom, temperance, justice and courage above such matters as health and beauty.[47] In like vein Lactantius often propounds the Stoic theme that evils and vice are necessary for the development of virtue.[48] Such attitudes may well have deterred educated Christians in the pre-Nicene period from taking much interest in healing ministry.

In contrast to the pre-Nicene situation, Greer declares further, 'The miraculous only occupies center stage after the Constantinian revolution'.[49] Was there then a resurgence of interest in healing ministry after Nicea? Indeed, by then certain inhibiting factors had been removed. Christians were no longer a despised minority needing to avoid the charge of magic. Again, no more challenged to accept the pains of martyrdom, they need have no embarrassment in seeking cures for the pains of sickness. Furthermore, several of the Fathers of this period held up for admiration monks and other saintly figures, readily admitting their miraculous powers. Perhaps in so doing they were consciously promoting devotion to the cult of the saints as an acceptable alternative to the practice of magic. These monks undoubtedly performed great healings, though their methods tended to be rather more protracted than in the earlier period, taking sometimes hours or even days to be completed,[50] and temptation to pride clearly posed a

---

42   *Ibid.* 38.9-10, cf. Basil, *Longer Rule* 55; see also Amundsen's summary of the general standpoint of the Fathers, 'Medicine and Faith', 341.
43   Greer, *Fear of Freedom*, 2-3.
44   Clement, *Misc.* 7.46.4.
45   Origen, *Prayer* 17.1.
46   Eusebius, *D.E.* 3.4.30-31.
47   Eusebius, *P.E.* 12.16.3, quoting Plato, *Laws* 631A.
48   Lactantius, *D.I.* 5.23, 7.5 *et passim.*
49   Greer, *Fear of Freedom,* 3.
50   E.g. that of Macarius of Alexandria reported by Palladius in his *Lausiac History* 18.22 (embellished with legendary elements, it seems), and Martin of Tours, *Life* 16 (details above in ch.6).

considerable problem for them.[51] In monastic circles too mortification of the flesh was commonly seen to be of spiritual benefit and a monk's sickness could be viewed in that light.[52] Such an attitude must in time have inhibited their offering healing ministry to others.

In the post-Nicene period it seems oil was widely used for sacramental healing. It appears that people went to church for ministry from the bishop or other clergy, unless they were chronically ill in which case they were ministered to at home.[53] Others anointed themselves.[54] In time, however, the emphasis on healing was lost and, by the ninth century, anointing had become largely preparation for a 'good death', healing beyond the grave.[55]

Healings at baptism and through participation in the eucharist[56] are also attested in the post-Nicene period, and a popular, new locus of healing was provided by the shrines of the martyrs, the faithful flocking to the cemeteries or to churches containing their remains to ask the prayers of the deceased saints and touch their holy relics. Many healings are attested,[57] God responding to the faith and awe of the petitioner. But such awe easily invested the relics with quasi-magical powers. Is it then surprising that some at least of those who visited the shrines of the martyrs saw nothing wrong with wearing amulets bearing prayers and texts from the Scriptures and engaging in other magical practices condemned by the Fathers of this period?[58] Here indeed we find syncretism.

The Fathers of the Post-Nicene Church were positive about medical science, Basil in his *Epistle* 189 going so far as to imply it is the chief means of physical healing and, though they maintained that all healing comes from God, and a healthy soul is even more important than a healthy body, this prepared for the ultimate 'takeover' of the field of healing by the medical profession.

It does then seem that Frost's sketch of the history of healing in the Early Church is basically correct, though she paints it with quick brush strokes whereas the actual picture was more complex and the time-scale extended. Greer too would appear correct when he says miracles were

---

[51] Athanasius, *Life of Antony* 38, Cassian, *Coll.* 15.1, 7.

[52] Horden, 'Death of Ascetics'.

[53] See above ch. 6, 'Bishop, Presbyter and Deacon' and 'Healing elements'.

[54] Chrysostom, *Hom. Mk.* 32:9, Innocent, *Ep.* 25.

[55] Puller, *Anointing,* 199.

[56] Augustine, *City of God* 22.8, cf. Serapion, *Sacramentary* (see discussion above in ch. 6, 'Healing Elements').

[57] The majority of the healings quoted by Augustine in *City of God* 22.8 are from contact with the relics of saints.

[58] Cyril, *Cat.* 19.8, Chrysostom, *Hom. Col.* 8.5, Augustine, *Tract. Jn.* 7.6.

more common in the Post-Nicene Church than before, but living practitioners had to some extent lost sight of the simplicity of the methods of the earlier age, and dead ones could not encourage repentance and faith in Christ.

Exorcism – A Venture into Reality?

Let us now turn specifically to the subject of exorcism. If Paul's approach in Ac.16:18 is typical of the Apostolic Church, the method resembled that of Jesus himself: a command addressed to the possessing spirit to leave the person at once. Whereas Jesus used his own authority the apostles used his name.[59] Gradually, it seems, the procedure acquired new elements. Justin brings in credal statements.[60] Origen says that the commanding of evil spirits to leave a person or thing in the name of Jesus is accompanied by the recital of *historia* (perhaps gospel narratives or credal statements), a ministry generally performed by uneducated people acting in sincerity and faith.[61] Sometimes there appears to have been a dialogue with the spirit first,[62] and the whole process might be protracted, or even fail[63] and need the further grace of baptism.[64] Lactantius mentions the use of the sign of the cross,[65] and eventually written exorcisms were used at least in some places.[66] In general, however, we have no reason to believe that, as practised in the mainstream of the Patristic Church, exorcism ceased to retain a simplicity and directness that contrasted markedly with the use of sonorous spells, fumigations and the other rituals of pagan practitioners of magic and Jewish exorcists.[67]

---

[59] See above ch. 2, nt. 83.
[60] Justin, *2 Apol.* 6.5-6, *Dial.* 85.1-2.
[61] *C.C.* 1.6, 7.4, see my discussion above, pp. 101-3.
[62] Tertullian, *Shows* 26.1-2, Cyprian, *Dem.* 15.
[63] Origen, *Hom. Josh.* 24.
[64] Cyprian, *Ep.* 69.15-16.
[65] Lactantius, *D.I.* 4.27.1-3.
[66] See p.135 above.
[67] We have noted Josephus' account of the first-century Jewish exorcism of Eleazar in his *Ant.* 8.45-49 (above pp. 12-13) and the statement of Justin that Jewish exorcisms were, in their ritual, indistinguishable from their pagan counterparts (*Dial.* 85.3). As representative of pagan magical exorcisms we have looked at PGM IV.1227-64 and various amulets (pp. 145-48). Further information is given by Twelftree, *Name of Jesus*, 36-44, revealing his considerable knowledge of this field. But his tendency later in his book to say that Christian exorcisms closely resembled their non-Christian counterparts (culminating in his conclusion 4, p. 290) runs quite contrary to the findings of this present study. His own discussions of Justin

The minor order or exorcist arose, it seems, and become widespread in the Church from the first half of the third century,[68] but in the post-Nicene period it tended to be subsumed by the higher clerical offices.[69] The repetitious baptismal exorcism of the *Apostolic Tradition* (the first instance in Christian literature) may represent the practice of the late fourth or early fifth-century Syrian church rather than the early third-century church in Rome[70] for there is no clear evidence of its use elsewhere at that time.[71]

In the pre-Nicene period exorcism is mentioned in our sources far more frequently than physical healing, not principally, it seems, because of the drama it entailed, but because of its apologetic value. The pre-Nicene Latin Fathers repeatedly declared that the gods whom non-Christians worship have been unmasked through Christian exorcism and shown to be mere deceitful demons.[72] As MacMullen points out, what happened in exorcism was seen to be a contest of strength:

> The winner was the 'true' god; for truth in that regard must be established precisely through the demonstration of commands given by one and obedience yielded by another...exorcism was thus a demonstration of a theological position and thereby a missionary instrument. It made converts.[73]

Undoubtedly this was true.[74] Indeed miraculous cures generally played a significant part in evangelism,[75] though their role remained secondary to preaching.[76]

(pp. 241-42) and Irenaeus (pp. 253-54) highlight the *differences* from pagan practice, and I have already taken issue with his deductions from some of the charges of Celsus emphatically denied by Origen, see above ch. 4, nt. 147. He claims that, because Christians use the *name of Jesus* in their exorcisms and thus call on an 'external power authority', this puts them in the same category as pagans, though the latter invoke their gods in a quite different way and with magical rituals.

[68] See p. 80, nt. 55 and p. 89 above.

[69] See pp. 135-6 above.

[70] See pp. 87-88 above.

[71] Thraede ('Exorzismus', 77, 98-99) tries hard to show Tertullian's references to baptism imply baptismal exorcism, but his arguments fail to convince as none of Tertullian's descriptions are explicit in this matter. For further discussion see my unpublished London University Ph.D. thesis 'The Healing Ministry in the Pre-Nicene Church', 174.

[72] Tertullian, *Apol.* 23, Cyprian, *Dem.* 15, Lactantius, *D.I.* 2.15.2-5 *et passim*.

[73] R. MacMullen, 'Two Types of Conversion to Early Christianity', VC 37 (1983), 180-81.

[74] Irenaeus, *A.H.* 3.32.4, Cyprian, *Ep.* 16.1, Origen, *Hom. Sam.* 1.10, Lactantius, *D.I.* 5.21 22.

But what in reality were, or indeed are 'demons'? In his monograph *Possession and Exorcism in the New Testament and Early Christianity* Eric Sorensen puts forward an interesting definition of demonic possession: 'A culturally shared belief in the potential for a maleficent spiritual being to disrupt, often in a way observable to others, the well-being of an unwilling host'.[77] But is a 'maleficent spiritual being' just a 'culturally shared belief'? Is it a way of thinking rather than an objective reality? Sorensen does not commit himself, but there are plenty of others in our modern era who have been prepared to do so, perhaps none more tersely than Rudolf Bultmann:

> Now that the forces and laws of nature have been discovered, we can no longer believe in spirits, whether good or evil...Sickness and the cure of

---

[75]   As MacMullen stresses in both his article 'Two Types of Conversion' and his book *Christianizing the Roman Empire AD 100-400* (Yale: University Press, 1984) pointing to Origen, *C.C.* 1.46, Eusebius, *H.E.* 3.37, Jerome, *Life of Hilary* 8.8-9 *et passim*.

[76]   As seen even in the Apocryphal Acts and Clementine Homilies. R.Lane Fox, seeking to correct what he felt was MacMullen's overemphasis on the effect of miracles, suggests that, as in the apostle Paul's day, the winning of true converts remained a long process of preaching and persuading people (*Pagans and Christians*, 329-30). Twelftree's study of the New Testament, and particularly his noting that no exorcisms are described in the Fourth Gospel, has led him to conclude that exorcism diminished in importance in the life of the Early Church. He deduces also from some early patristic literature that demons could be overcome another way: by a person's responding to the truth of the Gospel (conversion), being baptized, and undertaking the disciplines of the Christian life – see his studies of Hermas (*Name of Jesus*, 212-14), the *Epistle of Barnabas* (*ibid.*, 223-26), Clement of Alexandria (*ibid.*, 257-59) and his final conclusion (*ibid.*, 290). It is a pity his study did not cover more of Origen's prolific work, for there it is evident that these two approaches are not alternatives but complementary. Those *possessed* continue to need exorcism (*C.C.* 1.6, 1.25, 3.36 7.4, 7.67 *et passim*); Christians *afflicted* by demons through temptations and the obstacles they pose in day to day life can gain victory over them by prayer, fasting, Bible reading, the eucharist, and virtuous living. Origen likens this to the struggles of Israel in their wilderness wanderings (*Hom. Ex.* 2, *Hom. Lev.* 6.2, 6.6.5, 16.65, *Hom. Josh.*, 1.7, 8.7, 20 *et passim*). To be fair, Origen admits exorcism was not always effective in expelling demons (*Hom. Josh.* 24.1). In such cases, according to Cyprian, baptism was necessary (*Ep.* 69.15-16). But baptism was not the normal treatment for possession; many of those exorcised were pagans not then seeking admission to the Church, e.g. the cases referred to by Tertullian in *Scap.* 4.

[77]   Sorensen, *Possession,* 1.

disease are likewise attributable to natural causation; they are not the result of daemonic activity or of evil spells.[78]

But are we to say then that when Justin appeals to common knowledge that 'numberless demoniacs' in Rome and throughout the world have been expelled by Christians (2 *Apol.* 6.5-6), when Tertullian taunts the Roman magistrates by saying, "Who would rescue you from those secret enemies that every where lay waste your minds and your bodily health?" if Christians withheld their exorcistic services (*Apol.* 37.9), and when Cyprian speaks of these spirits as 'struggling, howling, groaning' as an exorcist demands (in the name of Christ) their departure (*Don.* 5), it is all in the realm of fantasy? Such a verdict might speak more of the inexperience of the one who passes judgement.

It is frequently stated that the Jews inherited their belief in demons from Persian Zoroastrianism during the time of their exile.[79] May it not rather have been that encounter with Zoroastrianism sharpened their understanding of a hitherto unexplained reality. Earlier, from their acute sense of the sovereignty of their God, they were prepared to believe that he had sent the evil spirit that troubled Saul (1 Sam.16:14, 19:9), but no such explanation was possible to account for those of their nation who turned to worship the gods of other nations, a move denounced in the first two of the Ten Commandments (Ex.20:3-5). The realisation that this was inspired by *alien* spiritual forces had, however, broken upon the Jews by the time the Hebrew Old Testament was translated into the Greek Septuagint (begun in the early third century BC) for Ps.95:6 which read in the Hebrew, 'The gods of the peoples are idols', was rendered here in the Greek, 'The gods of the peoples are *demons*'.

Sorensen declares that, prior to the impact of Judaism and Christianity in the first century of our era, demons were viewed in the Greco-Roman world, not as malicious spirits, but simply as intermediaries between gods and mortals.[80] Plato had indeed said that,[81] and the view persisted in the late second century AD, for Celsus complains that the Christian 'impiously divides the kingdom of god and makes two opposing forces' (*C.C.* 8.11). Yet, in his study of ancient demonology, Everett Ferguson has pointed out that by the later Hellenistic age (the early centuries of our era) the general trend was to

---

[78] Bultmann, 'New Testament and Mythology, tr. R.H. Fuller, 4-5.
[79] E.g. Hull, *Hellenistic Magic*, 29; Vermes, *Jesus the Jew*, 61; cf. Sorensen, *Possession*, ch. 2.
[80] Sorensen, *Possession*, 78.
[81] Plato, *Symp.* 202E – 203A.

attribute evil to demons.[82] He refers, for instance, to Plutarch (c.AD 50-120) quoting a current saying, 'What is most helpful? God. What is most harmful? Demons.' (Moralia 153A)

Sorensen goes on to point out that in ancient Greek literature possession by gods or by spirits serving them is a well-known theme. Dionysus, Pan, Hecate and other gods (and we must add Apollo at the oracle of Delphi and elsewhere) are said to 'enthuse' (ἐν θεῷ, 'in God'), i.e. take control of people. Resisting the frenzy thus generated was said to cause pain to the human concerned. In Greek tragedy the Olympian gods are depicted as possessing and afflicting people. Such possession is said to be the consequence of a god's being offended; in retaliation, he causes madness to the miscreant. But there was no recourse to exorcism; the sufferer could only offer sacrifices and petition the chastiser for relief.[83] Statements by Lactantius suggest that, in the early fourth century of our era, such phenomena were no mere literary fiction but translated into reality in the activities of the demons:

> They cling to individual men and they seize all homes...Men honour them in their inner chambers, and daily pour out wines [for them]... (*D.I.* 2.14.12) They harm, but they harm those by whom they are feared. (2.15.2)

The same could surely be said of earlier centuries. If so, here was indeed a problem but one people had to put up with as no effective means of relief was available. Sorensen may be right in his assertion that the Early Church, in its exorcisms, had to overcome suspicion because exorcism in the Greco-Roman world was associated with magicians, but he is surely wrong to say it offered a service for which there was no demand.[84] There appears to have been a potential demand ready to be awakened.

One further point needs to be born in mind: our sources imply that the presence of the God of the Jews and Christians, or his preached word, had the power to force evil spirits present to disclose themselves. According to Mark, it was as Jesus began to preach in the synagogue in Capernaum, an unclean spirit within one present cried out in protest (Mk.1:21-8.) More than two centuries later, as Origen was preaching and spoke out the words of Hannah, "My heart exults in the Lord" (1 Sam.2:1, *Hom. Sam.* 1.10) demonic cries of protest broke from a

---

[82] E. Ferguson, *Demonology of the Early Christian World* (Lewiston, NY: Mellen Press, 1984), 49-51.

[83] Sorensen, *Possession*, 117.

[84] Sorensen, *Possession*, 6.

listener, an insight it seems into the impact of the preaching of the patristic age.[85] How many other such instances went unpublicised?

The decline in awareness of evil spirits today may be, in part the result of our long Christian heritage which has broken the dominance of such powers; in part the prevalent materialistic worldview, inherited ultimately from the eighteenth-century European Enlightenment, which assumes such spirits are not real. What was once known as spirit possession is now attributed to a person's own mental disorganisation resulting from severe pressure, the repression of deep innate desires and so on, and that person labelled 'schizophrenic', 'hysterical' or 'a victim of multiple personality disorder';[86] but sometimes medicine and therapy are powerless to cure such conditions.[87] Even within the Church, we are somewhat amused today to hear Origen and other Fathers speak of the Christian life as a constant battle against demons ('sin demons', to use H.A. Kelly's quaint phrase). We are happier, and perhaps in reality healthier,[88] to think of it simply as a struggle against temptations and difficulties. But the battle remains no matter how we depict it, and we need the same resources as the early Christians: prayer, Bible reading, the sacraments, fasting on occasion, and so on. Kelly thinks the concept of sin demon came from pre-baptismal exorcisms such as found in the *Apostolic Tradition*, which may in turn have come from Valentinian Gnosticism.[89] Baptismal exorcism may in fact, however, have developed independently within the Early Church from the widespread belief that an evil spirit was associated with every pagan from birth through the

---

[85] As P. and M.T. Nautin comment, *Hom. Sam.* (SC 32), 67.

[86] See for instance S.V. McCasland, *By the Finger of God: Demon Possession and Exorcism in Early Christianity in the Light of Modern Views of Mental Illness* (New York: MaMillan, 1951), especially chs. 2 and 3, though he does not use the term 'multiple personality disorder'.

[87] Francis MacNutt tells of a case where a Christian psychiatrist, unable to bring relief to a woman with 'severe obsessive-compulsive neurosis and deprivation neurosis', rather finding himself becoming a victim of uncontrollable anger in therapy sessions, called in MacNutt who prayed for the woman's deliverance, resulting in, he says, several spirits leaving quietly and the woman's behaviour then showing a marked improvement - *Deliverance from Evil Spirits: A Practical Manual* (London: Hodder 1995), 63-64.

[88] Cf. the much quoted opening words of C.S. Lewis' classic *The Screwtape Letters* (London: Bles, 1942): 'There are two equal and opposite errors into which our race can fall about the devils. One is to disbelieve in their existence. The other is to believe, *and to feel an excessive and unhealthy interest in them*' (p. 9, my italics).

[89] H.A. Kelly, *Devil*, 55-61, considering Clement of Alexandria's *Excerpts from Theodotus*.

rituals of idolatry.[90] Most of us today are spared that background, but vestiges of an exorcistic prayer are found even in modern liturgies of baptism, suggesting that still from birth we are confronted by evil spirit powers over which only the God and Father of our Lord Jesus Christ can ensure victory.

---

[90] Cf. Irenaeus, *A.H.* 3.82, Tertullian, *Soul* 39, 57, *Didascalia* 26.

Appendix

Some Pointers for Today's Church

I have drawn these points from my study of the Early Church supplemented by my own experience from involvement in personal and parish healing ministry during the last twenty or so years. They are by no means exhaustive, and some may be seriously challenged, but I hope they will at least provide a basis for profitable discussion.

1. Jesus preached the arrival of the kingdom of God and pointed to his exorcisms as visual signs that the kingdom of Satan was being driven back (Mt.12:28, Lk.11:20). Should we not view the whole healing ministry today as providing visual signs of the advancement of God's kingdom? Healing can demonstrate the power of the one proclaimed.

2. The legitimacy of large-scale healing rallies should be questioned. Jesus never made a show of his healing powers and often, if we may accept the evidence of Mark's Gospel, preferred to keep his miracles unpublicised. Large rallies should rather be for evangelistic preaching, if desired, in which healing may sometimes perhaps play a subsidiary part.

3. In an age that has, in some measure, reaffirmed the centrality of the Holy Spirit in the life of the Church, should we not, like the early Christians, be encouraging all who are consciously committed to Christ's cause to pray to God for spiritual gifts, including healing, that they may be more effective in the life and witness of their church? This may take extended prayer, for the gifts are precious and will only be granted to those who will use them with care and humility.

4. As seems to have been the case in the Early Church, the ministry of healing by prayer, laying on of hands and anointing should be viewed as a normal part of the life of every local church today. All clergy should see it as an important part of their work but should share it with those laity who particularly care to bring relief to those suffering. By prayer and in faith the healing power of God should be called into every area of pain and incapacity, leaving the outcome to God.

5. The evidence for the reality of evil spirits should be made known, but not exaggerated so that every disturbing trifle is attributed to them and people unnecessarily frightened. People need to know that,

· no matter how strong the forces of evil, the power of Jesus is stronger still, and his name and the sign of his cross can be used by any Christian for protection. But, faced with someone evidently psychically disturbed, it is always wisest, if we can, to summon the help of someone with greater experience and wisdom than our own.

6. If we may follow the Early Church, those involved in exorcism should be strong in faith, constant in prayer, and willing sometimes to fast; they need not necessarily have a high degree of education. They must be persistent in demanding the departure of the alien spirits until this is achieved, but must realise that, in some cases perhaps, baptism may be necessary to complete the deliverance.

7. Healing and deliverance ministry in the name of Christ should not be supplemented by resort to magic, the occult or spiritism. The temptation to do so is probably greatest in developing countries. We do well to remember the first Commandment, 'You shall have no other gods beside me.'

8. The acquired knowledge and skills of the medical profession must be respected as ultimately coming from God (Ecclus.38:1-14). It is quite legitimate to pray *and* seek medical help. But the reality of sin and the need for repentance must not be forgotten.

9. When prayers for healing appear unanswered, as in the case of Paul's 'thorn in the flesh' (2 Cor.12:7-9), it is important not to sink into resentment and bitterness but to acknowledge that God is sovereign. We must hold on to his unchanging love and, if we can, pray that he may be glorified even in our weak state. It may be that, unlike Paul's, our malady will be temporary. We do well to remember though that ageing is a natural process, and there is an 'allotted span' of life for us all. Death, when it comes, will provide the ultimate healing of release into God's nearer presence.

Bibliography

Primary Sources

Ancient Pagan Works

Diodorus Siculus, *Bibliotheca historia*, ed. and tr. C.H. Oldfather *et al*, 10 Vols (Loeb Classical Library; London: Heinemann, 1933-67).

Herodotus, *Historiae*, ed. and tr. A.D. Godley, 4 Vols (Loeb Classical Library; London: Heinemann, 1921-4).

Philostratus, *The Life of Apollonius of Tyana*, ed. and tr. F.C. Conybeare, 2 Vols (Loeb Classical Library; London: Heinemann, 1912).

- *Life of Apollonius*, tr. C.P. Jones, ed. G.W. Bowerstock (Harmondsworth: Penguin Classics, 1970).

Plato, 'Symposium' in *Plato*, vol. 5, ed. and tr. W.R.M. Lamb (Loeb Classical Library; London: Heinemann, 1925).

Pliny, *Natural History*, ed. and tr. H. Rackham and D.E. Eichholz, 10 Vols (Loeb Classical Library; London: Heinemann, 1938-62).

Plutarch, 'Obsolescence of Oracles' in *Moralia*, ed. and tr. F.C. Babbitt (Loeb Classical Library; London: Heinemann, 1936).

Suetonius, *Lives of the Caesars*, ed. and tr. J.C. Rolphe, 2 Vols (Loeb Classical Library; London: Heinemann, 1913-14).

Tacitus, *Histories*, ed. and tr. C.H. Moore, 2 Vols (Loeb Classical Library; London: Heinemann, 1931-7).

Ancient Jewish Works

Josephus, *Jewish Antiquities* I-IV, ed. and tr. H.St.J. Thackeray (Loeb Classical Library; London: Heinemann, 1930).

Mishnah, tr. H. Danby (Oxford: University Press, 1933).

Talmud
- *Babylonian*, tr. I. Epstein, 35 Vols (London: Soncino Press, 1935-52).
- *Jerusalem*, tr. J. Neusner *et al*, 35 Vols (*Talmud of the Land of* Israel; Chicago: University Press, 1982-).

Testament of Solomon, tr. D.C. Duling in *The Old Testament Pseudepigrapha*, vol. 1, ed. J.H. Charlesworth (London: DLT, 1983).

Tosephta tr. ed. J. Neusner *et al*, 6 Vols (New York: Ktav, 1977-86).

Bible

Septuagint, ed. A. Rahifs, 2 Vols (Stuttgart: Deutsche Bibelstiftung, 1935).

Novum Testamentum Graece, 27th edn. K. Aland *et al* (Nestle-Aland; Stuttgart: Bibelgesellschaft, 1993).

The Holy Bible and the Apocrypha (Revised Standard Version; London: Nelson, 1959).

Ancient Christian Works

Ambrose, *Some of the Principle Works of St. Ambrose*, tr. H. de Romesti *et al*, (NPNF 10; 1896, repr. 1994).
- *Life of St. Ambrose by Paulinus his Scribe*, tr. M.S. Kaniecka, (Catholic University of America Patristic Study 16; Washington: Catholic University of America, 1928).

Apocryphal Acts
- *Acta Apostolorum Apocrypha* vol. 1-2.2, ed. R.A. Lipsius and M. Bonnet (Leipzig: Mendelssohn, 1891-1903).
- Eng. tr. in *New Testament Apocrypha* II, ed. E. Hennecke, tr. from Ger. R.McL. Wilson, rev. ed. W. Schneemelcher (Cambridge: J. Clarke, 1992);
- Eng. tr. in *The Apocryphal New Testament: A Collection of Apocryphal Christian Literature in an English Translation*, ed. J.K. Elliott (Oxford: University Press, 1993).
- *Acts of Andrew* – Gk. text ed. and comm. J-M. Prieur, 2 Vols (CCSA 5-6.
- *Acts of Thomas* – Eng. tr. from Syriac A.F. Klijn (Leiden: Brill, 1962).

Apostolic Constitutions, tr. J. Donaldson (ANF 7; 1886 (1995)).

Arnobius, *Against the Heathen* (*Nations*), tr. H. Bryce and H. Campbell (ANF 7; 1886, repr. 1995).

Athanasius, *On the Incarnation*, tr. A. Robertson (NPNF 2nd ser., vol. 4; 1892, repr. 1995).
- *The Life of Antony and the Letter to Marcellinus*, tr. R.C. Gregg (New York: Paulist, 1980).

Augustine, *City of God*, tr. P. Schaff (NPNF 1st ser., vol. 2; 1886, repr. 1995).
- *Homilies on the Gospel of John*, tr. J. Gibbs and J. Innes (NPNF 1st ser., vol. 7; 1886, repr. 1995).
- *Homilies on the Psalms*, tr. P. Schaff (NPNF 1st ser., vol. 8; 1888, repr. 1989).
- *Letters*, tr. J. G. Cunningham (NPNF 1st ser., vol. 1; 1886, repr. 1995).
- *Retractions*, tr. M.I. Bogan (FOC 60; 1968).
- *True Religion* in *Earlier Writings*, tr. J.H.S. Burleigh (Library of Christian Classics, vol. VI; London: SCM, 1953).

Bardaisan, *The Book of the Laws of Countries*, tr. H.J.W. Drijvers (Assen: Van Gorcum, 1965).

Basil, *Longer Rule*, tr. M.M. Wagner (FOC 9; 1950).
- *Letters*, ed. and tr. R.J. Defferon, 4 Vols (Loeb Classical Library; London: Heinemann, 1926-34).

Cassian, *The Institutes, The Conferences, On the Incarnation of the Lord*, tr. E.C.S. Gibson (NPNF 2nd ser., vol. 11; 1894, repr. 1994).

Chrysostom, *Homilies on the Acts of the Apostles and the Epistle to the Romans*, tr. J. Walker et al, (NPNF 1st ser., vol. 11; 1889, repr. 1995).
- *Homilies on Galatians...Philemon*, tr. G. Alexander *et al*, (NPNF 1st ser., vol. 13; 1889, repr. 1995).
- *Homilies on the Gospel of Saint Matthew*, tr. G. Prevost, (NPNF 1st ser., vol. 10; 1888, repr. 1995).
- *Homilies on the Gospel of Saint John and the Epistle to the Hebrews*, tr. P. Schaff and F. Gardiner (NPNF 1st ser., vol. 14; 1889, repr. 1995).

- *Homilies on the Statues*, rev. tr. W.R.W. Stephens (NPNF 1st ser., vol. 9; 1889, repr. 1989).
Clement of Alexandria, *The Exhortation to the Greeks, The Rich Man's Salvation and a fragment of an address entitled 'To the Newly Baptized'*, tr. G.W. Butterworth (Loeb Classical Library; London: Heinemann, 1919).
- *Exhortation* [*Protreptikos*], ed. and Fr. tr. A Plassart *et al*, 2nd edn (SC [2]; 1949).
- *Teacher* [*Paidagogos*], ed. and Fr. tr. H-I. Marrou *et al* (SC 70, 108, 158; 1960-70).
- *Miscellanies* [*Stromateis*], bks 1-6, ed. O. Stählin, (GCS; 1960); bks 7-8, ed. O. Stählin, rev. L. Früchtel (GCS; 1970).
- *Collected Works*, tr. W. Wilson (ANF 2; 1885, repr. 1995).
Clement of Rome, *Epistles 1, 2* in J.B. Lightfoot, *Apostolic Fathers*, rev. ed. I.II (London: Macmillan, 1890).
Clement, Pseudo, *Homilies*, tr. T. Smith *et al* (ANF 8; 1886, repr. 1995).
- *Recognitions*, tr. T. Smith (ANF 8; 1886, repr 1995).
- *Epistles to the Virgins*, tr. B.P. Pratten (ANF 8; 1886, repr. 1995).
Councils, Canons, Eng. tr. W.R. Clark in C.J. Hefele, *A History of the Christian Councils (of the Church) from the original documents*, 5 Vols (Edinburgh: T & T Clark, 1872-96).
Cyprian, *Works*, tr. R.E. Wallis (2 Vols, ANF 5; 1886, repr. 1995).
- *Letters*, tr. G.W. Clarke (ACW 43-4, 46-7; 1984-9).
Cyril of Jerusalem, *Catechetical Lectures*, tr. E.H. Gifford (NPNF 2nd ser., vol.7; 1894, repr. 1994).
Didache, Eng. tr. in *Early Christian Writings: The Apostolic Fathers*, tr. M. Staniforth (Harmondsworth: Penguin Classics, 1968).
Didascalia Apostolorum: The Syriac Version translated and accompanied by the Verona Latin Fragments, R.H. Connolly (Oxford: University Press, 1929).
Eusebius of Caesarea, *Against Hierocles*, ed. and Fr. tr. É. des Places *et al* (SC 333; 1986).
- Eng. tr. with *Life and Letters of Apollonius of Tyana*, ed. and tr. F.C. Conybeare (Loeb Classical Library; London: Heinemánn, 1912).
- *Demonstration of the Gospel*, ed. I.A. Heikel (GCS; 1913).
- Eng. tr. W.J. Ferrar, *The Proof of the Gospel*, 2 Vols (London: SPCK, 1920).
- *Ecclesiastical History*, ed. and Fr. tr. G. Bardy (SC 31, 41, 55, 73; 1952-60).
- Eng. trs. K. Lake and J.E.L. Oulton, 2 Vols (Loeb Classical Library; London: Heinemann, 1926-32); G.A. Williamson (Harmondsworth: Penguin Classics, 1965).
- *Life of Constantine*, tr. and comm. A. Cameron and S.G. Hall (Oxford: University Press, 1999).
- *Preparation for the Gospel*, tr. E.H. Gifford, Evangelicae Praeparationis, vol. 3 (Oxford: University Press, 1903).
Gregory of Nyssa, *Life of Gregory Thaumaturgus* [*De vita beati Gregorii*] in MPG 46, 893-958.
- Tr. M. Slusser (FOC 98; 1998).
Hermas, *Shepherd*, tr. F. Crombie (ANF 2; 1885, repr. 1995).
Hilary of Poitiers, *Trinity*, tr. S. McKenna (FOC 25; 1954).
Hippolytus, *Apostolic Tradition*, ed. and Fr. tr. B. Botte, 2nd edn (SC 11; 1968).

- Eng. trs. G. Dix (London: 1937, repr. with preface by H. Chadwick; London: SPCK, 1968); G.J. Cuming, Grove Liturgical Study 8, 2nd edn (Nottingham: Grove Books, 1987).

Hippolytus, *Canons*, tr. P.F. Bradshaw (Grove Liturgical Study 50; Nottingham: Grove Books, 1987).

Ignatius, *Epistles*, tr. J.B. Lightfoot, in *Apostolic Fathers* (London: Macmillan, 1885); and in *Early Christian Writings: The Apostolic Fathers*, M. Staniforth (Harmondsworth: Penguin Classics, 1968).

Innocent 1, *Opera* in MPL 20, 457-636.

Irenaeus, *Against the Heresies*, ed. and Fr. tr. A. Rousseau *et al*, (SC 100, 152-3, 210-11, 263-4, 293-4; 1965-82).

- Eng. tr. A. Roberts and W.H. Rambaut, 2 Vols (ANCL 5, 9; 1868-9).
- *Demonstration of the Apostolic Teaching*, tr. J. Armitage Robinson (London: SPCK, 1920).

Jerome, *Opera* in MPL 22-30.

- *Commentary on St. Matthew*, ed. and Fr. tr. E. Bonnard (SC 242, 259; 1977-9).
- *On Illustrious Men*, tr. E.C. Richardson (NPNF, 2nd ser., vol. 3; 1892).
- *Letters and Select Works* (incl. *Life of Hilarion*), tr. W.H. Fremantle *et al* (NPNF 2nd ser., vol. 6; 1893, repr. 1995).

Justin, *Opera* in MPG 6 (1857).

- Tr. M. Dods *et al* (ANF 1; 1885, repr. 1995).

Lactantius, *Opera* in MPL 6-7.

- *Divine Institutes*, 1, 2, 4, 5 ed. and Fr. tr. P. Monat (SC 204-5, 326, 337, 377; 1973-92).
- Eng. tr. M.F. McDonald (FOC 49; 1964).
- *Epitome*, ed. and Fr. tr. M. Perrin (SC 335; 1987).
- Eng. tr. W. Fletcher (ANF 7; 1886, repr. 1995).
- *On the Anger of God*, tr. W. Fletcher (ANF 7; 1886, repr. 1995).
- *On the Workmanship of God*, tr. M.F. McDonald (FOC 54; 1965).

Minucius Felix, *Octavius*, ed. and tr. G.H. Rendall (Loeb Classical Library; London: Heinemann, 1966).

Novatian, *Opera*, ed. G.F. Diercks (CCSL 4; 1972).

- Eng. tr. R.E. Wallis (ANF 5; 1886, repr. 1995).

Odes of Solomon, tr. J.H. Charlesworth in *Old Testament Pseudepigrapha* II (London: DLT, 1985).

Origen, *Commentary on the Gospel of St. Matthew*, vol. 1 (bks. 10, 11), ed. and Fr. tr. R. Girod (SC 162; 1970).

- Eng. tr. bks.1-2, 10-14 J. Patrick (ANCL addnal. vol.; 1897).
- *Commentary on the Gospel of St. John*, ed. and Fr. tr. C. Blanc (SC 120, 157, 222, 290, 385; 1966-92).
- Eng. tr. R.E. Heine (FOC 80; 1989).
- *Against Celsus* [*Contra Celsum*], ed. and Fr. tr. M. Bonnet (SC 132, 136, 147, 150, 227; 1967-76).
- Eng. trs. F. Crombie (ANF 4; 1885, repr. 1995); H. Chadwick, 2nd edn (Cambridge: University Press, 1980).
- *Homilies on Leviticus*, tr. G.W. Barkley (FOC 83; 1990).
- *Homilies on Numbers*, ed. and Fr. tr. A. Méhat (SC 29; 1951).

- *Homilies on Joshua*, ed. and Fr. tr. A. Jaubert (SC 71; 1960).
- *Homilies on 1 Samuel*, ed. and Fr. tr. P. and M-T. Nautin (SC 328; 1986).
- *Homilies on the Gospel of St. Luke*, ed. and Fr. tr. H. Crouzel *et al* (SC 87; 1962).
- *On First Principles* [*Peri archon*], ed. and Fr. tr. H. Crouzel and M. Simonetti (SC 252-3, 268-9, 312; 1978-84).
- Eng. tr. G.W. Butterworth (London: Butterworth, 1936).
- *On Prayer* [*Peri euches*] in *Origenes Werke* II, ed. P. Koetschau (GCS; 1899).
- Eng. tr. E.G. Jay (London: SPCK, 1954).
- *Philocalia* 21-27, ed. and Fr. tr. E. Junod (Sur le Libre Arbitre, SC 226; 1976).
- Eng. tr. G. Lewis (Edinburgh: T & T Clark, 1911).

Pachomius, *Life* [*Pachomian Koinonia*], Eng. tr. from Bohairic, Greek and Sahidic, A. Veilleux (Kalamazoo, MI: Cistercian Publications, 1980-82).

Palladius, *The Lausiac History*, tr. R.T. Meyer (ACW 34; 1965).

Polycarp, *Epistle to the Philippians*, ed. and tr. J.B. Lightfoot, *Apostolic Fathers* II (London: Macmillan, 1885).

Serapion, *Sacramentary*, tr. and comm. R.J.S. Barrett-Lennard (Alcuin/Grow Liturgical Study 25; Nottingham: Grove Books, 1993).

Socrates, *Ecclesiastical History*, tr. A.C. Zenos (NPNF 2nd ser., vol. 2; 1890).

Sulpicius Severus, *Life of St. Martin and Dialogues*, tr. A. Roberts (NPNF, 2nd ser., vol. 11; 1894).

Tatian, *Address to the Greeks*, ed. and tr. M. Whittaker (Oxford: University Press, 1982).

Tertullian, *Opera*, ed. E. Dekkers et al (CCSL 1-2; 1954).
- Tr. P. Holmes et al (ANF 3-4; 1885, repr. 1995).
- *Apology, On the Shows*, ed. and tr. T.R. Glover (Loeb Classical Library; London: Heinemann, 1966).

Theodoret of Cyrrhus, *A History of the Monks of Syria* [*Historia religiosa*] tr. R.M. Price (Kalamazoo, MI: Cistercian Publications, 1985).

Theophilus of Antioch, *To Autolycus*, ed. and tr. R.M. Grant (Oxford: University Press, 1970).

Secondary Sources

Amundsen, D.W., 'Medicine and Faith in Early Christianity', *BHM* 56.3 (1982), 326-50.
- 'Tatian's 'rejection' of medicine in the second century', in *Ancient Medicine in its Sociological Context*, ed. Van der Eijk, vol. 2.3 (Amsterdam: Rodopi, 1995).

Barnard, L.W., *Justin Martyr: His Life and Thought* (Cambridge: University Press, 1967).
- 'The Origins and Emergence of the Church in Edessa during the first two Centuries AD', *VC* 22 (1968), 161-75.

Barnes, T.D., 'Tertullian's Scorpiace', *JTS* 20 (1969), 105-32.

- *Tertullian: A Historical and Literary Study* (Oxford: University Press, 1971, 1985).
- *Constantine and Eusebius* (Harvard: University Press, 1981).

Barrett, C.K., *The Gospel according to St. John* (London: SPCK, 1955).

- *A Commentary on the First Epistle to the Corinthian* (London: A & C Black, 1968).
- *A Commentary on the Second Epistle to the Corinthians* (London: A & C Black, 1973).

Barrett-Lennard, R.J.S., *The Sacramentary of Serapion of Thmuis: A Text for Students, with Introduction, Translation and Commentary* (Alcuin/Grow Liturgical Study 35; Nottingham: Grove Books, 1993).

- *Christian Healing after the New Testament: Some Approaches to Illness in the Second, Third and Fourth Centuries* (Lanham: University Press of America, 1994).
- 'The Canons of Hippolytus and Christian Concern with Illness, Health, and Healing', *JECS* 13 (2005), 137-164.

Benson, E.W., *Cyprian: His Life, His Times, His Work* (London: Macmillan, 1897).

Bernard, J.H., *The Odes of Solomon* (Cambridge: University Press, 1912).

Betz, H.D., *The Greek Magical Papyri in Translation including the Demotic Spells* (Chicago: University Press, 1986).

Botte, B., *Hippolyte de Rome, La Tradition Apostolique: d'après les anciennes versions*, 2nd edn. (SC 11; Paris: Édit du Cerf, 1968).

Bowersock, G.W. (ed.), *Philostratus: Life of Apollonius*, tr. C. P. Jones (Harmondsworth: Penguin Classics, 1970).

Bradshaw, P.F., *The Search for the Origins of Christian Worship* (London: SPCK, 1992).

Bradshaw, P.F., M.E. Johnson and L.E. Phillips, *The Apostolic Tradition: A Commentary* (Minneapolis: Fortress Press, 2002).

Brown, P., *The Cult of the Saints* (London: SCM, 1981).

Bruce, F.F., *Commentary on the Book of Acts* (London: Marshall, 1954).

- *The Acts of the Apostles: The Greek Text with Introduction and Commentary*, 3rd edn. (Grand Rapids, 1990).
- *The Epistle to the Hebrews* (Grand Rapids: Eerdmans, 1964).

Budge, E.A.W., *Egyptian Magic* (London: Kegan Paul, 1901).

Bultmann, R., *The History of the Synoptic Tradition*, tr. J. Marsh, 2nd edn. (Oxford: University Press, 1968) from *Die Geschichte der synoptischen Tradition*, 2nd edn. (Göttingen, 1931).

- 'New Testament and Mythology', tr. R.H. Fuller, in *Kerygma and Myth: A Theological Debate*, ed. H.W. Bartsch, vol. 1, 2nd edn. (London: SPCK, 1964) from Ger. 'Neues Testament und Mythologie' (1941).

Cadbury, H.J., *The Making of Luke-Acts*, 2nd edn. (London: SPCK, 1958).

Chadwick, H., 'Justin Martyr's Defence of Christianity', *BJRL* 47 (1965), 275-

297.
- *Origen: Contra Celsum*, 2nd edn. (Cambridge: University Press, 1980).
Charlesworth, J.H. ed., *The Old Testament Pseudepigrapha*, 2 Vols (London: DLT, 1983-5).
Clarke, G.W., *The Letters of St. Cyprian of Carthage*, 4 Vols (ACW 43-4, 46-7; New York, 1984-9).
Connolly, R.H., *Didascalia Apostolorum: The Syriac Version Translated and accompanied by the Verona Latin Fragments* (Oxford: University Press, 1929).
Crislip, A.T., *From Monastery to Hospital: Christian Monasticism and the Transformation of Health Care in Late Antiquity* (Ann Arbor: University of Michigan Press, 2005).
Crouzel, H., *Origen*, tr. A.S. Worrall (San Francisco: Harper, 1989).
Cumming, G.J., *Hippolytus: A Text for Students*, 2nd edn. (Grove Liturgical Study 8; Nottingham: Grove Books, 1987).
Daunton-Fear, A., 'The Healing Ministry in the Pre-Nicene Church' (London University Ph.D. Dissertation, 2000).
Davies, J.G., 'Deacons, Deaconesses and the Minor Orders in the Patristic Period', *JEH* 14 (1963), 1-15.
Dibelius, M., *From Tradition to Gospel*, tr. B.L. Woolf (London: Nicholson, 1934) from Ger. *Die Formegeschichte des Evangeliums* (Tübingen, 1933).
- *Studies in the Acts of the Apostles*, ed. H. Greeven, tr. M. Ling (London: SCM, 1956) from Ger. *Aufsätze zur Apostelgeschichte* (Göttingen, 1951).
- *James*, tr. M.A. Williams (Philadelphia: Fortress Press, 1976) from Ger. *Der Brief des Jakobus*, 11th edn. H. Greeven (Göttingen, 1964).
Dix, G. (ed.), *The Treatise on the Apostolic Tradition of St. Hippolytus of Rome*, with corrections and additional material by H. Chadwick (London: SPCK, 1968).
Donaldson, S.A., *Church Life and Thought in North Africa AD 200* (Cambridge: University Press, 1909).
Dunn, J.D.G., 'The Messianic Secret in Mark', *Tyn. Bull.* 21 (1970), 92-117.
Edelstein, E.J. and L., *Asclepius: A Collection and Interpretation of the Testimonies*, 2 Vols (Baltimore: John Hopkins Press, 1945).
Edelstein, L., 'Greek Medicine in its Relation to Religion and Magic', in *Ancient Medicine: Selected Papers of Ludwig Edelstein*, ed. O. and C.L. Temkin (Baltimore: John Hopkins Press, 1967).
Ehrhardt, A., 'Justin Martyr's two Apologies', *JEH* 4 (1953), 1-12.
Elliott, J.K. (ed.), *The Apocryphal New Testament: A Collection of Apocryphal Christian Literature in an English Translation* (Oxford: University Press, 1993).
Fee, G.D., *The First Epistle to the Corinthians* (Grand Rapids, MI: Eerdmans, 1987).
Ferguson, E., *Demonology of the Early Christian World* (Lewiston, NY: Mellen Press, 1984).

Ferrar, W.J., *The Proof of the Gospel being the Demonstratio Evangelica of Eusebius of Caesarea* (London: SPCK, 1920).

Fitzmyer, J.A., *The Gospel according to Luke*, 2 Vols (New York: Doubleday, 1981-5).

Fox, R.L., *Pagans and Christians* (Harmondsworth: Penguin, 1986).

Frend, W.H.C., *The Rise of Christianity* (Philadelphia: Fortress Press, 1984).

Frost, E., *Christian Healing: A Consideration of the Place of Spiritual Healing in the Church of Today in the Light of the Doctrine and Practice of the Ante-Nicene Church* (London: Mowbray, 1940).

Fuller, R.H., *Interpreting the Miracles* (London: SCM, 1963).

Fung, R.Y.K., *The Epistle to the Galatians* (Grand Rapids, MI: Eerdmans, 1988).

Grandjean, Y., *Une Nouvelle Arétologie d'Isis à Maronée* (Leiden: Brill, 1975).

Grant, R.M., *Theophilus of Antioch Ad Autolycum* (Oxford: University Press , 1970).

Greer, R.A., *The Fear of Freedom: A Study of Miracles in the Roman Imperial Church* (Pennsylvania: University Press, 1989).

Grout-Gerletti, D., 'Le vocabulaire de la contagion chez Cyprian', *in Maladie et maladies dans les texts latins antiques et médiévaux*, ed. C. Deroux (Brussels: Latomus, 1998), 228-46.

Haenchen, E., *The Acts of the Apostles: A Commentary* (Oxford: University Press, 1971), tr. from the 14th Ger. edn.

Harris, C., 'Visitation of the Sick: Unction, Imposition of Hands and Exorcism', in *Liturgy and Worship: A Companion to the Prayer Books of the Anglican Communion*, ed. W.K. Lowther Clarke and C. Harris (London: SPCK, 1932), 472-540.

Harvey, A.E., *Jesus and the Constraints of History* (The Bampton Lectures, 1980; London: Duckworth, 1982).

Henneck, E., (ed.), *New Testament Apocrypha*, rev. W. Schneemelcher, tr. from Ger. R.McL. Wilson, vol. 2: *Writings Relating to the Apostles, Apocalypses and Related Subjects* (Cambridge: J. Clarke , 1992).

Herford, R.T., *Christianity in Talmud and Mishnah* (London: Williams & Norgate, 1903).

Hesse, M., 'Miracles and the Laws of Nature', in *Miracles*, ed. C.F.D. Moule (London: Mowbray, 1965).

Horden, P., 'The Death of Ascetics: sickness and monasticism in the early Byzantine Middle East', *Studies in Church History*, ed. W.J. Shiels, vol. 22 (1985), 41-52.

Horbury, W., 'The Benediction of the Minim and early Jewish Christian Controversy', *JTS* 33 (1982), 19-61.

Hull, J.M., *Hellenistic Magic and the Synoptic Tradition* (London: SCM, 1974).

Jackson, M., 'Miracles and 'Spiritual Correctness' in the Theology of St. Augustine', *SP* 38 (2001), 184-89.

James, M.R., *The Apocryphal New Testament* (Oxford: University Press, 1924).

Jones, F.S., 'The Pseudo-Clementines, A History of Research', *Second Century* 2 (1982), 1-33, 63-96.

Kalmin, R., 'Christians and Heretics in Rabbinic Literature of Late Antiquity', *HTR* 87.2 (1994), 155-69.

Kee, H.C., *Miracle in the Early Christian World* (Yale: University Press, 1983).

- *Medicine, Miracle and Magic in New Testament Times* (Cambridge: University Press, 1986).

Kelly, H.A., *The Devil at Baptism: Ritual, Theology and Drama* (New York: Cornell University Press, 1985).

Kelly, J.N.D., *Early Christian Creeds* (London: Longmans, 1950).

Klijn, A.F.J., *The Acts of Thomas: Introduction, Text, Commentary* (Leiden: Brill, 1962).

Kydd, R.A.N., 'Charismata to 320 AD: A Study of the Overt Pneumatic Experience of the Early Church' (St. Andrew's University Ph.D. Dissertation, 1973).

- *Charismatic Gifts in the Early Church* (Peabody, MA: Hendrickson, 1984).

Lampe, G.W.H., 'Miracles in the Acts of the Apostles', in *Miracles*, ed. C.F.D. Moule (London: Mowbray, 1965).

- 'Miracles and Early Christian Apologetic', in *Miracles*, ed. C.F.D. Moule (London: Mowbray, 1965).

Latourelle, R., *The Miracles of Jesus and the Theology of Miracles*, tr. by M.J. O'Connell (New York: Paulist Press, 1988) from Fr. *Miracles de Jésus et Théologie des Miracles* (Paris, 1986).

Laws, S., *A Commentary on the Epistle of James* (London: A & C Black, 1980).

Légasse, S., 'Les Miracles de Jésus selon Matthieu', in *Les Miracles de Jésus*, ed. X. Léon-Dufour (Paris: Édit du Seull, 1977).

Léon-Dufour, X. (ed.), *Les Miracles de Jésus selon le Nouveau Testament* (Paris: Édit du Seull, 1977).

Lewis, C.S., *The Screwtape Letters* (London: Bless, 1942).

Lilla, S.R.C., *Clement of Alexandria: A Study in Christian Platonism and Gnosticism* (Oxford: University Press, 1971).

Lockton, W., 'The Martyrdom of St. John', *Theology* 5 (1922), 80-3.

MacMullen, R., 'Two Types of Conversion in Early Christianity', *VC* 37 (1983), 174-92.

- *Christianizing the Roman Empire AD 100-400* (Yale: University Press, 1984).

Maconachie, C.L., 'Anointing and Healing' (Greenwich University Ph.D. Dissertation, 1990).

MacNutt, F., *Deliverance from Evil Spirits* (London: Hodder & Stoughton, 1993).

Marshall, C.D., *Faith as a Theme in Mark's Narrative* (Cambridge: University Press, 1989).

Marshall, I.H., *Luke: Historian and Theologian* (Grand Rapids, MI: Eerdmans, 1970).

Martin, R.P., *James* (Word Biblical Commentary, vol.48; Waco, Texas: Word Books, 1988).

McCasland, S.V., *By the Finger of God: Demon Possession and Exorcism in Early Christianity in the Light of Modern Views of Mental Illness* (New York: Macmillan, 1951).

Méhat, E., 'Saint Irénée et les Charismes', *SP* 17 (1982), 719-24.

Meyer, M. and R. Smith (eds.), *Ancient Christian Magic: Coptic Texts of Ritual Power* (San Francisco: Harper, 1994).

Mills, M.E., *Human Agents of Cosmic Power in Hellenistic Judaism and the Synoptic Tradition* (Sheffield: University Press, 1990).

Montefiore, H.W., *A Commentary on the Epistle to the Hebrews* (London: A & C Black, 1964).

Morgan-Wynne, J.E., 'The Holy Spirit and Christian Experience in Justin Martyr', *VC* 38 (1984), 172-77,

Morris, L.L., *Studies in the Fourth Gospel* (Grand Rapids, MI: Eerdmans 1969).

Nautin, P., *Origène: Sa Vie et Son Oeuvre* (Paris: Beauchnesce, 1977).

Nautin, P. and M-T., *Origène: Homélies sur Samuel* (SC 328; Paris: Édit du Cerf, 1986).

Parker, D.C., *The Living Text of the Gospels* (Cambridge: University Press, 1997).

Peterson, P.M., *Andrew, Brother of Simon Peter: His History and His Legends* (Leiden: Brill, 1963).

Phillips, E.D., *Greek Medicine* (London: Thames & Hudson, 1973).

Polkinghorne, J., *The Way the World Is: The Christian Perspective of a Scientist* (London: SPCK, 1983).

- *Science and Providence: God's Interaction with the World* (London: SPCK, 1989).

Powell, D., 'Tertullianists and Cataphrygians', *VC* 29 (1975), 33-54.

Prieur, J-M., *Acta Andreae: Praefatio, Commentarius, Textus*, 2 Vols (CCSA 5-6; Turnhout, 1989).

Princivalli, E., 'Hippolytus, Statue of', in *EEC*, ed. A. di Berardino (Cambridge: University Press, 1992).

Puller, F.W., *The Anointing of the Sick in Scripture and Tradition: with some Considerations on the Numbering of the Sacraments*, 2nd edn (Church Historical Society lxxvii; London: SPCK, 1910).

Quasten, J., *Patrology*, 3 Vols (Utrecht: Spectrum, 1950-60).

Rankin, D., *Tertullian and the Church* (Cambridge: University Press, 1995).

Ramsay, Sir W., *The Bearing of Recent Discovery on the Trustworthiness of the New Testament* (London: Hodder, 1915).

Rayner, S. L., 'The Early Church and the Healing of the Sick' (Durham University M.A. Dissertation, 1973).

Reed, A.Y., 'The Trickery of the Fallen Angels and the Demonic Mimesis of the Divine: Aetiology, Demonology, and Polemics in the Writings of Justin Martyr', *JECS* 12.2 (2004), 141-71.

Richardson, A., *The Miracle-Stories of the Gospels* (London: SCM, 1941).

Scarborough, J., *Roman Medicine* (London: Thames & Hudson, 1969).

Schneemelcher, W., (ed.), *New Testament Apocrypha*, see Hennecke, E.

Schweitzer, E., 'Observances of the Law and Charismatic Activity in Matthew', *NTS* 16 (1969-70), 213-230.

Segelberg, E., 'The Gospel of Philip and the New Testament', in *The New Testament and Gnosis*, ed. A.H.B. Logan and A.J.M. Wedderburn (Edinburgh: T & T Clark, 1983).

Sherwin-White, A.N., *Roman Society and Roman Law in the New Testament* (Oxford: University Press, 1963).

Sherwin-White, S.M., *Ancient Cos: An Historical Study from the Dorian Settlement to the Imperial Period* (Göttingen: Ven den Loeck & Ruprecht, 1978).

Simmons, M.B., *Arnobius of Sicca: Religious Conflict and Competition in the Age of Diocletian* (Oxford: University Press, 1995).

Siniscalco, P., 'Minucius Felix', in *EEC*, ed. A. Berardino (Cambridge: University Press, 1992).

Smith, Morton, *Jesus the Magician* (Wellingborough: Aquarian Press, 1978).

Speigl, J., 'Die Rolle der Wunder im vorkonstantinischen Christentum', *ZKTh* 92 (1970), 287-312.

Sorensen, E., *Possession and Exorcism in the New Testament and Early Christianity* (Tübingen: Mohr, 2002).

Strack, H.L. and Billerbeck, P., *Kommentar zum neuen Testament aus Talmud und Midrash*, 4 Vols (Munich: C.H. Beck, 1922-8).

Strauss, D.F., *Leben Jesus* (Tübingen: Osiander, 1835), Eng. tr. George Eliot (1846, repr. 1994).

Telfer, W., 'The Culture of St.Gregory Thaumaturgus', *HTR* 29 (1936), 225-344.

Temkin, O., *Hippocrates in a World of Pagans and Christians* (Baltimore: John Hopkins Press, 1991).

Temkin, O. and C.L. (eds), *Ancient Medicine: Selected Papers of Ludwig Edelstein* (Baltimore: John Hopkins Press, 1967).

Thiselton, A.C., *1 Corinthians: A Commentary on the Greek Text* (Grand Rapids, MI: Eerdmans, 2000).

Thomas, J.C., *The Devil, Disease and Deliverance: Origin of Illness in New Testament Thought* (Sheffield: University Press, 1998)

Thraede, K., 'Exorzismus', in *Reallexikon für Antike und Christentum* (Stuttgart: Hersmann, 1969).

Trigg, J.W., *Origen* (London: Routledge, 1998).

Twelftree, G., *Jesus the Exorcist: A Contribution to the Study of the Historical Jesus* (Tübingen: Mohr, 1993).

- *Jesus the Miracle Worker* (Downess Grove, Il: IVP, 1999).

- *In the Name of Jesus: Exorcism among Early Christians* (Grand Rapids, MI: Baker Academic, 2007).

Vermes, G., *Jesus the Jew: A Historian's Reading of the Gospels*, 2nd edn (London: SCM, 1983).

Vogt, H.J., 'Novatian', in *EEC*, ed. A. di Berardino (Cambridge: University Press, 1992).

Wallace-Hadrill, D.S., *Eusebius of Caesarea* (London: Mowbray, 1960).

Warfield, B.B., *Counterfeit Miracles* (Edinburgh: Banner of Truth Trust, 1918, repr. 1983).

Wilkinson, J., 'Healing in the Epistle of James', *Scot.JT* 24 (1971), 326-45.

Woolley, R.M., *Exorcism and the Healing of the Sick* (London: SPCK, 1932).

Wrede, W., *The Messianic Secret*, tr. J.C.G. Grieg (Cambridge: J. Clarke, 1971) from Ger. *Das Messiasgeheimnis in den Evangelien* (Göttingen, 1901)

General Index

Studies in Christian History and Thought
(All titles uniform with this volume)
Dates in bold are of projected publication

David Bebbington
Holiness in Nineteenth-Century England
David Bebbington stresses the relationship of movements of spirituality to changes in their cultural setting, especially the legacies of the Enlightenment and Romanticism. He shows that these broad shifts in ideological mood had a profound effect on the ways in which piety was conceptualized and practised. Holiness was intimately bound up with the spirit of the age.
2000 / 0-85364-981-2 / viii + 98pp

J. William Black
Reformation Pastors
Richard Baxter and the Ideal of the Reformed Pastor
This work examines Richard Baxter's *Gildas Salvianus, The Reformed Pastor* (1656) and explores each aspect of his pastoral strategy in light of his own concern for 'reformation' and in the broader context of Edwardian, Elizabethan and early Stuart pastoral ideals and practice.
2003 / 1-84227-190-3 / xxii + 308pp

James Bruce
Prophecy, Miracles, Angels, *and* Heavenly Light?
The Eschatology, Pneumatology and Missiology of Adomnán's Life of Columba
This book surveys approaches to the marvellous in hagiography, providing the first critique of Plummer's hypothesis of Irish saga origin. It then analyses the uniquely systematized phenomena in the *Life of Columba* from Adomnán's seventh-century theological perspective, identifying the coming of the eschatological Kingdom as the key to understanding.
2004 / 1-84227-227-6 / xviii + 286pp

Colin J. Bulley
The Priesthood of Some Believers
Developments from the General to the Special Priesthood in the Christian Literature of the First Three Centuries
The first in-depth treatment of early Christian texts on the priesthood of all believers shows that the developing priesthood of the ordained related closely to the division between laity and clergy and had deleterious effects on the practice of the general priesthood.
2000 / 1-84227-034-6 / xii + 336pp

Anthony R. Cross (ed.)
Ecumenism and History
Studies in Honour of John H.Y. Briggs
This collection of essays examines the inter-relationships between the two fields
in which Professor Briggs has contributed so much: history—particularly
Baptist and Nonconformist—and the ecumenical movement. With contributions
from colleagues and former research students from Britain, Europe and North
America, *Ecumenism and History* provides wide-ranging studies in important
aspects of Christian history, theology and ecumenical studies.
2002 / 1-84227-135-0 / xx + 362pp

Maggi Dawn
Confessions of an Inquiring Spirit
Form as Constitutive of Meaning in S.T. Coleridge's Theological Writing
This study of Coleridge's *Confessions* focuses on its confessional, epistolary and
fragmentary form, suggesting that attention to these features significantly affects
its interpretation. Bringing a close study of these three literary forms, the author
suggests ways in which they nuance the text with particular understandings of
the Trinity, and of a kenotic christology. Some parallels are drawn between
Romantic and postmodern dilemmas concerning the authority of the biblical
text.
2006 / 1-84227-255-1 / approx. 224 pp

Ruth Gouldbourne
The Flesh and the Feminine
Gender and Theology in the Writings of Caspar Schwenckfeld
Caspar Schwenckfeld and his movement exemplify one of the radical
communities of the sixteenth century. Challenging theological and liturgical
norms, they also found themselves challenging social and particularly gender
assumptions. In this book, the issues of the relationship between radical
theology and the understanding of gender are considered.
2005 / 1-84227-048-6 / approx. 304pp

Crawford Gribben
Puritan Millennialism
Literature and Theology, 1550–1682
Puritan Millennialism surveys the growth, impact and eventual decline of
puritan millennialism throughout England, Scotland and Ireland, arguing that it
was much more diverse than has frequently been suggested. This Paternoster
edition is revised and extended from the original 2000 text.
2007 / 1-84227-372-8 / approx. 320pp

Galen K. Johnson
Prisoner of Conscience
John Bunyan on Self, Community and Christian Faith
This is an interdisciplinary study of John Bunyan's understanding of conscience across his autobiographical, theological and fictional writings, investigating whether conscience always deserves fidelity, and how Bunyan's view of conscience affects his relationship both to modern Western individualism and historic Christianity.

2003 / 1-84227-223-3 / xvi + 236pp

R.T. Kendall
Calvin and English Calvinism to 1649
The author's thesis is that those who formed the Westminster Confession of Faith, which is regarded as Calvinism, in fact departed from John Calvin on two points: (1) the extent of the atonement and (2) the ground of assurance of salvation.

1997 / 0-85364-827-1 / xii + 264pp

Timothy Larsen
Friends of Religious Equality
Nonconformist Politics in Mid-Victorian England
During the middle decades of the nineteenth century the English Nonconformist community developed a coherent political philosophy of its own, of which a central tenet was the principle of religious equality (in contrast to the stereotype of Evangelical Dissenters). The Dissenting community fought for the civil rights of Roman Catholics, non-Christians and even atheists on an issue of principle which had its flowering in the enthusiastic and undivided support which Nonconformity gave to the campaign for Jewish emancipation. This reissued study examines the political efforts and ideas of English Nonconformists during the period, covering the whole range of national issues raised, from state education to the Crimean War. It offers a case study of a theologically conservative group defending religious pluralism in the civic sphere, showing that the concept of religious equality was a grand vision at the centre of the political philosophy of the Dissenters.

2007 / 1-84227-402-3 / x + 300pp

Byung-Ho Moon
Christ the Mediator of the Law
*Calvin's Christological Understanding of the Law as the Rule of Living
and Life-Giving*
This book explores the coherence between Christology and soteriology in
Calvin's theology of the law, examining its intellectual origins and his position
on the concept and extent of Christ's mediation of the law. A comparative study
between Calvin and contemporary Reformers—Luther, Bucer, Melancthon and
Bullinger—and his opponent Michael Servetus is made for the purpose of
pointing out the unique feature of Calvin's Christological understanding of the
law.

2005 / 1-84227-318-3 / approx. 370pp

John Eifion Morgan-Wynne
Holy Spirit and Religious Experience in Christian Writings, c.AD 90–200
This study examines how far Christians in the third to fifth generations (c.AD
90–200) attributed their sense of encounter with the divine presence, their sense
of illumination in the truth or guidance in decision-making, and their sense of
ethical empowerment to the activity of the Holy Spirit in their lives.

2005 / 1-84227-319-1 / approx. 350pp

James I. Packer
The Redemption and Restoration of Man in the Thought of Richard Baxter
James I. Packer provides a full and sympathetic exposition of Richard Baxter's
doctrine of humanity, created and fallen; its redemption by Christ Jesus; and its
restoration in the image of God through the obedience of faith by the power of
the Holy Spirit.

2002 / 1-84227-147-4 / 432pp

Andrew Partington,
Church and State
The Contribution of the Church of England Bishops to the House of Lords during the Thatcher Years

In *Church and State*, Andrew Partington argues that the contribution of the Church of England bishops to the House of Lords during the Thatcher years was overwhelmingly critical of the government; failed to have a significant influence in the public realm; was inefficient, being undertaken by a minority of those eligible to sit on the Bench of Bishops; and was insufficiently moral and spiritual in its content to be distinctive. On the basis of this, and the likely reduction of the number of places available for Church of England bishops in a fully reformed Second Chamber, the author argues for an evolution in the Church of England's approach to the service of its bishops in the House of Lords. He proposes the Church of England works to overcome the genuine obstacles which hinder busy diocesan bishops from contributing to the debates of the House of Lords and to its life more informally.

2005 / 1-84227-334-5 / approx. 324pp

Michael Pasquarello III
God's Ploughman
Hugh Latimer: A 'Preaching Life' (1490–1555)

This construction of a 'preaching life' situates Hugh Latimer within the larger religious, political and intellectual world of late medieval England. Neither biography, intellectual history, nor analysis of discrete sermon texts, this book is a work of homiletic history which draws from the details of Latimer's milieu to construct an interpretive framework for the preaching performances that formed the core of his identity as a religious reformer. Its goal is to illumine the practical wisdom embodied in the content, form and style of Latimer's preaching, and to recapture a sense of its overarching purpose, movement, and transforming force during the reform of sixteenth-century England.

2006 / 1-84227-336-1 / approx. 250pp

Alan P.F. Sell
Enlightenment, Ecumenism, Evangel
Theological Themes and Thinkers 1550–2000

This book consists of papers in which such interlocking topics as the Enlightenment, the problem of authority, the development of doctrine, spirituality, ecumenism, theological method and the heart of the gospel are discussed. Issues of significance to the church at large are explored with special reference to writers from the Reformed and Dissenting traditions.

2005 / 1-84227-330-2 / xviii + 422pp

Alan P.F. Sell
Hinterland Theology
Some Reformed and Dissenting Adjustments
Many books have been written on theology's 'giants' and significant trends, but what of those lesser-known writers who adjusted to them? In this book some hinterland theologians of the British Reformed and Dissenting traditions, who followed in the wake of toleration, the Evangelical Revival, the rise of modern biblical criticism and Karl Barth, are allowed to have their say. They include Thomas Ridgley, Ralph Wardlaw, T.V. Tymms and N.H.G. Robinson.
2006 / 1-84227-331-0 / approx. 350pp

Alan P.F. Sell and Anthony R. Cross (eds)
Protestant Nonconformity in the Twentieth Century
In this collection of essays scholars representative of a number of Nonconformist traditions reflect thematically on Nonconformists' life and witness during the twentieth century. Among the subjects reviewed are biblical studies, theology, worship, evangelism and spirituality, and ecumenism. Over and above its immediate interest, this collection provides a marker to future scholars and others wishing to know how some of their forebears assessed Nonconformity's contribution to a variety of fields during the century leading up to Christianity's third millennium.
2003 / 1-84227-221-7 / x + 398pp

Mark Smith
Religion in Industrial Society
Oldham and Saddleworth 1740–1865
This book analyses the way British churches sought to meet the challenge of industrialization and urbanization during the period 1740–1865. Working from a case-study of Oldham and Saddleworth, Mark Smith challenges the received view that the Anglican Church in the eighteenth century was characterized by complacency and inertia, and reveals Anglicanism's vigorous and creative response to the new conditions. He reassesses the significance of the centrally directed church reforms of the mid-nineteenth century, and emphasizes the importance of local energy and enthusiasm. Charting the growth of denominational pluralism in Oldham and Saddleworth, Dr Smith compares the strengths and weaknesses of the various Anglican and Nonconformist approaches to promoting church growth. He also demonstrates the extent to which all the churches participated in a common culture shaped by the influence of evangelicalism, and shows that active co-operation between the churches rather than denominational conflict dominated. This revised and updated edition of Dr Smith's challenging and original study makes an important contribution both to the social history of religion and to urban studies.
2006 / 1-84227-335-3 / approx. 300pp

Martin Sutherland
Peace, Toleration and Decay
The Ecclesiology of Later Stuart Dissent
This fresh analysis brings to light the complexity and fragility of the later Stuart Nonconformist consensus. Recent findings on wider seventeenth-century thought are incorporated into a new picture of the dynamics of Dissent and the roots of evangelicalism.

2003 / 1-84227-152-0 / xxii + 216pp

G. Michael Thomas
The Extent of the Atonement
A Dilemma for Reformed Theology from Calvin to the Consensus
A study of the way Reformed theology addressed the question, 'Did Christ die for all, or for the elect only?', commencing with John Calvin, and including debates with Lutheranism, the Synod of Dort and the teaching of Moïse Amyraut.

1997 / 0-85364-828-X / x + 278pp

David M. Thompson
Baptism, Church and Society in Britain from the Evangelical Revival to
Baptism, Eucharist and Ministry
The theology and practice of baptism have not received the attention they deserve. How important is faith? What does baptismal regeneration mean? Is baptism a bond of unity between Christians? This book discusses the theology of baptism and popular belief and practice in England and Wales from the Evangelical Revival to the publication of the World Council of Churches' consensus statement on *Baptism, Eucharist and Ministry* (1982).

2005 / 1-84227-393-0 / approx. 224pp

Mark D. Thompson
A Sure Ground on Which to Stand
The Relation of Authority and Interpretive Method of Luther's Approach to Scripture
The best interpreter of Luther is Luther himself. Unfortunately many modern studies have superimposed contemporary agendas upon this sixteenth-century Reformer's writings. This fresh study examines Luther's own words to find an explanation for his robust confidence in the Scriptures, a confidence that generated the famous 'stand' at Worms in 1521.

2004 / 1-84227-145-8 / xvi + 322pp

Carl R. Trueman and R.S. Clark (eds)
Protestant Scholasticism
Essays in Reassessment
Traditionally Protestant theology, between Luther's early reforming career and
the dawn of the Enlightenment, has been seen in terms of decline and fall into
the wastelands of rationalism and scholastic speculation. In this volume a
number of scholars question such an interpretation. The editors argue that the
development of post-Reformation Protestantism can only be understood when a
proper historical model of doctrinal change is adopted. This historical concern
underlies the subsequent studies of theologians such as Calvin, Beza, Olevian,
Baxter, and the two Turrentini. The result is a significantly different reading of
the development of Protestant Orthodoxy, one which both challenges the older
scholarly interpretations and clichés about the relationship of Protestantism to,
among other things, scholasticism and rationalism, and which demonstrates the
fruitfulness of the new, historical approach.
1999 / 0-85364-853-0 / xx + 344pp

Shawn D. Wright
Our Sovereign Refuge
The Pastoral Theology of Theodore Beza
Our Sovereign Refuge is a study of the pastoral theology of the Protestant
reformer who inherited the mantle of leadership in the Reformed church from
John Calvin. Countering a common view of Beza as supremely a 'scholastic'
theologian who deviated from Calvin's biblical focus, Wright uncovers a new
portrait. He was not a cold and rigid academic theologian obsessed with probing
the eternal decrees of God. Rather, by placing him in his pastoral context and by
noting his concerns in his pastoral and biblical treatises, Wright shows that Beza
was fundamentally a committed Christian who was troubled by the vicissitudes
of life in the second half of the sixteenth century. He believed that the biblical
truth of the supreme sovereignty of God alone could support Christians on their
earthly pilgrimage to heaven. This pastoral and personal portrait forms the heart
of Wright's argument.
2004 / 1-84227-252-7 / xviii + 308pp

Paternoster
9 Holdom Avenue,
Bletchley,
Milton Keynes MK1 1QR,
United Kingdom
Web: www.authenticmedia.co.uk/paternoster

July 2005